LEARNING FROM COUNTERNARRATIVES IN TEACH FOR AMERICA

LEARNING FROM COUNTERNARRATIVES IN TEACH FOR AMERICA

Studies in the
Postmodern Theory of Education

Shirley R. Steinberg
General Editor

Vol. 472

The Counterpoints series is part of the Peter Lang Education list.
Every volume is peer reviewed and meets
the highest quality standards for content and production.

PETER LANG
New York • Bern • Frankfurt • Berlin
Brussels • Vienna • Oxford • Warsaw

Sarah Matsui

LEARNING FROM COUNTERNARRATIVES IN TEACH FOR AMERICA

Moving from Idealism Towards Hope

PETER LANG
New York • Bern • Frankfurt • Berlin
Brussels • Vienna • Oxford • Warsaw

Library of Congress Cataloging-in-Publication Data

Matsui, Sarah.
Learning from counternarratives in Teach For America:
moving from idealism towards hope / Sarah Matsui.
pages cm. — (Counterpoints: Studies in the Postmodern
Theory of Education; v. 472)
Includes bibliographical references and index.
1. Teach for America (Project)—Evaluation. 2. Teachers—Training of—United States—
Evaluation. 3. Teaching—United States. 4. Education, Urban—United States.
5. Education, Rural—United States.
6. Educational equalization—United States. I. Title.
LB1715.M3425   370.71'1—dc23   2015008447
ISBN 978-1-4331-2813-4 (hardcover)
ISBN 978-1-4331-2812-7 (paperback)
ISBN 978-1-4539-1591-2 (e-book)
ISSN 1058-1634

Bibliographic information published by **Die Deutsche Nationalbibliothek**.
Die Deutsche Nationalbibliothek lists this publication in the "Deutsche
Nationalbibliografie"; detailed bibliographic data are available
on the Internet at http://dnb.d-nb.de/.

Cover design by Hannah Perrine Mode

The paper in this book meets the guidelines for permanence and durability
of the Committee on Production Guidelines for Book Longevity
of the Council of Library Resources.

Printed in the United States of America

CONTENTS

ACKNOWLEDGMENTS

This is an abridged note of acknowledgment, since adequate thanks would be a longer text than the entirety of this book.

There are many people of overlapping identities—students, colleagues, educators, CMs, helping professionals, academics, writers, friends—who helped this book come into being. I want to extend heart-held thanks:

To the staff at Peter Lang for providing me the formal opportunity and support to write and publish my first book. And to Hannah Mode, an incredibly talented artist, for collaborating with me and creating my cover.

To the academics who have fostered my growth outside of a PhD program. You have been generous with your time, and your ongoing support has been exceptional. In particular, Alice Ginsberg, my thesis advisor, was the first person to encourage me to write this book. I think I laughed when you first suggested it. Thank you for planting that idea, for your follow-ups, and for both your mentorship and friendship. Paul Thomas, who I have yet to meet in person, has acted as a sort of fairy godmother in the new world of academic publishing—helping me to navigate an unfamiliar space, providing quick responses to my range of questions, and inviting me to think more deeply about the social context of my work. Your contributions helped my book grow into itself.

To former students and educator colleagues. You are among the most human, dynamic, resilient, resourceful, and thoughtful people I know. My former students, I feel more grateful than I can articulate for the ways you've shaped my life. You have pushed the bounds of what I imagine possible in the world, in the best way possible, and I am so proud of what we accomplished together. I hope I have been a similarly positive presence in your lives. Courtney Lemon-Tate, Brenda Garcia, Caitlin Nelson, Alia Bukhowa, Allison McClain, Meghan Swanson—you are beautiful people, and I learned a new kind of camaraderie working alongside you. Joseph Dugan and Charles Jackson, I can only hope to be as brilliant and as much myself in whatever I do as each of you are brilliant and yourselves in your classrooms.

To my extended community and friends who, through my years in the corps, cooked meals for me, drove me home on snowy days, graded papers competitively and jokingly tracked their hours on the star chart, offered words of prayer and encouragement for me and my students, served as a sounding board for various lesson plan ideas, wrestled with and mourned the reality of injustices I encountered, affirmed and celebrated the reality of the good I experienced, gave me a space to rest over the summer, and more. People who, through this writing process, read drafts and provided feedback, tracked with my web of disparate thoughts, listened to my insecurities and concerns, reminded me of what I knew but was unsure of how to claim, nudged me towards and helped me practice self-care through this process, and more. There were many, though to name a few: Elizabeth Nicolas, Stephanie Wheeler, April Ognibene, Taryn Nakamura, Sascha Murillo, Lee Vandivier, Heather Miki, Russell Trimmer, Susanne Flood, Nicholas McAvoy, Emily Carter, Ashley Umberger, PJ Raduta, Matt Lanza, Joshua Roddy, Sister Thérèse De Balincourt, Vineyard Community Church's West Philly Small Group and Restore, my mom, and Richard. I don't deserve you. But I'm thankful you choose to stick around.

To Liz, my anam cara, thought partner, the ENFP to my INFJ, and my most diligent reader. You have examined more drafts than I would have thought possible. Your way reminds me to be myself, nothing more and nothing less.

To Taryn, my 300%. Thank you for sitting up with me 'til various deadlines and doing word check after word check. The bias is mutual.

To Steph and April. The Amish honey wheat bread and the leopard headband exist in memory as symbols of what I experience regularly in our friendships. Who needs Patagonia when I have you two.

To Sascha and Lee. My thought process is not an easy one to decipher. It/I require commitment. As you noted, good thing that years of listening to my stream of consciousness primed you to tease out my early outline.

To my brother, Richard. You are, regardless of circumstance or differences in opinions, always on my team. I won the brother lottery. I would not have been able to write this book without you. I'm always for you, too.

Lastly, to the CMs who, despite enormous workloads and pressures, made time to speak with me and entrusted me with hearing their narratives. Your honest reflections, resistance to the powers and principalities, commitment to being yourselves in the struggle, and critical deconstructions have made this book possible. Thank you.

· 1 ·

COUNTERNARRATIVES AND THE COMPLEXITY OF A FULLER TRUTH

"In sum, successful teaching in urban and rural areas requires all the same approaches that transformational leadership in any setting requires. It requires extraordinary energy, discipline and hard work. What is encouraging is that there is nothing elusive about it."
—Wendy Kopp, founder of Teach For America, 2011, p. 33

Seated in a corner of a Starbucks in Philadelphia Center City East, Susie and I met informally over a quick cup of coffee.

"Hey, how are you? How's Philly life going for you?" I asked.

"Ahh well, that's what I wanted to talk to you about. Because it's been so rough. To be honest, I've had so many thoughts about quitting. I'm legitimately so miserable," Susie responded.

It was Monday, October 8, 2012, and we had each been using the Indigenous Peoples' Day[1] holiday to catch up on planning lessons and grading papers. Susie was a month into her first year teaching, and I was a month into my second. She was a 2012 Teach For America[2] (TFA) corps member (CM) and a friend of a friend. TFA is a national teacher corps which selects graduates from many of the nation's most selective universities and places them in urban and rural schools serving predominantly poor students of color.

Though we did not know each other very well, when Susie reached out to talk through some of her first-year experiences, I said I would be happy to listen.

Just four months prior, Susie had graduated from Yale, where she had excelled academically, held various positions of leadership, worked a part-time job, and also served as an active member in her small church community. Our mutual friend introduced us over e-mail, noting that Susie was going to be new to Philly, and that "she's wonderful beyond belief" and "always looking out for everyone else." Though I found TFA included a range of backgrounds, beliefs, interests, and personalities, Susie typified many of the CMs I came to respect: an intellectually and socially accomplished individual actively committed to caring for others.

Closing her laptop, Susie began describing her first month:

> In my classroom, like every CM, I'm good at checking off boxes. My TFA Manager of Teacher Leadership and Development (MTLD) and my Mastery Charter School evaluator both checked me off as doing the right things. I can hang up my posters, write up an agenda board, make sure everyone's in their seat. On paper, all the boxes are checked. I've got all my boxes checked and I'm all boxed in. But it's not enough. I'm not enough.

With both fluidity and urgency, she proceeded to give examples of what seemed to make her work so challenging—culture shock, what she understood to be "disrespect" in her classroom, limited resources, inadequate support, incredibly long work hours which left little time for herself or her friends, and other commonly listed reasons for what makes "hard to staff" schools acquire that label (Ingersoll, 2001; Prince, 2003; Shernoff et al, 2011). Beyond the commonly listed reasons, however, Susie also struggled to identify exactly what it was that made this job harder than the various challenges she had overcome in her school, work, and personal life prior to the corps. That in itself—the inability to name what she was experiencing—seemed to present its own challenge:

> Am I supposed to be this sad? I don't know what it is. I'm not sure if I should quit. I've never been this miserable in my life. I cry every single day—no, really. Every single day. Is this normal? I feel like I don't have time to talk with anyone about this because I almost can't make space in my weekend, and this isn't something we can discuss in TFA sessions. But I also feel like I can't *not* talk about all of this.

Susie had started crying early in our conversation, but when she began recounting her feeling of isolation and failure, she "began sobbing."[3] On the surface, she was theoretically aligned with the narrative of idealism and looked successful on paper. In practice though—in the actions she took in her classroom and her scarce times of reflection afterwards—she was confronted with a notable discrepancy between the TFA-endorsed and compelling narratives and the harsh reality she was experiencing.

I was only a second-year CM, but many of the questions and experiences she shared felt familiar. Throughout that conversation, Susie expressed a persistent desire to know and understand her experiences, and to know if she was not alone in wanting to quit and feeling like a complete failure. I could hear her wrestling with questions about her identity, power, and agency, and wondering what actual hope looked like in the reality of her first month teaching.

In her honesty, Susie contributed to my own growing set of questions.

Susie was not the only CM to experience cognitive dissonance between what she thought she should be experiencing and the reality of what she was experiencing in day-to-day teaching. During my time in TFA, I continued in a practice of journaling specific observations and questions. I noticed internally within myself and externally among my peers that—despite the idealism prevalent in the corps culture and the meritocratic language of reform—many CMs' experiences were not aligned with the TFA-endorsed narratives presented to us about who we are, who our students are, who we should be, who our students should be, and so forth.

Many of TFA's narratives about both students and teachers emphasize the singular power of hard work to overcome injustice—a simple equation founded on the principles of meritocracy and idealism (see Chapters 2 and 7).

In contrast to TFA's formula of unrelenting hard work directly yielding clear positive outcomes, I noticed many of my peers in the high-achieving corps experiencing mixed outcomes and struggling to articulate their experiences that did not align with the popular education reform narrative.

Fellow CMs were only broaching the subject of trauma and changes in their behavioral health through telling jokes and sharing nightmares. For example, during the summer after our first year teaching, friends in the corps joked, "I'm so worn out I can't even get off of the couch or stop watching TV" or "Oh my god, it's like I've got PTSD or something."

At our first All-Corps Saturday mandatory training of our second year, a small group of six CMs clustered informally in the hallway and began discussing their nightmares and the reflected shared experiences of trauma. Every person who walked by the conversation joined in and contributed that they had woken up some time in the middle of the night before their first day back in the classroom. These dreams included being attacked by bloodied knives and guns wielded by no one, drowning without anyone to rescue or even witness the drowning, shouting to be heard and yet ignored, waking up repeatedly in seemingly inexplicable cold fear, or not being able to fall asleep from anxiety.

Many CMs were also drinking to black out multiple times a week out of a need and with an intensity and frequency they had not experienced in college or any time prior to TFA. Both CMs and people outside the corps have observed this behavior in CMs. A friend in the 2011 corps began experiencing unusual, persistent abdominal pain and decided to visit her doctor. She had acid reflux disease. She learned that it was most likely caused by her alcohol consumption, and her doctor explained that her new drinking habits would easily be characterized as "binge drinking." She had enjoyed drinking socially during her undergraduate years, but prior to the corps she had never been addicted to alcohol or felt that she "had to drink" the way she felt while teaching in TFA. Her doctor asked about how these patterns developed and expressed both concern and understanding when she shared she was a TFA teacher.

When I raised the concern about binge drinking in one of our second-year TFA Penn classes, there was an immediate response of loud, awkward, uncomfortable laughter—people were familiar with the pervasive phenomenon of drinking to black out because of new teacher stress, but no one knew how to respond to it in a healthy way. Another TFA colleague was angered by this and quietly told the class that she did not think this was a laughing matter, and that "mental health is not something to be laughed at." Our class ended on that note, and throughout my two years in the corps, that was the first and last time I heard teacher mental health addressed in a large group conversation until I presented CMs' survey responses at the end of the year. Unacknowledged by the institution of TFA, some CMs described this disquieting trend in the corps as their own form of "self-medication." CMs were having difficulties being present to their realities, many opting instead to regularly drink to black out.

In private conversations, a few closer friends shared that they had started seeing a counselor or taking antidepressants after joining the corps. A friend in the corps and I shared the same school placement and, similar to many other teachers there, she began seeing a counselor and taking prescribed medications after working at our school. She came into my room in tears after a typical day at our school, "I do not think I can do this. I don't know if I can make it through the year at this place with my mental health intact."

I observed that in contrast to the various ways TFA as an institution presented a dominant narrative about CMs' identities, there was little structured space for CMs to ask questions constructively or discuss their more complex lived realities. A tension existed between narratives designated by TFA as an organization and actual narratives lived by the subjects of these stories. CMs were grappling with their realities, but with little to no structured spaces to have these needed, honest discussions, these alternative perspectives emerged in informal settings, if at all.

I wondered, "What makes talking about the subjective experiences of teaching so difficult?" Focusing on the experiences of CMs as reflections of potential patterns of young, inexperienced teachers in urban, under-resourced schools, my initial questions included:

- How and where do teachers ask themselves questions about their identity, including: Can I do this? Do I want to do this? What effect does my work environment have on me?
- What do teachers name as life-giving and life-draining in their work?
- In what ways (direct and indirect) does the stress manifest itself?
- What unnamed factors make the job so difficult and where does TFA as an organization fit into this?

Official, grand, sweeping narratives often impose a single story and exclude the lived experiences of those who do not assimilate to this claim to universal experience (Giroux, 1996, pp. 2–4). Various aspects of CMs' experiences were not captured by TFA's official narratives. Further, CMs noted that TFA's metanarratives were limited in their application not only to CMs, but also to veteran teachers, to new teachers who came through non-TFA pathways, and to their students.

In order to be an egalitarian movement working towards educational equity, TFA's epistemology needs to seek out rather than exclude perspectives of those directly affected by its claims. Epistemology is a theoretical claim to knowledge which validates and privileges certain authors, perspectives, experiences, values, audiences, and purposes. Both individuals and institutions—consciously or subconsciously—have an epistemology and set of underlying ideological beliefs which drive their actions. Though simple reform slogans may assert otherwise, neither schooling nor education reform is a straightforward equation. Schools are not removed from the dynamics and history of power; rather, schools are "contested spheres that embody and express a struggle over what forms of authority, types of knowledge, forms of moral regulation and versions of the past and future should be legitimated and transmitted to students" (Giroux, 2004, p. 210). To address the particular dynamics of power which foundationally reinforce educational inequity, it is critical to make the unconscious conscious and acknowledge the complex, historically and structurally rooted, politicized experiences of schools and school reform.

Overview

This book examines the gap between the designated and actual narratives within Teach For America. Taking an inquiry stance, I surveyed and interviewed 26 of my fellow CMs in the Greater Philadelphia region. These CMs presented their counternarratives which collectively problematize TFA's standard reform discourse. Many CMs are working hard and are seeking to care for others, but their stories and challenges are complex, elusive, and commonly self-described with the words "shame," "failure," and "isolating." CMs reported experiencing new levels of fatigue, alcohol dependency, depression, and trauma during their two-year service commitment with TFA.

Postmodern counternarratives function as a constructive critique to the grand metanarratives common to the dominant discourse on education reform and social change. Counternarratives are essentially "little stories" of individuals and groups of people whose knowledge and histories have been excluded from the telling of official narratives (Giroux, 1996, p. 2). These localized "little stories" have the power to interrupt the grandiosity of the metanarrative and advocate for a more truthful representation of reality. The primary purpose of counternarratives is not to negate the dominant narrative, though this may also occur; the primary purpose is to construct a fuller historical account of events and permit new practices to emerge (Foucault, 1977, p. 9).

The shared work of individual and corporate critical reflection is a vital feedback loop for both individuals and the institution. CMs' narratives explicitly or implicitly point to shortcomings of the current dominant narrative and thereby propose more ethical alternatives. Jane posited, "I think TFA really needs to change because they preach self-reflection, but they need to look at the whole picture—not just data, not just who they recruit, not just the success that they're seeing in some schools, but they also need to think about the people that they're bringing into this organization and think about—is this healthy? And is this actually what's best for kids? And what about me? I love my kids, but what about me?" Jane raised the concern that without honest self-reflection on a fuller data set, unacknowledged negative effects can become obstructions to TFA's original social mission. For CMs themselves, the students they serve, and the mission and institution of TFA, exploring counternarratives is a necessary step towards developing a more humanizing epistemology and theory of change. Adopting an inquiry stance and naming CMs' positionality allows CMs to recognize ways they can be excluded by and also exclude others in the telling of official narratives, ways CMs can both resist and still be dehumanized by or unwittingly collude in systems of oppression. This is not to discourage attempts to help others; rather, it is an invitation to reflect on and improve the quality of "help" we in professional positions of "helping" extend. Reflecting on who we are, the effects of our actions, and how we are affected by our context is integral to working along-side with rather than for people in the movement towards greater social equity and justice.

Working in the abstract *for* others is another way of holding power over another; it reifies a power dynamic which objectifies both professional helpers and those in their care by reducing them to their static role of the helper and the helped. Working alongside *with* others involves a commitment to reciproc-ity and dignity; it acknowledges the interconnected nature of the struggle for liberation from systems of oppression. Working in solidarity alongside those who are oppressed aligns the means with the ends; this egalitarian method affirms the inherent humanity and agency of all people. This method requires, among other things: acknowledging the positionality of professional helpers in systems of power, making explicit the power relations and the specific prac-tices which bolster these dynamics, engaging in the praxis of continual action and reflection, and listening to the people professional helpers are seeking to serve.

TFA does an excellent job of recruiting idealists and promoting an idealis-tic narrative. Idealism has its strengths: it can highlight the potential for pos-itive change, provide a rudimentary vision of what needs to be accomplished, and remind individuals of their power and capacity. However, there are limits to idealism.

Prescribing idealistic narratives can have damaging effects on individuals and systems. Idealistic narratives misstate the challenges at hand, skew what resources are needed to address these challenges, and set unrealistic expecta-tions of what can be accomplished through the prescribed method. Burning through people has individual and systemic repercussions. Individually, CMs are valuable as people and as new teachers. Systemically, burning through peo-ple wastes the precious resources of CMs, promotes teacher burnout and attri-tion, contributes to the transience and instability of what is already often an unstable environment, and can cause harm where the intentions were to help.

One of the central limits of idealism is that it treats structural inequity as a result of individual failure that can be wholly overcome by individual heroic effort. Idealism decontextualizes educational inequity from its relationship to historic and present power structures; this narrative presents the euphemized problem of "the achievement gap" without questioning how this gap was created. In response to the injustices it witnesses, idealism curtails difficult, needed conversations by highlighting the need of the victim without asking how this need came to be. Focusing on students' disenfranchisement without recognizing the intent, agent, mechanism, or beneficiaries of the disenfranchisement leaves a lot of space for uninformed interpretations and encourages blaming students for their disenfranchisement or scapegoating structural inequity on individual educators.

Idealism is insufficient to dismantle structural inequity. TFA's hero narrative calls for CMs to overcome the obstacles of structural oppression, institutional racism, and historic inequity through their individual hard work and caring, and in doing so, it minimizes the need for systemic change. Educational inequity is socially constructed, and it needs to be addressed as such. Despite their best efforts, individual CMs are unable to "close the achievement gap" or "ensure that all children can receive an excellent education" (TFA: Our Mission, 2014). Scaling up even the best of intentions is insufficient to dismantle structural, historically rooted inequity.

Relevant to helping professionals and people working to address constructed systems of inequity, this book ultimately advocates for a more honest, contextualized, egalitarian approach to reform—one that recognizes both individual and systemic realities. CMs' lived realities help to articulate a need for change and illuminate a better way forward. This work is grounded in the belief that hope does not come from idealistic, popular ideology, but from acknowledging and grappling with individual and systemic reality.

Background on TFA as a Powerful Institution in the Educational Landscape

Founded in 1989 by Wendy Kopp with a stated mission to address educational inequities facing children in low-income communities across the U.S., TFA recruits college seniors and graduates to provide teachers to under-resourced schools and produce "future leaders" committed to "closing the achievement gap" (TFA: Achievement Gap, 2014). With thousands of students from top universities applying to the corps every year, an impressive list of corporate and individual supporters, and over 32,000 alumni, Teach For America is now a powerful force in the dominant discourse on educational and social change.

A popular employment option for recent graduates from elite universities, TFA recruits from over three hundred colleges across the U.S. (Decker, Mayer, & Glazerman, 2004), and at more than 122 of these colleges, over 5% of the senior class applied to the corps, including 13% of Princeton's senior class (TFA: Our Mission, 2013). Across various majors and backgrounds, TFA recruits individuals "who have demonstrated outstanding achievement, perseverance, and leadership." The program is highly selective, with an acceptance rate of only 12% of 46,000 applicants for the 2010 corps (TFA, 2010). According to a 2004 Mathematica study on TFA, CMs are known for being high academic achievers, with an average SAT score of 1310 and an average grade point average of 3.5 (Decker et al., 2004). Additionally, according to TFA, 89% of CMs have "significant leadership experience" prior to joining the corps (TFA, 2010). As a group, TFA is comprised of high-achieving individuals.

TFA has established partnerships with a wide range of powerful institutions across various fields in both the private and public sector. Financial powerhouses ranging from large banks to the Bill and Melinda Gates Foundation provide TFA with institutional support. According to a *Forbes* piece, "The 50 Largest U.S. Charities," Teach For America's revenue totaled $318 million in November 2013. Graduate schools and employers also partner with TFA and actively recruit and extend special benefits to CMs. Graduate schools across the fields of business and finance, education, law, medicine and dentistry, policy, STEM, and social services offer partial and full scholarships as well as other benefits to TFA alumni. Google, Deloitte, PricewaterhouseCoopers, Ernst and Young, General Electric, Bain and Company, JP Morgan Chase, and McKinsey & Co. are listed as TFA's top employer deferrals, meaning these companies support their new hires in deferring their job offers for two years to join TFA. Top alumni recruiters who actively participate in TFA's Full-Time Business Resume Program include Deloitte, Pearson, Target, Morningstar, Parthenon Group, Boston Consulting Group, and Capital Group (TFA: Graduate School and Employer Partnerships, 2013).

TFA's thousands of alumni occupy a range of positions, and some famous alumni include former chancellor of D.C. Public Schools, Michelle Rhee, and founders of the Knowledge Is Power Program (KIPP) network of public charter schools, Mike Feinberg and Dave Levin. According to TFA's autobiographical history, "Our corps members and alumni have helped accelerate the pace of change as teachers, principals, elected officials, social entrepreneurs, and leaders in all fields" (TFA: Our History, 2013).

Beginning with a corps size of 500 recent college graduates, TFA has since grown to include 33,000 participants who have taught over 3 million children (TFA: Our History, 2013), and it is continuing to expand aggressively. In the 2013–14 school year, over 10,000 CMs taught 750,000 students in 48 regions across the country (TFA: Application, 2013). Factors including TFA's compelling vision, opportunities, and aggressive marketing team yielded a record high of 57,000 applicants in 2013 (Serko, 2013). Taking a corporate recruitment strategy, there are multiple TFA campus coordinators at each of the elite colleges who are rigorous, intense, and thorough in pitching to classes, posting TFA advertisements across campus, and individually e-mailing individuals with invitations to meet with a TFA recruitment associate (Timmerman, 2011). Oftentimes, university alumni who completed TFA will be enlisted to help with campus recruitment efforts. TFA is seeking to increase its applicant pool—in the spring of 2013, TFA announced that it would expand to allow college junior applicants. The University of Pennsylvania is included in the pilot program. TFA is already one of the University of Pennsylvania's top employers, coming second only to Goldman Sachs in hiring members of the Class of 2012 (Serko, 2013). In a speech to the American Council of Education, U.S. Secretary of Education Arne Duncan cited TFA as a "proven strategy ready to go to scale" (U.S. Department of Education, 2009).

Though TFA's impacts on American public education are debated (Barnum, 2013; Blanchard, 2013; Boyle, 2013; Naison, 2011; Osgood, 2013; D. Ravitch, 2014b; Royal, 2013; Rubinstein, 2011; Students Resisting Teach For America, 2014; Tennyson, 2013), because TFA recruits people from elite institutions, partners with elite institutions, and has alumni in positions of power across different fields and sectors, TFA has inarguably become an established, powerful institution in the American public education landscape. The way TFA defines change is both rooted in and also shapes the dominant discourse on education—people from positions of power join a powerful institution which then has even greater collective power in the dominant discourse to define "change."

TFA's intended "changes" are often affiliated with the corporate reform movement which emphasizes market-based reforms, data-driven accountability for teachers, and plenary commitment to the power of decontextualized high expectations and hard work (Crawford-Garrett, 2013; Miner, 2010;

Rubinstein, 2013b). TFA's slogans which characterize their institutional culture and ethos are further explored in Chapter 2.

Many of the published studies on TFA evaluate the organization primarily through test scores and report mixed results (Boyd et al., 2006; Darling-Hammond et al., 2005; Decker et al., 2004; Laczko-Kerr & Berliner, 2002). Considering TFA's increasing scope of public influence, it is essential to consider various aspects and impacts of the organization, including the internal experiences of those in the corps.

The Local Context: Challenges in Philadelphia's Public Education Landscape

An overview of the challenges in Philadelphia's public education landscape helps to contextualize this study.

Philadelphia is the eighth-largest school district in the country, and 79% of its public students are eligible for free or reduced-price lunch. Philadelphia's high school graduation rate is 64% and fewer than half of students scored proficient or above on the 2013 Pennsylvania State Standards Assessment (Broussard, 2014). In Philadelphia, per pupil expenditures were $9,299 per pupil for the city's 79% black and Latina/o population, while just over the city's boundaries into Lower Merion, part of the inner ring of Philadelphia suburbs, the per pupil expenditure was $17,261 for a 91% white population (Ladson-Billings, 2006, p. 6). During the time of this study from January 2013 to July 2014, Philadelphia was undergoing a significant period of structural transition, including, though not limited to: a budget crisis, a change in school district superintendent, a shift towards charter schools and the closure of 23 district schools. In June 2013, nearly 4,000 school district educators and support staff were laid off (Royal, 2013).

Philadelphian and urban education professor Camika Royal (2013) describes public education in her hometown as a "man-made disaster" and states:

> Yet Teach For America brought new corps members here, most of whom are now teaching in charter schools that are run by charter management organizations that feed off the destruction of the district. Philadelphia and school districts like it need systemic changes, not tweaks, not tacit support for the expansion of charters while our traditional public school system is starved, robbed, and cheated by those who hope that it will die. Urban public school systems need more than temporary

solutions like TFA. Supplying teachers by relying heavily on TFA with its two-year commitment and incentives for people to leave the profession is deeply flawed. In districts and cities where people have, for decades, experienced constant experimentation in schools, classrooms, and district governance and are now struggling to cope with school closings and mass educator layoffs, these districts, cities, communities, and families must rely on teachers who, for the most part, have limited understanding of their historical and cultural contexts and little to no long-term investment in the sustaining and improving of the community, city, or district. It could be that accepting TFA means that a district has given up on finding real, sustainable, permanent solutions to our woebegone situations.

A former 1999 TFA CM and self-identified "critical friend" to TFA, Royal describes the various ways she sees TFA as an institution engaging with Philadelphia's complex, systemic challenges; she contextualizes individuals' efforts in the historical backdrop of the city's reform movements and calls for a longer-term solution than what TFA currently offers. In her work, she recognizes that Philadelphia's resources and needs do not necessarily equate to a need for TFA to expand. It is important to question the range of TFA's impacts and considers what part TFA can play in the pre-existing movement for educational justice and equity.

Data Collection and Methods

Part of TFA training involves evening and weekend coursework towards either certification or an M.Ed. in the Greater Philadelphia region, and TFA partners with the University of Pennsylvania's Graduate School of Education. I initially began this study in January 2013 for my Penn M.Ed. thesis during my second year in the corps.

All participants of the study were either 2011 or 2012 CMs[4] from Teach For America's Greater Philadelphia (TFAGP) region. Though TFA does not yet make public the exact numbers of those who began in the corps and those who finish their commitment, a TFAGP spokesperson stated that TFAGP had 252 total teachers in the 2011 school year and that decreased 46% to 115 total teachers during the 2012 school year. In 2012, 20 CMs were placed in traditional School District of Philadelphia schools and the other 95 were placed in charter schools (Clozel, 2012; Muse, 2013).

Unlike the mandatory TFA surveys which CMs must complete to be given their AmeriCorps education award, participation in this survey was voluntary. An initial survey link was e-mailed to the 2011 and 2012 corps and posted in the private corps Facebook groups. Twenty-six active CMs opted into this study and completed this initial survey.

Of these 26, another 13 self-selected into one-on-one interviews: nine women and four men; eight 2011 CMs and five 2012 CMs; and placed in 11 different schools teaching across a range of grades and subjects. The age range of these 13 CMs at the time of their first interview was 21 to 46, though most, as reflective of the corps demographics, were recent college graduates in their twenties. Many had worked a part-time or full-time job prior to joining TFA. Two of these 13 took on positions of leadership within TFAGP while active in the corps. Seven of these 13 were nominated for the prestigious national Sue Lehmann Excellence in Teaching Award.

From early 2013 to mid-2014, these interviews were conducted in person or over Skype. Each of these 13 participants was interviewed anywhere from one to four separate times. Each interview session ranged from 30 minutes to 150 minutes. Given permission, these interviews were audio-recorded and transcribed to ensure accuracy and integrity of data. Short e-mails were occasionally exchanged to clarify points made during interviews, but the primary data includes the initial survey and subsequent interviews. While some CMs were open to having their name attached to this study, the majority preferred anonymity. To ensure all CMs had the option to be as open as possible without any potential repercussions, all surveyed and interviewed CMs in this study are listed by a first-name pseudonym. As these interviews were conducted over a period of a year and a half, those who were interviewed more than once reflected back on their earlier responses; edits were made to reflect the changes in their understanding of their experiences.

There is currently no adequate control group, so in order to identify what changes CMs attributed to their time in the corps, particular attention was given to how these CMs identify and interpret their personal and professional experiences prior to, during, and in some cases, after their two years in the corps.

This study includes the counternarratives of CMs who—despite extremely challenging situations and conflict with TFA's metanarratives—chose to complete their two-year commitment with TFA. Some former CMs who dropped out of the corps prior to completion contacted me and asked to be interviewed. I regretfully declined in order to focus on the range of experiences within active CMs. However, a separate study could easily be done on the experiences of those who dropped out of the Greater Philadelphia corps. Though it was not within my capacity to pursue their narratives in this study,

I am sure that both as individuals and as a sizable group they would have much to contribute to the discussion on TFA and reform movements.

Research Positionality

"It is in the knowledge of the genuine conditions of our lives that we must draw our strength to live and our reason for acting."
—Simone de Beauvoir, 1947, p. 9

The questions explored in this study are born directly from issues I have encountered, phenomena I have witnessed, or discussions I have participated in (see Appendix B: Journal Reflection). To make myself visible in this work and from the belief that words are not alienated from their speaker, it is important to note some aspects of my positionality which have shaped this work.

My identity is a collection of various dominant identities, subdominant identities, and their intersections: half-Taiwanese and half-Japanese, recent immigrant roots, born and raised in Hawai'i where there is no racial majority, from a middle-class background, now part of the church though not raised in the church, Penn undergraduate and graduate school educated, woman. Depending on space, these identities hold different social significance. Various dominant identities have granted me many systemic privileges and sometimes blinded me to ways I collude in systems of oppression. Various subdominant identities have often positioned me in power structures' margins, which has made marginalized perspectives deeply and increasingly important to me.

As a 2011 CM, my relationship to TFA is multi-faceted: TFA has influenced and shaped various aspects of my personal and professional identity. There are ways I am part of and still separate from the institution of TFA. My experiences in TFA have also credentialed and further developed my identity as a helping professional. It is from this positionality that I consider the role of helping professionals in their relationship to their institutions and the people they serve.

My observations of and conversations with fellow CMs at our ACS meetings, TFA meetings, and Penn classes both shaped the questions asked and influenced my relationship to interviewees. Because I took classes and worked alongside some CMs, CMs occasionally referenced events and conversations with which I had assumed familiarity. Familiarity with the basic subject matter allowed me to ask in-depth questions and gain a fuller understanding of

CMs' experiences with TFA. An established relationship with some of the CMs prior to interviews also allowed for honest discussion and a developing co-construction of understanding. The topics discussed were not vague, idealized abstractions; rather, discussions sprang from particular lived occurrences, manifestations of the ideologies experienced in TFA, individuals' personal and professional identities, and what methods and beliefs CMs brought into their classrooms. At times I grappled with my nebulous, sometimes overlapping roles as an interviewer, researcher, friend, and fellow CM. I faced some of the same thematic challenges, but I was also an outsider invited into knowing particular details of CMs' lives.

Organization of the Book

This book is organized around a set of overlapping themes which emerged from surveys and interviews. Examining CMs' narratives and interpretations of their experiences both aids in CMs' individual growth and presents a trenchant, constructive critique of how powerful institutions such as TFA "help" the communities they serve. The following chapters examine CMs' and TFA's roles and narratives through the lens of educational philosophy, critical pedagogy, psychology, sociology, and anthropology (see Appendix C for more details on data analysis).

Chapter 2 explores the oversimplification of complex, structurally rooted challenges to what CMs called "the TFA script." This chapter problematizes the designated "TFA script" and specific TFA slogans.

Chapter 3 provides a thick description of negative changes CMs experienced while in TFA, including alcohol dependency, physical fatigue, major weight changes, strained relationships, needing professional counseling, and needing prescription medications for depression, anxiety, or trauma.

Chapter 4 identifies CMs' experiences with varying levels of trauma, secondary trauma, Post-Traumatic Stress Disorder (PTSD), compassion fatigue, and vicarious traumatization. This chapter provides language to discuss trauma and explores CMs' feelings of helplessness, isolation, their avoidance behaviors and tipping points, and the limited space and resources they had in TFA to process these experiences.

Chapter 5 investigates the pervasive culture of guilt and shame in TFA. CMs described interactions in which they felt attacked, guilty, or ashamed for ways they differed from TFA messaging, staff, and culture. This chapter delineates the differences between individual and systemic work, explores the limits of CMs' agency, explores the negative effects of guilt and shame narratives, and raises questions about TFA's responsibility for its narrative and for the well-being of its CMs.

Chapter 6 outlines the nature of identity development as a complex, politicized process. This chapter explores both the general challenges of developing a professional teacher identity and the particular constraints CMs faced in TFA relating to complex racial, cultural, and political dynamics. Many CMs felt they lacked the language, time, and support to engage meaningfully in understanding their own identities in relationship to their students' identities. CMs struggled to identify their social location or unpack their prejudices and privileges, and they struggled with TFA's instructions to teach their students to be "racially aware."

Chapter 7 explores the limits of TFA idealism and the hero teacher narrative. Many CMs entered TFA as idealists, and TFA's messaging and programming perpetuated an idealistic narrative. This chapter identifies a gap between CMs' designated idealistic hero narrative that they expected and the actual, disillusioning reality that they experienced. The hero teacher narrative has individual and systemic repercussions. Idealism can cause harm where it intends to help, and idealism falls short in addressing complex, systemic challenges.

Chapter 8 provides a summary of key questions and findings.

Intentions of This Study

As any discussion related to TFA and public education reform is highly politicized and charged, I want to make a statement about my intentions in writing this book.

I conducted this study out of the belief that carefully examining thematically shared, challenging experiences can both reveal problems in the current status quo and illuminate a better way forward. I want to affirm the reality that these counternarratives exist and develop a shared language for describing and learning from these experiences. This study is not intended to be a comprehensive account or a single story of all TFA CMs in every city or of all CMs in the Greater Philadelphia region. It is an expository account and analysis of a volunteer, sample group of CMs with an intentional focus on the aspects of their narratives that are often omitted from the dominant discourse.

Overall, I appreciate TFA; I am thankful for the opportunities TFA gave me to be in my classroom and for the people I met through the program. I know many CMs and people on staff whom I respect. I am critically investigating problems within TFA, but my intentions are not to condemn TFA or provide critiques for the sake of critique. I could write a book on the merits of TFA. But there are already teams of people (TFA's marketing department, TFA's leaders, other vested interests) whose job it is to narrate, document, and promote TFA's merits. And I believe there are things to be learned from exploring both current strengths and growth edges.

Exploring CMs' counternarratives nuanced and deepened my own understanding of education inequity, reform, and the differences between individual- and systemic-level work. I began this research to better understand why CMs were struggling to honestly narrate their lived experiences and with a focus on how TFA could better support its CMs. Through conversations with CMs and exploring their individual attempts to address a systemic, man-made inequity, it became impossible to ignore the political implications of CMs' experiences. Patterns emerged from this process and presented both individual and systemic implications: CMs' counternarratives have direct implications on TFA's responsibilities to its CMs, and CMs' counternarratives also problematize the dominant discourse on education reform and social change.

I understand that this is a high-stakes conversation to students, communities, educators, education reformers, and investing institutions because of the common recognition of a terrible injustice. This injustice dehumanizes various people and groups of people; it must be addressed. However, the injustice is complex and the reform process will need to address this complexity. In the discourse on education reform, high-stakes and urgency require neither blithe idealism nor incendiary language. Contrary to TFA's popular discourse, suggesting another way or presenting a constructive critique is not necessarily "backing down" from injustice, taking a stance against education, complacently believing that "the education system is 'fine' as it is," positing that students "don't need high standards" or "are probably not going to college anyway," or somehow claiming that "kids in low-income communities can't reach the same performance as affluent kids" (Villanueva Beard & Kramer, 2014).

I do not personally know anyone who is consciously, actively "against education." Analogous to Geoffrey Canada positing in *Waiting for "Superman"* that there is no one superhero for the public education system, I believe also that there is no one villain against the public education system. There are systemic forces at play; often we as individuals know not what we do. But if we as helping professionals are to meaningfully participate in a movement towards educational equity and justice, how we engage and how we "help" matters. It is critical to examine our motivations, actions, and the range of our effects to improve the quality of care and "help" we as individuals and also as an institution extend.

In a discussion on TFA's future, TFA CEO Elisa Villanueva Beard (2014) boldly repeated that TFA is a "force for good." TFA is not an unequivocal good; we should not conflate people with good intentions with an entirely good result, should not approach an institution as infallible or beyond constructive critique even as it calls on the higher powers of "for the children." Everyone is theoretically for children and education, in practice, some with more wisdom than others.

Because TFA is such a powerful institution with a wide-reaching impact on policies, people, and the public consciousness, these realities should also be addressed publicly. TFA is part of and strongly influences the dominant discourse, and this is an opportunity for honest, needed growth.

There are consequences to the programs and policies in place. I am calling for us to begin looking at some of the hidden costs, inclusive of the costs to those joining this movement, as I believe this is only part of a much greater cost. For CMs as people, teachers, and future leaders being groomed to "lead an educational revolution in low-income communities across the country" (TFA: Our Mission, 2014), and for the value of the work CMs are engaging in, it is concerning that the reality of trauma and these other problematic struggles are for the most part unaddressed and ignored in the dominant discourse on education reform. It is difficult to discuss relevant solutions without first acknowledging some of the true conditions of many CMs' experiences. Before expanding their current model, TFA needs to reflect: if these meritocratic-heavy reform narratives are falsely descriptive of so many high-functioning CMs who have already attended top universities—the very same resource and achievement TFA is seeking to make accessible to disadvantaged students— will promoting individual education access sufficiently dismantle structural educational inequity? If CMs who are recruited for track records of grit and accomplishment are having these experiences in the public education system, how does this reality challenge TFA and the dominant discourse? In what ways does this challenge the meritocracy behind the words of simply working hard to get smart? In a meritocracy, people are where they are because they deserve to be there; it is a simple equation of merit plus effort equals outcome (Fiske, 2010). Why would TFA impose this narrative on other teachers and students without considering how their own CMs are affected by this same logic and theory of change? This reform model requires reform.

It is from a position of working in solidarity that I invited CMs to identify their lived experiences and grapple with how they did or did not align with the dominant narrative. Both CMs as individuals and TFA as an institution need to listen, learn, contextualize themselves, recognize the politicized nature of educational inequity, and develop a stance of working alongside rather than for the students and communities they serve. Through a process of critical action-reflection, I hope my and others' trendy idealism can grow into a more sustainable, mature, nuanced, contextualized, responsive hope. Designated narratives do not have to be divorced from actual narratives. Rather, genuine hope which acknowledges and grapples with actual human conditions trumps idealism which is contrived from imagined human conditions.

As TFA CMs, ours is not the only perspective. But our lived stories are also significant and, alongside our students and the communities we serve, we have power to identify our experiences, even if it breaks silence or conflicts with the dominant narrative put forth by TFA. From the truths of lived experiences, CMs have power to constructively shape and challenge TFA, other institutions of power, and the dominant discourse on education reform and social change. Rather than oversimplified soundbites or idealism, we need the realities of our experiences and the personal as political to illuminate our choices (Lorde, 1984, p. 113).

In considering potential audiences, it is my deep hope and intention for this work to be redemptive. I do not want this to be co-opted or reduced into a demand for TFA to fold. The findings on the limitations of meritocratic reform narratives are not exclusive to TFA. International aid organizations, religious institutions like churches, other alternative teaching certification programs, and other helping institutions face thematically similar challenges in reconciling how to extend help without reinforcing pre-existing inequities or creating deficit ideologies (Crawford-Garrett, 2013; Easterly, 2006; Fikkert & Corbett, 2009; Polman, 2011). If able to wrestle with the tensions between their designated and actual narratives, TFA can make a significant contribution to the dominant discussion on how to support social justice movements that are already in existence, leading other institutions to better recognize and respond to the costs and reality of systemic injustice.

I am concerned primarily with how we position and approach change, individually and systemically. As we take up a common cause, ignoring our own ethics, needs, or goals is less likely to help others and more likely to wound both others and ourselves. Acknowledging and addressing individual and systemic realities is a necessary—albeit challenging—requisite to developing equity-oriented perspectives and ethically engaging in the work of applied development.[5] To the best of our individual and institutional capacities, I hope we can make the unconscious conscious and know our own ethics and positions to reduce the likelihood of hurting ourselves and those we are intending to help, and meaningfully partner with those already working towards justice.

Notes

1. The federal holiday is officially referred to as Columbus Day in Philadelphia. Three states, Hawai'i, Alaska, and South Dakota, do not celebrate Columbus Day, and an increasing number of cities are renaming the holiday Indigenous Peoples' Day (Chappell, 2014; Gandhi, 2013).
2. See Appendix A: Titles & Acronyms for a brief description of the titles and acronyms used in the book.
3. When I asked Susie for permission to share part of her story here, this is how Susie described her recollection of this moment.
4. As a group, CMs are named and referred to by the year they joined TFA.
5. Applied development is the overall work in the related fields of counseling, clinical practice, social work, education, youth work, and applied research (Nakkula & Ravitch), 1998. I use the terms "applied developmentalists" and "helping professionals" interchangeably in this book.

· 2 ·

EXAMINING THE "TFA SCRIPT"

"I think so much about it, like the mission and the script is really what drew me in, but then experiencing it for myself, I realized that the script is inaccurate—it's flawed and it has nothing to do with the reality of the situation."

—Lola

There is a dominant discourse, narrative, metanarrative—both explicitly spoken and also embedded into the structure of TFA—that many CMs have identified as the "TFA script," "TFA Kool-Aid,"[1] or "TFA brand."

TFA endorses a set of thematically similar slogans, including:

- "Nothing Elusive"
- "Closing the Achievement Gap"
- "Work Hard, Get Smart"
- "No Excuses" & "We Don't Back Down"
- "More"
- "Data-Driven"
- "One Day" & "New Civil Rights Movement"

TFA's metanarrative is ubiquitous. When asked what messages he perceived from TFA, Bennett began by stating, "We've seen [TFA's script] a thousand times." This narrative is explicitly communicated through TFA's slogans, the slogans of schools and other institutions associated with TFA, TFA's website, recruitment materials, speeches given by TFA leaders and selected representatives, e-mail blasts from the local and national office, and the videos CMs are given to watch in Summer Institute; much of TFA's marketing and messaging is spoken from the vocabulary of this dominant discourse. This narrative is also embedded into the very structure of TFA: the pedagogy CMs are instructed in, how CMs are evaluated and interpreted by their Manager of Teacher Leadership and Development (MTLD), the style of All-Corps Saturday trainings, the content of programming, the people who are highlighted or brought in to speak to CMs, who is recruited to become a CM, and criteria of prestigious awards like the Sue Lehmann Award. This narrative is common and influences both CMs and students: "If you look at the videos they show us, those model classrooms, the very KIPP model and all the students are raising their hands and repeating kind of a recited script. The students sound very Teach For America" (Lola).

TFA's messaging both communicates and shapes TFA's ideology. This narrative is an expression of an institutional identity and purpose, and also helps to impress the institution's core message upon people within and outside of the institution. Since "we do not really see through our eyes or hear through our ears, but through our beliefs" (Delpit, 1988, p. 46), the beliefs captured and encouraged by TFA's narrative have power to shape peoples' perceptions of reality. Narrative involves an implicit interpretation of reality. For example, the TFA slogan "Work Hard, Get Smart" is not only an encouragement to work hard—it is also an interpretation of how the world works. This implicit interpretation is a kind of filter, one which influences both perceptions and practices. Because the process of interpretation is woven into the spoken narrative and embedded into the practices of an institution, the underlying ideology of an institution's narrative can remain hidden and yet still influence and direct peoples' understandings and actions (Žižek, 1989, pp. 27–30).

There are benefits to having a consistent, dominant message. From a theoretical perspective, TFA's narrative is both an expression of and also reifies TFA's identity. From a practical perspective, consistent narrative and identity facilitate the establishment, growth, and survival of the institution. Narrative and identity in the form of branding and marketing attract new recruits and donors. Lola and Nicole identify recruitment and fundraising as practical reasons for a consistent TFA script: "That is the stuff that sounds good. To people who are going to invest, and to donors, and to potential people who want to be in it, it sounds good. It really does draw people in—it drew me in" (Lola). Similarly, Nicole commented, "If they're going to keep this organization alive, they have to promote short sayings like that (e.g., "Work Hard, Get Smart"). They need funding. And they're not going to get funding from people if they're like, 'Do your best. Please realize that you're situated in this broader social context.'" Lola and Nicole both highlight ways the TFA-endorsed narrative is "the stuff that sounds good" and draws people to invest their funds, their resources, and themselves in TFA. Narrative in the form of branding and marketing may be critical to TFA's survival. Consistent messaging and actions which are aligned to this messaging promote a cohesive institutional identity and can be used to convey a sense of purpose, rally support, and establish TFA's mission.

To an extent, some kind of script is needed. However, CMs identified problems with both TFA's general script and TFA's specific sound bites.

CM Critiques of TFA's General Script

A majority of CMs identified messages from TFA as inaccurate and problematic; they had issues related to authorship, content, and effects of TFA's messaging. CMs challenged the authorship of TFA's messaging and questioned who should have the power to interpret students' and CMs' experiences. CMs commonly critiqued the content of the "TFA script" as alienated from reality, oversimplified, equivalent to Kool-Aid, and unresponsive to their needs or students' needs.

Jane, Jordan, Lola, and Elliott identified a disconnect between TFA-endorsed messages and their own experience. Jane openly questioned whether TFA is accomplishing what their narrative claims they are working towards: "Their whole mission 'One day every child will whatever,' I mean, that's great, but they're not doing that." Similarly, Jordan described TFA's narrative as "out of touch with reality." Lola noted that she was initially drawn to the content of TFA's message, but that she ultimately found TFA's messaging to be disconnected from reality: "I think so much about it. The mission and the script is really what drew me in, but then experiencing it for myself, I realized that the script is inaccurate—it's flawed and it has nothing to do with the reality of the situation."

When asked to identify what messages he perceived from TFA, Elliott responded, "It's Orwellian. It reminds me of *1984*." In Orwell's dystopian novel *1984*, "doublethink" and "newspeak" are tools the ruling party uses to indoctrinate, manipulate, and control the public. These tools involve euphemizing and keeping language intentionally ambiguous to distort reality. The ruling party inverts words to convey messages opposite of the word's original meaning, as evidenced by their slogan, "War is peace. Freedom is slavery. Ignorance is strength" (Orwell, 1950, p. 6). Other CMs also identified ways TFA's messaging is a form of doublespeak: heavily euphemized, coded, and oftentimes invisible if not carefully evaluated. A forthcoming analysis of specific sound bites explores the gap between the designated script and actual experiences.

In addition to the script's alienation from reality, many CMs also found the script to be oversimplified. Even when CMs thought the script was connected to reality, CMs noted that the TFA script is promoted as collectively exhaustive, but in reality, the slogans at best only capture partial truths. As Nicole reflected on TFA's script, she took issue with the arrogance of this oversimplified, partial-truth culture:

> I understand why they do it. I just wish they were a little bit more humble about it. A little bit more like, "We're trying our best and we realize that we're a *part* of the solution." But TFA doesn't want to do that. They want to say they're actually shifting inequality in the city. And it's just crazy to me. It's just crazy.

Nicole observed that presenting an oversimplified message is understandable, but ultimately problematic. She felt TFA ignored "broader social context" in a way that limited TFA's efficacy and also promoted a self-important theory of change for the institution's benefit.

Nicole is one of several CMs who referred to TFA's messaging using the specific descriptor "Kool-Aid," referring to beliefs that are widely accepted without critical reflection or constructive challenge. When asked what messages they perceived from TFA, Nicole, Bennett, and Aiden each began using the phrase "Kool-Aid":

> Messages from TFA: 1. If students are not parroting "I am doing my work, because I want to go to college" then I am not really making a positive impact. 2. If I refuse to sip the TFA Kool-Aid, I don't care about kids. (I.e. I believe that for real change to occur for our students, there needs to be massive structural changes … I do not believe that my year of teaching is really "changing the trajectory" for my students. I think that's really naive and I am made to feel guilty for not buying it.) (Nicole)

> We've seen the Kool-Aid a thousand times. And I respect what TFA does, I believe in the mission, I do. Do I think that everything they do is the best method for solving the issue at hand? No, obviously not. (Bennett)

People come in having drunk the Kool-Aid. And I think you see an erosion of belief in that. (Aiden)

Nicole, Bennett, and Aiden believed that there is an "issue at hand," and they were invested in contributing to a solution. However, they questioned TFA's methodology and acknowledged a gap between TFA's messaging and many CMs' realities. Nicole noted a formula to TFA's approach, one that involved both her students' and her own compliance. Further, if she did not adopt this formulaic approach, rather than discuss her actions or the reason behind her decisions, members on TFA staff challenged her commitment to her students. Nicole was not ignoring her students' needs or not caring about her students; rather, she was questioning TFA's definition of "positive impact" and the means to achieve "real change." Similarly, Bennett acknowledged wanting to find a "best method" to achieve TFA's mission. Like many of their colleagues, Nicole, Bennett, and Aiden grappled with how to best address the inequities they witnessed. Aiden explained that his experiences problematized TFA's messaging: "Personally, I still fully believe my kids can achieve at the highest level, but I've come to far more deeply understand how rooted and entrenched many of the forces are that do hold my kids where they are, and how critical school systems and structures are that I have limited influence over." Aiden acknowledged ways CMs come into the corps with their own idealized commitment to TFA and formulaic methods of changing students' trajectories, but he described how he and many other CMs became disillusioned with TFA's messaging after gaining work experience.

Other CMs affirmed the same concept that the TFA script is pervasive and demands blind ideological faith in the institution and its actions. Dionne appreciated the opportunity TFA gives to its CMs, but wanted TFA to acknowledge and address the dynamics of power which create and sustain educational inequity: "I'd love to have an organization that provides a similar opportunity but has a more critical lens on the educational landscape that we're in."

CMs described TFA's script as pre-made and applied haphazardly regardless of the specific context or situation. Without active reflection and revision, TFA's script has no incentive or means of evolving, and remaining unresponsive to its environment ultimately limits its effectiveness. Rather than serve as a panacea, TFA, confined by its script, is as likely to inflict harm as help in complex social situations. Lola critiqued the TFA script for this quality of being canned and unresponsive to CM or student needs:

I feel like everyone in TFA has a script and they follow it to a tee. So I know that whatever I say, they're going to have one of five responses. They give the same response no matter what situation. It could be like, "hold up a mirror" or "think about your commitment" or they just have these five lines that they say over and over to the point where they're not even real people. They're robots reciting a script. Whenever I feel like I'm open and honest about my situation and what's going on at my school, they don't listen. They just give me one of their pre-written answers. It's not human to me … When the script is not going as planned and when things are not going as promised that they would go, then they need to step in and be supportive.

My MTLD, she just doesn't know anything. My MTLD kept asking me, "I need your assessment data. I need your assessment data." After I had a real conversation with her asking, "How do you use assessment data for a non-skill class like history class?" … Instead of saying that she understood my concerns, she said, "It's really important that we see growth in your students." Yeah, but they're not growing. And it's like talking to a brick wall. She was reading off of that script. Even after that conversation, instead of working out a way where I could have more meaningful assessments, which is probably what I need, she kept asking me for assessment data. This is not valuable data. What are you doing with this data. It means nothing. (Lola)

Lola summarized what many CMs expressed: the TFA script is often "pre-written," blind in its application, unsupportive, dehumanizing, and ultimately ineffective. Lola felt like she was hearing "robots reciting a script" or speaking to a "brick wall" when she needed to problem solve with responsive, critically constructive individuals. This canned approach of giving "the same response no matter what situation" was "not human." In Lola's experience, the pre-made TFA script was alienated from reality, and this scripted approach then alienated her. Rather than help Lola help her students, the refusal or inability of her MTLD to talk off-script resulted in what was at best an unproductive conversation.

The following subheadings examine specific sound bites from the "script" and CMs' reflections on these TFA-endorsed messages.

"Nothing Elusive"

"Nothing Elusive" characterizes TFA's posture towards educational inequity and education reform work. Founder Wendy Kopp stated the following:

In sum, successful teaching in urban and rural areas requires all the same approaches that transformational leadership in any setting requires. It requires extraordinary energy, discipline and hard work. What is encouraging is that there is nothing elusive about it. (Kopp, 2011, p. 33)

The "Nothing Elusive" narrative presents a simple problem with a straight-forward, formulaic solution that TFA can provide. The "Nothing Elusive" narrative is pervasive in TFA.

For example, a typical e-mail from a TFA recruiter to a Penn student on September 10, 2010 read, "Teach, and no matter what you choose to do with the rest of your life, you will always know that you spent two years doing something irreproachably good." In responding to critiques of the organization, TFA Co-CEO Elisa Villanueva Beard insisted, "I am certain of this—we are a force for good" (2014).

This narrative seeks to place TFA beyond constructive critique due to the grand nature of TFA's ideals and ambitions. Additionally, phrases such as "Nothing Elusive," "no matter what," "irreproachably good," and "I am certain of this" insist on absolutes and impose a single story narrated by TFA rather than inviting students, CMs, other teachers, and other stakeholders to identify and interpret their lived heterogeneous experiences.

CMs' experiences with what they called the "TFA script" reveal a critical skepticism towards TFA's "Nothing Elusive" metanarrative. In contrast to "Nothing Elusive," CMs identified negative life changes from serving in TFA (Chapter 3), the reality of trauma in TFA (Chapter 4), identity development as a process (Chapter 6), and complex dynamics involving race, class, and identity politics (Chapter 6). CMs experienced a range of unexpected challenges and often struggled to make sense of their experiences. Dionne explained that TFA in some ways has a "positive success-driven culture," but that emphasis in messages such as "Nothing Elusive" can invalidate the realities that CMs experience:

> Coming into the corps there is such a culture that people expect to make this transformational change, and it really is a positive, success-driven culture. However, that can lead to the situation when people are feeling real emotions, because the culture is not inviting of those things, anything that is contrary to that, any experience contrary to that culture, is sort of not acceptable—even though the majority of people could be experiencing it. The messaging of it would make it so that we would never know. (Dionne)

Dionne, Nicole, Elliott, Robin, Bernadette, Ariel, and Adrian were all nominated for the prestigious national Sue Lehmann Award; their experiences highlight some of the shortcomings of the "Nothing Elusive" narrative. TFA's Sue Lehmann Award "celebrates excellence in teaching and leadership. Each year, regional staff across the country nominate second-year corps members who have inspired their students to achieve remarkable success. Finalists are selected based on the belief that their students are on an enduring path to expanded life opportunities due to major academic and personal growth" (Sue Lehmann, 2013). Sue Lehmann nominees who participated in this study described their new experiences with depression, anxiety, trauma, fatigue, therapy, and medication while serving in TFA. Meeting TFA's metrics for success does not somehow preclude a reality of internally deeply grappling with the very context in which a person is overtly succeeding. Even though these CMs achieved some clear markers of success by TFA's metrics, they experienced costs and effects outside of the formula requirements of "extraordinary energy, discipline, and hard work." These CMs identified a gap between the official narrative of "Nothing Elusive" and their complex lived experiences.

In addition to CMs' empirical evidence, certain realities undercut the TFA narrative of "Nothing Elusive:" TFA as an institution is 25 years old; educational inequity existed before TFA and still persists; historically, many people, including students, parents, teachers, policy makers, and community members, have worked for social justice in the school system; and 20% of teachers at high-poverty schools leave every year, a rate 50% higher than that of more affluent schools (Seidel, 2014). Theoretically, if the development of our educational system to its current state of class and racial segregation was a complex political and intentional movement, then the revision and reform would also need to be political, intentional, and nuanced. Acknowledging the complexity of the struggle for educational equity does not necessitate a lessening of immediacy or reduction of the importance of the struggle in any way. Rather, it explores a needed shift in posture and suggests a change in how to work together towards educational equity.

"Closing the Achievement Gap"

TFA conceptualizes and labels educational inequity in the U.S. as "the achievement gap." Researchers began using the phrase "achievement gap" in the 1960s to describe a disparity between educations and educational outcomes between poor black, Latino, American Indian, and Asian immigrant students and their wealthier white counterparts (Ladson-Billings, 2006; Lee, 2002). TFA's website describes the achievement gap and acknowledges disparities by class: "In America today, an academic achievement gap separates kids growing up in poverty from their peers in higher-income communities" (TFA: Achievement Gap, 2014). Language encouraging potential TFA recruits,

CMs, and TFA's partners to "close the achievement gap" is used on TFA's web-site, in TFA's trainings, in TFA's promotional materials, and in conversations among TFA's members. Bennett stated, "The mission of TFA in its most basic form is to close the achievement gap," and he described TFA's staff, CMs, and affiliates as "people who are committed to closing the achievement gap."

Though there are likely good intentions behind TFA's acknowledgment of educational inequity and TFA's efforts to call individuals to action, the phrase "achievement gap" is problematic in its promotion of a label without grappling with what that label means or how educational inequity came to be, its blurred definitions of individual and systemic work, and the way this phrase is applied in TFA.

TFA positions "the achievement gap" as a straightforward problem with a straightforward solution. Dionne expounded, "TFA's always like, 'Do you think the achievement gap can be closed?' I feel they raise this question to have more people to answer yes to it … they want you to say that the achieve-ment gap can be closed, because they want you to have this idealistic view of the world." TFA asserts that it recruits committed recent college graduates and professionals, trains these teachers to have an immediate positive impact on their students, and fosters the leadership of its extensive network to close the achievement gap (TFA: Achievement Gap, 2014). If race is mentioned, it is mentioned in the past tense and without an acknowledgment of how racism in America has shaped American notions of race (Coates, 2014c). TFA narrates systemic racism as a relic of the past, and TFA focuses on the heroism and power of individual TFA teachers to provide a "transformational education" through high expectations, hard work, and heart. For example, the TFA: Achievement Gap webpage features a TFA video, titled A New Man-date for Public Schools (2014), which presents the breakthroughs of individual teachers and students as models for success. The video begins with black and white photos of segregation and explains, "For decades, children's race and economic backgrounds have determined their educational outcomes." It then quickly moves to the present and describes the progress individuals have made through "providing a transformational education" while showing clips of TFA teachers with poor students of color:

> Today in our growing number of classrooms and schools students are moving on two completely different trajectories. Now our challenge is to build on those successes by providing a transformational education that fundamentally alters students' academic and life prospects. Not just in a school but across whole districts, already we are seeing evidence of substantial progress in places many had given up on: places like New York

City, Washington, D.C., New Orleans, and the Rio Grande Valley in Texas. They are showing that it is possible to give kids growing up in poverty an excellent education.

Place aside for a moment that this video ignores the reality that communities of color have worked and continue to work to educate themselves (Ladson-Billings, 2006, p. 6) and instead claims that people gave up on entire cities like New York City, Washington, D.C., and New Orleans in order to highlight TFA's alleged progress; this video positions systemic racism as a relic of the past, it describes children's races rather than racist policies as determining their educational opportunities, and it narrates addressing educational inequity as the work of hardworking individuals who prove that "kids growing up in poverty [can have] an excellent education." This narrative presents a theory of change that focuses on the power of the individual without addressing a created systemic injustice that still exists presently.

Labeling educational inequity as the "achievement gap" obviates the uncomfortable realities of systemic racism in America (Coates, 2014a); the intergenerational effects of education inequity (Wolfe & Haverman, 2001); and the historic, economic, sociopolitical, and moral decisions and policies that created a national education debt to historically oppressed people (Ladson-Billings, 2006, p. 5). Educational inequity has a legacy in the U.S.: students were historically advantaged or disadvantaged based on socially constructed systems of race, class, and gender (Anderson, 1989; Ladson-Billings, 2006; Fultz, 1995; Tyack, 2004). Some of these inequities have lessened in severity, but these systems still exist. Education historian Ladson-Billings (2006) provides examples of the systems that have advantaged and disadvantaged people based on race; she describes a national debt owed to students of color. Ladson-Billings describes the historic, economic, and sociopolitical aspects of the national educational debt; to provide a few examples:

- Historically, students of color have been barred equal access to education. Cases such as *Plessy v. Ferguson* in 1896 guaranteed national, legal, racist segregation of public facilities, and segregation persisted even after official desegregation of schools with *Brown v. Board* in 1954 (Anderson, 1989, p. 192; Tyack, 2004, p. 84). Black students in the South did not have universal access to secondary schooling until 1968 (Anderson, 2002). Native Americans also have a history of oppression, forced assimilation, and dispossession from American society and systems (Ladson-Billings, 2006). Latino students experience disparities in American education dating back to 1848; a class-action lawsuit was filed in the 1946 *Mendez v. Westminster* on behalf of Mexican American students in California to address school segregation (Ladson-Billings, 2006; Valencia, 2005). Race-conscious policies remain necessary to address both the ongoing effects and current reality of racially discriminatory policies established over the course of American history (Beckert, 2014; Coates, 2014a; Rothstein, 2012a). Communities of color have worked to educate themselves and to advocate for their rights in the face of these racist injustices, but it is critical to recognize the systems that advantage and disadvantage groups of people based on racist policies and practices. Both the effects of past inequities and current systems of oppression affect people in the present.

- Economically, separate school districts and funding education through property taxes facilitates differential funding. The School District of Philadelphia's (SDP) "adequacy gap," a term referring to the difference in what funding a district needs for all its students to achieve academically and what it actually spends, was calculated to $5,478 per student (Steinberg & Quinn, 2014, pp. 11–16). In Philadelphia, per pupil expenditures were $9,299 per pupil for the city's 79% black and Latina/o population, while just over the city's boundaries into Lower Merion, part of the inner ring of Philadelphia suburbs, the per pupil expenditure was $17,261 for a 91% white population (Kozol, 2005, p. 322; Ladson-Billings, 2006, p. 6). Other major cities follow similar patterns of segregation and correlating funding disparities; educational segregation often mirrors neighborhood segregation. Writer Coates (2014a) details how housing segregation—blockbusting, redlining, segregated public housing, the G.I. Bill, etc.—has economically disadvantaged black people and further contributed to disparities in education and educational opportunities. According to a study conducted by the Joint Center for Political and Economic Studies, concentrated poverty has risen substantially since 2000 and is home to highly disproportionate numbers of black Americans; racially segregated, high-poverty neighborhoods have not only persisted, but spread (Davies, Freiman, & Pitingolo, 2011, pp. 2–3; Ellen, 2010). According to an Economic Policy Institute briefing paper, policies such as countrywide discriminatory mortgage lending caused an epidemic of foreclosures, which worsens racial and class segregation for minority communities (Rothstein, 2012a).
- Sociopolitically, people of color have been excluded from America's civic process (Ladson-Billings, 2006). Both federal and local laws

have disenfranchised people of color from legislative representation. For example, even though black people legally gained the right to vote under the 15th Amendment in 1870, restrictive local laws such as poll taxes and literacy tests made it nearly impossible for black people to vote, thereby further disenfranchising black people and ensuring unequal schooling for black students (Anderson, 1989). Ladson-Billings (2006) presents the Voting Rights Act of 1965 as a proactive attempt to address the nation's longstanding sociopolitical debt to people of color. Though people of color have been gaining sociopolitical access, policy outcomes are still biased towards the status quo and "strongly reflect the preferences of the most affluent and bear virtually no relationship to the preferences of poor or middle-class Americans" (Gilens, 2005, p. 778).

Labeling educational inequity the "achievement gap" presents a historically-rooted problem as if it were a natural phenomenon. TFA repeatedly points to the disenfranchisement of poor students of color without questioning how this disenfranchisement came to be. Counterstories of TFA teachers of color explore how TFA trainings focus on the decontextualized alleged deficits of students of color without acknowledging racism or white privilege; these CMs of color described how questions of race in TFA trainings were only about students' race and not about CMs' race (Lapayese et al., 2014). Jane, Lola, Dionne, Nicole, and Elliott expressed similar frustration over TFA's non-existent to superficial engagement with structural racism, white privilege, and the cultural and racial stereotypes that are held within TFA. Jane described her own participation in believing and perpetuating stereotypes about her students, and explained how both the trainings and structure of TFA do not facilitate critical examination of these assumptions: "During institute, TFA really makes it easy to make assumptions about your kids … The whole program really makes you make assumptions about the people you're going to be working with. And two, you're so overwhelmed your first year, you may not have time to understand the people—the kids—that you're serving."

Educational inequity in the U.S. is a man-made, systemic problem. Focusing primarily on the decontextualized "achievement gap" precludes a need for systemic change and promotes short-term solutions without addressing the underlying problem (Ladson-Billings, 2006, p. 4). This discourse places all responsibility on individual poor students of color and their individual educators to simply try harder and care more as opposed to a discourse that also holds the larger society accountable for its historic and present marginalization of people by race and class, to the education debt the American public has accumulated and owes to entire groups of people and their subsequent generations (Coates, 2014b; Ladson-Billings, 2007).

The "achievement gap" lends a narrative of explanation without engaging with the reality of historic and systemic oppression. The "achievement gap" precludes difficult discussions on race and class, and focuses the conversation on students' disenfranchisement without recognizing the intent, agent, mechanism, or beneficiaries of the disenfranchisement. Dionne expressed frustration over TFA's superficial engagement with systemic racism and described TFA as at best only acknowledging race and class as a label; this minimizes the role of students' voice in co-constructing meaning from their lived experiences, and it promotes short-term solutions to structurally-rooted problems. How a problem is positioned influences the type of solutions generated to address this problem. When asked how TFA relates to and talks about students' race and class backgrounds, Dionne responded:

> There's two pieces. One, we talk about the race and class of our students. However, I feel it's more spoken about as an identity marker as opposed to actually realizing what that means for our kids. I think it's more catchy to say, "Oh, they're reading about *institutionalized racism!*" and not actually discussing what that means in our classroom *for kids*. That's one piece. It's just labeling students. And they [TFA] basically label it and say, "This is the achievement gap!" We can talk about the achievement gap and not talk about race and class. I think it's useful to talk about it, but the way that they speak about race and class, it's like it shouldn't matter, or like it doesn't matter. (Dionne)

TFA's usage of the phrase "achievement gap" is further problematic in its distortion of individual and systemic work, causes, and effects. As teachers who are also tasked with "closing the achievement gap" (TFA: Achievement Gap, 2014), CMs straddle and blur more than most individual helping professionals the line between responsibility for individual and systemic change. TFA further obscures the definitions of individual versus systemic responsibilities. For example, as pre-work for summer institute, CMs read a lengthy case study on a TFA teacher, Ms. Lora, who is introduced as providing a "first-hand view of the achievement gap and a model for closing it" (Farr, 2009). Similarly, TFA's website features a testimony of a 2009 CM that reflects TFA's approach to addressing educational inequity: "I have seen the achievement gap close for individual students, even those with learning disabilities, when they are given high expectations and the educational opportunities they deserve" (TFA: Achievement Gap, 2014).

The achievement gap is presented as a phenomenon that exists only for individual students and presents amazing individual teachers as models for closing this gap. This narrative oversimplifies and misstates the problem at hand, the work CMs are doing during their TFA commitment as teachers, and the systemic changes needed to address systemic inequity.

TFA narrates educational inequity as a problem of individual access separate from a created systemic inequity. This is an inaccurate narrative. Educational inequity impacts individual students, but it is a systemic inequity. Promoting educational access to individual students is an admirable goal and needed work, but it does not address the system which disadvantages individual students. The problem of the "achievement gap" is not situated in individual students; giving "high expectations" to "individual students, even those with learning disabilities," is insufficient to dismantle structural inequity. Individual teachers and students can make incredible academic gains despite educational inequity, but educational inequity is not a problem of individuals' efforts or expectations, because it is not an isolated problem of individuals, but a collective, systemic problem.

TFA's narrative also misstates the responsibilities of CMs as teachers during their TFA commitment. CMs described how they as individual teachers were tasked with closing the systemic "achievement gap" during their TFA commitment. For example, in a classroom evaluation, Jane was faulted as an individual teacher for somehow widening the achievement gap—"My school on my formal evaluation rates me as highly effective, but according to TFA I am ineffective and I am widening the achievement gap." A professional tasked with individual-level work should not be interpreted as singlehandedly worsening a systemic inequity. Working on a systems level and an individual level are both valuable and needed to address the same problem of injustice, but one focuses on the structure of the man-made problem and the other on the effects of the man-made problem.

Teachers can serve as transformative intellectuals within their classrooms and support students' development of both functional and critical literacy (Giroux, 2004); however, TFA's trainings and structure do not position CMs to effect systemic change during their TFA commitment. Bennett described the connected but still distinct concepts of individual and systemic change; he described the difference between classroom changes and systemic changes:

> Even if you can effect significant change in that classroom, it doesn't really give you the tools you need to affect things beyond the classroom or connect and collaborate with the community to actually cause long-term, scalable change … In some ways

[in TFA], you can make a big difference, but long-term, I'm not sure if that alone will do the job. (Bennett)

Working alongside individual students who have been disadvantaged by systemic inequity is important, difficult, needed work. Teachers can serve a unique capacity by supporting students to grow academically and grow as advocates for educational equity (Freire, 1970; Giroux, 2004; Gutstein, 2006). However, educational inequity in the U.S. is not a problem of individuals' efforts or expectations, because it is not an isolated problem of individuals, but a collective, systemic problem. TFA's narrative is inaccurate and not only causes harm to its CMs (see Chapter 5), but it also skews the problem of systemic injustice and minimizes the need for actual systemic change. Utilizing labels such as "the achievement gap" can suggest greater familiarity without exploring in-depth what the problem is or whether the current solution is appropriate. It is important to recognize educational inequity not as a natural phenomenon or a problem of individual effort or caring, but as a created inequity with structural roots, so that it can be addressed accordingly.

"Work Hard, Get Smart"

CMs frequently referenced the TFA mantra, "Work Hard, Get Smart." Alex stated, "Main messages from TFA: 1. Hard work = success ... I disagree." Many CMs made similar statements describing TFA's iterations of "Work Hard, Get Smart," and the ways they wrestled with this messaging.

"Work Hard, Get Smart" is a reduction of the theory of malleable intelligence. The theory of malleable intelligence states that intelligence is not fixed and can be developed. CMs' and students' actions can have significant impact, and every person has the capacity to grow. This theory does not need to be taken in isolation from history or the politics of power. However, in isolation, "Work Hard, Get Smart" implies that CMs' and students' outcomes are a result of their efforts alone. This message was explicitly taught in TFA trainings and CMs then often communicated this slogan to their students. When asked what message she perceived from TFA, Robin responded, "If my students or I are not meeting TFA standards, we are not trying hard enough." "Work Hard, Get Smart" was applied to both CMs and students.

Jane, Alex, Aiden, Elliott, Leigh, Dionne, and Robin disagreed with the meritocratic ideology behind this TFA slogan and its application to students. Jane explained,

It's as if their whole education is happening in a vacuum, and it's not. The whole idea of "Work Hard, Get Smart" totally discounts poverty, it totally discounts health, it totally discounts all the things that come with living in poverty. And it also kind of defines what success is exactly, and that's not the best thing to do for students—you should let them decide that for themselves. There's nothing wrong with having a good work ethic, but "Work Hard, Get Smart"? No.

Jane explained that she wanted to hold "high expectations" for her students, but she struggled with the narrative overemphasis on individual responsibility for manifestations of a broader, systemic struggle.

Aiden, Ariel, Bernadette, Drake, Mark, Jane, Adrian, Kate, Stephen, Lola, and Taylor disagreed with this TFA slogan and its application to CMs. These CMs disagreed with the formulaic message and thought it did not align with their experiences. When asked what messages he perceived from TFA, Aiden responded:

If you don't succeed, you're not trying hard enough … When we look at it from the big picture, from a more objective perspective, it's hard to square that circle of these two competing realities. We're told legends of people who achieved unbelievable things in TFA in a very specific context. And those stories are passed on in a kind of lore. I certainly believe that they happened, but they're not at all the norm. And TFA talks like everyone should be that and can be that and the only difference between someone who is that and isn't that is effort. In terms of how TFA messages things, that's absolutely the case.

"Work Hard, Get Smart" is an alluring ideological solution to educational inequity because it is aligned to a broader national belief in the meritocracy. The "American Dream" is defined by the meritocratic ideal that all Americans have equal opportunity, regardless of their economic status at birth, gender, or race (Urahn et al., 2012). In dominant American culture, "When people become unemployed, need legal help, or develop emotional problems, we tend to see the cause as a lack of individual motivation. We recognize the influence of economic, political, or social factors, but we tend to think that people can "rise above" such obstacles if they just try" (Cherniss, 1995, p. 32). Under the ideological construct of the meritocracy, individuals' social contexts theoretically exist but are in practice irrelevant; in the meritocracy, all challenges can be overcome with merit and effort.

However, the U.S. is not a perfect meritocracy, and the meritocracy narrative ignores structural obstacles that individuals face based on their race and class. Past and current forms of institutional racism are systemic problems, not individuals' failures (Coates, 2014a; Thomas et al., 2014; Ture & Hamilton,

1992, pp. 3–6). Individual effort is one of many factors that impacts a person's social, economic, and political life. According to a Pew study, Americans raised at the top and bottom of the family income ladder are likely to stay there as adults, a phenomenon called "stickiness at the ends" (Urahn et al., 2012, pp. 1–6). This problematic reality is reflected in our education systems: in the nation's top 193 most selective colleges, only 14% of students came from the bottom half of Americans in terms of socioeconomic status; only 5% of students came from the lowest quartile (Carnevale & Strohl, 2010, p. 135).

While CMs acknowledged a need for constant improvement and the importance of their own and students' efforts, CMs described ways the "Work Hard, Get Smart" message falsely suggests a perfect meritocratic system. This euphemized endorsement of the meritocracy applied to public education is at best aspirational and not accurately descriptive of the current social reality; it treats as wholly individual what is in reality systemically rooted. To reinforce the meritocratic lie is dangerously akin to implying that the only reason why the "achievement gap"—more accurately described as an opportunity gap or education debt—exists is because poor students of color and their teachers have not been working hard enough, or implying that students are poor because they and their families have not worked hard enough to "get smart." Effort might be all a student or teacher feels he or she has in the moment to address historic injustice manifest in an individual's life, but there is a broader systemic reality that also needs to be addressed.

"No Excuses" & "We Don't Back Down"

Slogans such as "No Excuses" and "We Don't Back Down" are common in TFA evaluations of CMs, TFA press releases, and in the messaging of charter schools associated with TFA (Goodman, 2014; Rubinstein, 2013a; Villanueva Beard, 2014). UPenn Academic Director of the TFAGP program Joan Goodman (2014) stated that many TFAGP CMs teach in Charter Management Organizations (CMO) that are characterized by the "No Excuses" philosophy. TFA's "No Excuses" narrative ties into a broader "No Excuses" education reform discourse (Carter, 2000; Thernstrom & Thernstrom, 2004). An increasing number of urban minority students are being educated at "No Excuses" CMOs (Goodman, 2013). Similar to "Work Hard, Get Smart," the "No Excuses" slogans emphasize the driving power of effort in a way that characterizes TFA's ethos; they promote individual responsibility, high expectations, hard work, and tenacity.

However, in their emphasis on the clear possibilities opened through individual motivation, these slogans can also misinterpret all negative outcomes as a lack of individual motivation. These slogans are problematic in their applications to both students and CMs. CMs identified the "No Excuses" ideology as connected to issues of social reproduction, stereotypes, institutional racism, mental health struggles, and the sustainability of teaching as a profession.

In its application to students, "No Excuses" is part of a working-class pedagogy. Pedagogy and education are not static products, but active, dynamic processes. Research shows that these processes vary by social class: American researchers and educators Anyon and Finn studied the experiences of students across working-class schools, middle-class schools, affluent professional schools, and executive elite schools and posit that students develop respective relationships to work, economy, and authority through a hidden curriculum which varies by social class (Anyon, 1980; Finn, 1999).

Many CMs felt that they as TFA teachers and their employing schools operated under a working-class school model: socializing students to follow directions, teaching rote procedures, emphasizing conformity over critical thinking processes, enforcing authority for authority's sake, demanding submission and obedience, providing little opportunity for meaningful decision-making, and presenting a disjointed, isolated curriculum. Student feedback or questions were often not invited, and students were often not given opportunities to make sense of the world around them in a classroom setting. Some CMs expressed particular discomfort over their employing schools' emphasis on "merits" and "demerits" to force students to follow directions, a phenomenon that these CMs had not experienced when they were students in their middle-class, professional, or elite schools. The "No Excuses" hidden curriculum emphasizes teacher authority and positions teachers as holders of knowledge; "No Excuses" simultaneously demands students take responsibility for their surroundings while undermining students' authority to interpret their own lives.

All interviewed CMs believed in the broad TFA-endorsed mission of providing every student access to an excellent education. They diverged over the definition of an excellent education. CMs were conflicted about TFA's methods, such as empty chants on college attendance, heavy reliance on behavior management strategies, and dismissal of critical reflection. Many CMs questioned whether the working-class pedagogy prescribed by TFA and their employing schools would be apposite, effective means to providing their students with opportunities more commonly accessible to students from middle-class, professional, and elite schools.

Elliott, Lola, Dionne, Nicole, and Leigh experienced limits and contradictions in the "No Excuses" instructional model; they wanted an alternative to accepting the hidden curriculum of the working-class school model which ignores, reflects, and perpetuates inequity. For example, Elliott referenced Anyon and Finn's work during his interview as he explained some of his concerns about TFA's pedagogy and this "new rhetoric":

> The instructional model TFA follows is very rote, and it's very monotonous, and it reminds me of that study done on New Jersey public schools where the poor schools do rote exercises throughout and the very rich schools give their students complete autonomy. TFA is reinforcing stereotypes, and hand in hand with that is social reproduction. I'm a third-year teacher now and only now am I beginning to explore beyond just running the classroom. I did a little bit my second year. And I don't think TFA's into that at all ... Again, I don't want to confuse TFA with just this new rhetoric, but I do think the whole thing is a little dehumanizing, especially for marginalized students. (Elliott)

Elliott wrestled with what he experienced of TFA's hidden curriculum and working-class pedagogy, which he critiqued as "rote," "monotonous," and "dehumanizing, especially for marginalized students." Reflecting on TFA's hidden curriculum, Lola commented, "If you look at the videos they show us, those model classrooms, very KIPP model and all students are raising their hands and repeating kind of a recited script. The students sound very Teach For America. Are they just repeating and reciting a script or do they have critical thinking abilities?" Elliott and Lola questioned the means and objectives of the TFA pedagogy and instructional model. Elliott expressed concern that TFA's instructional model reinforces stereotypes and promotes social reproduction, two issues which are foundationally contrary to TFA's mission of educational equity. The way students are socialized through a hidden curriculum contributes to class culture perpetuation, the reproduction of social classes through schools which transfer class culture norms from one generation to the next (Finn, 1999, pp. 9–24). Utilizing a working-class pedagogy is unlikely to provide new opportunities to students who are marginalized; rather, it can simultaneously serve as a mechanism in social reproduction and blame students who are not breaking from this systemic pattern.

Similarly, Dionne thought the "No Excuses" model was applied in a way that ignored the reality of institutional racism and oversimplified historical inequity. She wanted models and narratives that would create space for rather than deter needed discussions:

> TFA's way is directly related to the "Excellence, No Excuses" model, like, "Institutional racism is not a reason for you to not succeed." And not in a, "Let's talk about this and work through it," but more like, "Let's ignore it—excellence, no excuses! I don't want to hear it!" TFA doesn't want to digest that. (Dionne)

Nicole also problematized TFA's message of "No Excuses" and its application to students' backgrounds. Nicole identified a tension of holding her individual students to high expectations and not dismissing students' experiences with institutional racism or structural poverty as "excuses":

> You know Mastery [CMO] is very much like TFA—"College! College! College! No excuses!" ... I struggle with that ... It's so clear that TFA's definition of success is college. College and numbers. With the background for your students being, "No excuses!" And I understand that it can't stop you from teaching, but at the same time [systemic injustice] is a huge factor in students' success, obviously. (Nicole)

Nicole identified that TFA and certain partnering schools share a "No Excuses" ideology that can be inadvertently dismissive of students' social realities. Nicole grappled with what educator Paul Thomas identifies as the tension between what is versus what should be—poverty should not be destiny, but currently the overwhelming majority of people in the U.S. remain in the social class in which they were born (Sawhill & Morton, 2007; Thomas, 2013; Urahn et al., 2012). This problematic reality is reflected in the U.S. education system (Carnevale & Strohl, 2010, p. 135). Nicole struggled with how to best support her students while acknowledging the reality of what many experienced. Seeing and experiencing aspects of their students' social context, CMs grappled with how the narrative of individual responsibility was being prescribed onto their students and the role they as teachers played in this process.

Dionne grappled with the limitations of the "No Excuses" ideology as applied to mental health struggles. She expressed tension between how to constructively push students to grow, but also acknowledge the reality of students' experiences and struggles in a human way. While Dionne believed in the power of individual effort and high expectations, she struggled with how mental illness fits into this narrative. Her student's suicide caused her to consider very seriously whether the "No Excuses" narrative enables students, families, or teachers to respond to the reality of mental illness:

> I actually thought about the "Excellence, No Excuses" model of teaching and how my feeling towards that model of teaching kids is that it doesn't validate struggles that kids go through. It'd be interesting to see if there's research around that "No Excuses"

model. If TFA's model is "No Excuses," how are legitimate mental illnesses or any-thing of that nature seen? Is it not allowed? And abuse and things that—especially as a child—impact your life greatly. And those things are very difficult to get through. And how especially with Will* passing, I feel like his mom and I still tried to hold him to certain standards, and I feel like we did our best to have an empathetic aspect to it, but there is a bit of guilt around being so hard on him and holding him to certain expectations every day. He still needs to do his work. He's bipolar and ODD. How do you recognize the limits of students around mental illness or special education for certain kids, but also hold them to a certain standard and push them. How do you balance that? (Dionne)

Dionne proceeded to question the effect of the "No Excuses" model on teachers:

How can this impact teachers as well? That's sort of what TFA promotes with "No Excuses." And Mastery and KIPP are schools that TFA has sort of doctored, at least in Philly, and they are the ones that use a lot of these "No Excuses" model. And those schools are also the schools that have very high turnover, very high burnout. They aren't in a sustainable model, in my opinion. They don't validate the humanity of teachers. Teachers can't really have families and still work there. That's very rare in those schools. (Dionne)

As Dionne observed, the "No Excuses" model is promoted by TFA and/or many partnering schools (Goodman, 2014; Rubinstein, 2013a). Dionne ques-tioned "No Excuses" and its impact on teachers' ability to have a personal life outside of school, noting that it is "very rare" to have teachers with their own families working at these "No Excuses," "very high turnover, very high burnout" schools. Dionne critiqued the culture bolstered by the "No Excuses" model as unsustainable and dehumanizing for teachers.

Leigh also challenged the impacts of the "No Excuses" narrative on both students and teachers. When asked what messages she perceived from TFA, Leigh responded, "Same as my school—no excuses. If a student fails, you need to examine your own practice because there is always something you can or should be changing. We can never be good enough, we must con-stantly improve. Not improving is not an option." In Leigh's example, the "No Excuses" narrative is applied first to understand a student's failure, and then it extends to their teacher's failure. Leigh experienced the "No Excuses" message as reducing all outcomes to a function of her students' and her own effort. Though teacher and student effort are crucial to student success, these are not the only factors affecting students' educational outcomes. As they examined their lived experiences, CMs problematized the meritocratic ideology behind the "No Excuses" narrative and how it is applied to students and teachers.

The slogan "We Don't Back Down" is an example application of the "No Excuses" ideology onto teachers and education reformers. On March 4, 2014, TFA hosted their "first ever coast-to-coast, corps-to-alumni, staff-to-supporter, student-to-parent, all-hands-on-deck live broadcast" in which TFA Co-CEO Elisa Villanueva Beard employed the "No Excuses" narrative and popularized the "We Don't Back Down" slogan:

> I will not back down from my beliefs … I will not back down when folks say the education system is 'fine' as it is … I will not back down when folks suggest that some kids—not their own, of course—don't need high standards, because "they are probably not going to college anyway" or "We're just setting them up for failure." No. I've seen what my students Laura, Brianda, Carlos, Anayeli, and Oscar could do—so when it comes to high standards and high expectations, I will not back down. When folks tell you that kids of color can't reach the same levels as white kids—do not back down. When folks try to tell you that kids in low-income communities can't reach the same performance as affluent kids—do not back down. Yes, poverty is crippling. Poor healthcare is debilitating. Child hunger is all too real. We know kids need good healthcare and nutrition. We know they need safe cities. This doesn't mean we STOP teaching with high expectations. It means we must KEEP teaching with high expectations … When folks say it can't be done—we will not back down. And as for Teach For America's role in all of this … We are a force for good. We will not back down from that, either.

Nicole, Elliott, and Dionne entered their fourth year teaching in the fall of 2014. None of them thinks the education system is "fine" as it is or that their kids are inherently inferior to white kids from affluent backgrounds. These CMs are not "backing down." Rather, they expressed concern about ways they think TFA can do unintentional harm by taking a dichotomous, reductive, "No Excuses" approach. As alumni and part of TFA, these CMs did not think that TFA was wholly a force for good.

CMs' experiences with this "No Excuses" approach point to a larger problem: TFA applies oversimplified formulas and dismisses as "backing down" or making "excuses" what really might be critical reflection, constructive feedback, or acknowledgment of systemic injustice. Utilizing working-class pedagogy to address educational inequity is problematic; it is questionable whether a tool used to establish and reinforce educational inequity can undo that structural injustice. While there may be value in acknowledging and affirming what learning processes could look like without systemic injustice, CMs struggled to support their students amidst the tension of what is versus what should be.

"More"

Various CMs challenged the definition of "more" they perceived from TFA. CMs noted that this definition was often buried in the rhetoric of "broaden your impact," "expand your scope," have a "transformative impact," do "more." For example, in a mandatory 2013 All-Corps Saturday meeting, then-TFAGP Executive Director Travis Jordan* told CMs that teachers are important, but TFA teachers can and need to do "more" by going on beyond the classroom after TFA.

While many CMs believed strongly in a systemic need for change and the need for leaders in the struggle for equity and justice, many like John, Dionne, Robin, and Elliott also believed there is an equally pressing need for consistent teachers who value teaching itself as leadership: "We really need a consistency of professional and very good teachers throughout all years to close the achievement gap. And I don't think on a very basic level that TFA sets it up for that" (Bennett).

Dionne and Robin thought TFA's definition of "more" denigrated teaching as lifelong work:

> The assumption is that you will not be a career teacher. To be ambitious you should find another job (administration, law, marketing, etc.) that pays more and has more prestige. If you stay, it is "noble and kind" because you could be doing something else that is "inherently more challenging and demanding" … TFA does not provide any sustainable model for [lifelong teaching] to happen. I feel like the premise is "just get through the two years," but what about the people for whom that's going to be 20 or 30 years? The message is discouraging. It does make me doubt the importance of my career choice and also the work I'm currently doing. Maybe because I want to be a lifelong teacher, I'm more in tune with it, but I wonder how it subconsciously affects other CMs … The rhetoric of TFA that we "should" … I think that messaging is very obvious: "After your two years of service you can have a greater impact by being a school leader, or going into policy, valuing or anticipating *more*." That's what's going to happen. But you're not going to stay in direct contact with students necessarily. (Dionne)

> There was definitely a pressure that I had to acknowledge coming from TFA to stay in education, although I was shocked by their blatant messaging about "moving up to higher-impact positions." By that, I guess they meant becoming an administrator. That was pretty upsetting to me as a teacher because it essentially devalues the profession as a stepping stone to loftier goals. (Robin)

Both CMs critiqued TFA-endorsed narratives for deemphasizing the immense challenge, ambition, and value of teaching beyond two years. Dionne thought

TFA's narrative pushed CMs to do something other than teach after TFA with the underlying message that teaching is not a legitimate option to do "more." Similarly, Robin thought TFA's "blatant messaging" was to move up to "higher-impact positions." As teachers who are committed to work in classrooms beyond their TFA commitment, Robin called TFA's theory of change "upsetting" and Dionne called it "discouraging." Robin also noted that this narrative "essentially devalues the profession as a stepping stone to loftier goals." Framing teaching as a less challenging or worthwhile career undermines teaching and the people inside and outside of TFA who make the choice to be lifelong teachers. Defining educational leadership outside of the classroom as necessarily "more" places a false value judgment that educational leadership in and from the classroom is necessarily less. Dionne and Robin critiqued TFA's narrow definition of "more" and the way it can inadvertently exclude career teaching as needed leadership. Emphasizing a need for systemic change does not necessitate devaluing teaching. Though CMs were required to read a book titled *Teaching as Leadership* (Farr, 2010) before entering the corps, TFA's messaging of "more" as school leadership, administration, or policy work undermines the significance of teaching as needed and legitimate leadership.

Similarly, Elliott thought the primary message from TFA is that he and his classroom work do not matter. He felt pushed to do "big things after the two years," another iteration of "more":

> Main message from TFA: "We don't give a crap about how good of a job you are doing in your classroom. Fulfill your commitment, don't make too much noise, and do big things after the two years." None of that is explicit of course, but I can read the writing on the wall.

> I have this perception based on a number of factors. We had those TFA get-togethers … and it's always profound to me how at such gatherings TFA brings in people who have very limited classroom experience and then went on to "do something," whether it was administrative or policy-level. You have the same kinds of figures being placed at panels. These panels happen frequently. I have not been to them all, but I hear other CMs say things like that. That's the overarching TFA organization that's organizing these events and putting figures before us that have recently left the classroom, were not there for very long, and went on to do something, quote-unquote, "more meaningful." It's the TFA institution, the TFA jargon—they wanted to "broaden their impact," "expand their scope," etc. That's the big picture. (Elliott)

This critique of TFA's depreciation of teaching as an invalid and lesser career option was also echoed by many first- and second-year CMs at the TFA

All-Corps Saturday "Teaching as Career" panel, in which CMs expressed frustration over the fact that all three people invited to speak on the panel that day were planning on leaving their classroom the next year. Two of three were also only third-year TFA teachers. The other had been teaching for fewer than five years. CMs questioned whether there is room for wanting and needing systemic change while still affirming the immense value of quality career teachers.

CMs who chose to leave their classrooms after two years also perceived similar messages from TFA. Some, like Sofia, expressed wanting to do more in the classroom but not being able to personally make this work sustainable. Though Sofia partly wanted to stay in her classroom and thought it would be one of the most challenging and productive uses of her time and effort, she stated that she was burnt out and needed to leave her classroom in an act of self-preservation. Additionally, Sofia discussed CMs who borrowed TFA's language of "more" during interviews by parroting the familiar narrative of, "I am leaving the classroom because I want to do more for my students in a new role at your institution." She noted that CMs sometimes use this line to apply to prestigious banks, consulting firms, and law schools.

The Assistant Dean of Yale Law School, Asha Rangappa, discussed the narrative trend of CMs using the language of "more." Rangappa writes a blog series on clichés to avoid in law school personal statements. Essays written by TFA alumni applying to Yale Law School were so ubiquitous and as a group predictable that she wrote a post on the "TFA Essay" phenomenon:

The TFA Essay follows a fairly predictable model, to wit: bright, ambitious, public service-minded college graduate decides to do TFA to make a difference in the world. S/he spends hours and hours preparing the perfect lesson for the first day of school, only to find that the first day doesn't go anything as planned. Things go downhill from there. The problems are epitomized, usually, by one very troubled student, [insert name of student here (we'll refer to her as Tanya)], who is bearing the brunt of one or more inner city/rural social ills (surrounded by drugs/violence/gangs, single-parent family, poverty, etc.), is practically illiterate/cannot do math, and a troublemaker in class, to boot. After a period of disillusionment and struggling to control the class, TFA applicant tosses original lesson plan out the window, works around the clock to connect with the students in new and original ways, and even makes a breakthrough with Tanya. The applicant's efforts are rewarded when the class, including Tanya, passes the state testing requirements, advancing three grade levels in reading/math. The students may or may not stand on their desks and recite "O Captain! My Captain!" The whole experience, while rewarding, makes the applicant realize that real change can only be effected at the policy level, and so s/he is applying to law school in order to enter the field of education policy. (Rangappa, 2012)

Through TFA's programming and messaging, CMs experienced TFA's promotion of a theory of change which does not include teaching as inherently intellectual and transformative work. Some CMs also furthered this narrative in their interviews and applications. The narrated definitions of "real change," "big things," "higher impact," and "more" as glittering euphemisms for leaving the classroom is at worst dishonest and damaging to those who choose to stay in classroom work and at best cliché. Insisting on a need for systemic change does not necessitate a value judgment on the relative importance and meaning of teaching.

Dionne, Elliott, and Robin thought that TFA exacerbates teacher-turnover problems in poorer schools under the imperative of "more." By indirectly messaging that teaching is less valuable work, positioning teaching as short-term work in TFA, and promoting teacher burnout culture, these CMs were concerned that TFA reinforced a pre-existing problem of high teacher-turnover rates in poorer schools. Working-class schools already tend to have predominantly young teachers with limited experience compared to wealthier schools (Anyon, 1980; Finn, 1999), and nearly 20% of teachers at high-poverty schools leave every year, a rate 50% higher than wealthier schools (Seidel, 2014). The revolving-door effect has enormous fiscal and student learning costs (Ingersoll, 2004; Murnane & Phillips, 1981; Rockoff, 2004). High teacher-turnover rates also negatively impact schools' cultures and investment in professional development (National Commission on Teaching and America's Future, 2003). Elliott challenged TFA's narrative interpretation of his choice to stay in the classroom: "The work we do matters, and you should try to keep me in the classroom ... where I would go is where I think I can best serve that community. And hopefully that means staying in the classroom and finding a place where you can *really*, quote-unquote, 'broaden your impact.'" From his perspective, Elliott viewed teaching as work that matters and his classroom as a place where he could grow as a professional educator, serve his community, and broaden his impact. He resisted TFA's and any CMs' messaging of teaching as a lesser option.

On an individual level, it is understandable that CMs who are applying to new jobs or trying to interpret themselves kindly might be inclined to claim they are off to do "more." And there is a need for systemic change and partner advocates. But politically and ideologically, it is problematic to claim "more." It very well might be needed work. But it is not inherently "more." Or maybe it needs to be specified: more of what and more for whom? It might be more *convenient*, more *needed for the* CM, more *appealing*, more *lucrative*, more *prestigious* than staying in teaching, or simply a better fit for that CM to leave the classroom. But it is *not* inherently more *valuable*, not when it comes to the shared movement for educational equity. There is significant work to be done in this movement both inside and outside of the classroom.

"Data-Driven"

TFA takes an explicitly "data-driven" approach to its work, CMs, and students (Villanueva Beard & Kramer, 2014; TFA: Research, 2014). This data includes a range of criteria used to evaluate TFA's impacts: student's scores on varying assessments, teacher retention rates, employing principals' evaluations of CMs, civic engagement rates of TFA alumni, and more (Boyd et al., 2006; Decker et al., 2004; Henry et al., 2012; Kovacs, 2011; McAdam & Brandt, 2009; TFA: Research, 2014). For TFA, CMs, and students, data can be a valuable tool in guiding growth and driving both individuals and institutions towards improvement. However, within and outside of the corps, TFA's "data-driven nature" (Villanueva Beard & Kramer, 2014) and the data claims about TFA's impacts have come under significant criticism (Barnum, 2013; Blanchard, 2013; Kovacs, 2011; Naison, 2011; Osgood, 2013; D. Ravitch, 2014a; Royal, 2013; Rubinstein, 2011; Students Resisting Teach For America, 2014).

Similarly, CMs in this study were ambivalent about TFA's "data-driven" narrative. Although many CMs like Elliott believed "our decisions should be data-driven" and stating expectations clearly is "really valuable," they took issue with various aspects of the "data-driven" narrative. Their concerns included: the legitimacy of data, the reduction of education to collection of a set of data specified by TFA, how this narrative is being used, and the impacts of this narrative.

Leigh, Jane, and Lola called into question the legitimacy of the data TFA collects. Data collection can be meaningless or harmful if it is "fudged," inaccurate, or manipulated, or if the data creators are put in a position where they feel they need to make up statistics:

> A lot of the data-driven focus seems out of touch with reality, especially at the public school where I work. There's no one supervising me to make sure my tests are up to standard, so I feel I can easily fudge results. (Leigh)

> Even if [TFA] sees results, they should question those results. Say, if TFA teachers do X, Y, and Z. Well, think about the teachers you're collecting this from, think about

their mental state, think about all the things they have to do today; can you really trust those statistics? Seriously! … Every e-mail where I send [my MTLD] my data, it's just blank. Like an attachment. I've got nothing to say. (Jane)

Even after that conversation, instead of working out a way where I could have more meaningful assessments, which is probably what I need, she kept asking me for assessment data. This is not valuable data. What are you doing with this data? It means nothing. It's just a number. I can make up any number. [My MTLD] asked me for my assessment data and kept five times that day asking for it. I just had two fights in my room. I had to break it up. You don't understand what goes on on a daily basis. Giving you some number that doesn't matter is not on the top of my priority list. (Lola)

From Leigh's perspective, "a lot of the data-driven focus seems out of touch with reality." Like many CMs, Leigh created lesson plans and assessments to the best of her abilities. However, as a new teacher beginning work with limited support or supervision, she struggled with the lack of resources available to her and acknowledged an arbitrary element to her results—they could be "fudged," as much accidentally as intentionally. Jane was similarly skeptical about CMs' claims of student gains, particularly after acknowledging the daily realities many CMs face. Whether it is because of a pressure to report significant gains to feel like they are making a difference or because other responsibilities were prioritized over submitting data reports to TFA, Jane introduced different aspects that could affect the legitimacy of data submitted, and questioned, "Can you really trust those statistics?" Lola explained her belief that this data was "not valuable … it means nothing." Many CMs brought up feeling like their data submissions were not used constructively to help their students grow or to help CMs become better teachers. From this perspective, submitting data felt needlessly secretarial, and like a waste of their already scarce time. There was limited incentive to engage in the "data-driven" approach as defined by TFA when they did not have the resources to do so or see productive reasons to submit data reports.

CMs also critiqued the "data-driven" approach for what they viewed as a reduction of teaching and student success to a specific set of numbers. When asked what messages they perceived from TFA, Sofia, Jane, and Alex responded:

Student success is measured one way—with tangible data on assessments." (Sofia)

We just want you for your data. (Jane)

Good teachers are like management consultants: They define a quantitative metric and work relentlessly to reach the quantitative goal … Non-TFA teachers aren't as good … Data-driven teachers are better than less data-driven teachers … Learning and schooling can largely be reduced to numbers. I disagree with all of [these messages]. (Alex)

CMs felt the process and language around data collection were reductive and at best the collected data only paints a partial picture. CMs advocated for a more complex understanding of learning.

John, Jane, and Maggie took issue with how the "data-driven" narrative was being applied:

When I left TFA, I got involved with the educational entrepreneurship community … That's a community that looks at failure differently than I think the TFA community did. There's this idea [outside of TFA] that failure is something you learn from and it makes you stronger in that you are constantly reevaluating your ideas and venture, and in that process you're making it better for whoever you're trying to serve. Failure and data are not supposed to be things you slap people around with, which is what they were in TFA. It's not about control. It's about feedback and it's about getting better. That's what this new community has done for me. (John)

I believe in feedback and criticism, and I think [TFA] does a great job at [criticism], but they rarely tell you anything positive, which is human relationships 101. Tell me how I can grow. Unfortunately this year, all they do is ask me for data. My school on my formal evaluation rates me as highly effective, but according to TFA I am ineffective and I am widening the achievement gap, when all I'm trying to do is do the best I can with the resources I'm been given, which I've found on my own. (Jane)

[TFA] is not looking at all these intersecting factors … All they want to talk about is scores. It's about control. The real narrative is too big, too messy. (Maggie)

John described experiencing a very different approach to data in his educational entrepreneurship community than in TFA. In his new community, he saw data being used for the purpose of improvement—"it's about feedback and it's about getting better." Contrastingly, in TFA he experienced failure and data punitively as "things you slap people around with." Both John and Maggie described TFA's data-driven approach as more about control than about constructive growth.

In addition to the way the data-driven narrative was being applied, CMs were also concerned about the effects of this narrative. Maggie explained that the narrative focus on scores ignored "intersecting factors" and eschewed the "real narrative." Lola described needing "more meaningful assessments" and wanted to work with her MTLD to develop better assessments for her students, but repeatedly had her request ignored. For Jane, TFA's data-driven approach shut down constructive dialogue and the data submissions were meaningless. Her development as a helping professional was not supported and she was further disinvested in TFA—in response to TFA's data-driven approach, Jane stated, "I've got nothing to say" to them.

There are ways the tension these CMs describe reflects a larger, systemic, ideological tension in the discourse and structure of public education in America. American students performed much lower than most other developed nations on the Program for International Student Assessment (PISA), a system of international assessments that compares outcomes of student learning (NCES, 2013). Elizabeth Green compared and contrasted the approaches of teachers by country as a lens for analyzing the American underperformance on standardized tests. In countries like Japan and Finland, whose students both significantly outperformed American students on the PISA, teachers taught for 600 or fewer hours each school year compared to the 1,100 hours American teachers were required to teach (Green, 2014). Japanese education reformers cited being influenced by American education reformers, but noted that these theories were largely not implemented in American classrooms. In contrast to their Japanese or Finnish counterparts, American teachers were given drastically less time to prepare, revise, and learn from their own or their colleague's teaching experiences. There were few opportunities to discuss their teaching methods, to watch one another teach, or to conduct lesson studies to improve their craft (Green, 2014). Green interpreted the phenomenon of American students underperforming compared to their OECD counterparts as a systemic problem: "Odds-defying individual teachers can be found in every state, but the overall picture is of a profession struggling to make the best of an impossible hand" (2014). Similarly, CMs noted that both they and their non-TFA teacher colleagues were often held entirely responsible as individuals for what was also a systemic failure. The data featured in the dominant discourse's "data-driven" approach often focuses on the scores of individual teachers and students without also considering contributing systemic factors, including though not limited to teachers' classroom teaching hours or pedagogies that vary by class. What data TFA uses to feature and position the problem of educational inequity influences the types of solutions generated to address educational inequity.

CMs were not inherently opposed to data. CMs described wanting to see a real change in their students' outcomes, as measured by test scores, available opportunities, and more, and they thought data-driven approaches have potential to provide constructive feedback and guide growth. However, CMs experienced the data-driven narratives as disconnected from their realities and therefore ineffective in helping to drive situated, meaningful change. How the data was being collected and the messaging behind the data was often not constructive or productive. CMs required time to revise and learn from their experiences, to engage in conversations with TFA and their colleagues about their lesson plans, to receive constructive feedback on how to improve. Further, unintended consequences of this data-driven narrative included disinvestment of CMs from TFA.

In examining what data is being collected, Aiden said of TFA: "They're not the best at collecting information even though they obsess over data." Even with a "data-driven" approach, TFA can overlook some of the important complexities of what knowledge gets collected and prioritized, and how phenomena are interpreted. Jane thought that despite TFA's identity as a "data-driven" organization, TFA was losing sight of their mission by not examining a fuller data set, inclusive of the range of its CMs' reflections.

CMs' counternarratives have power to inform how helping professionals are doing and speak to the complexity of the challenges at hand, contributing to the development of a more nuanced, responsive way forward. TFA Co-CEO Kramer said: "We commit to tempering our data-driven nature with a greater appreciation for the human stories in our work that tie us all together" (2014). These are some of the human stories from this work. CMs' counternarratives are another form of data that need to be considered in TFA's data-driven approach.

"New Civil Rights Movement" & "One Day"

TFA has been explicitly described by its leaders as the "New Civil Rights Movement" and borrows phrases popularized in the American Civil Rights Movement (Kopp, 2003; Washington, 1986).

In her book titled *One Day, All Children …*, Kopp is likely referencing Dr. King's 1963 "I Have a Dream" speech which positions "one day" as an imminent coming of radical racial justice and reconciliation in America (Washington, 1986). Borrowing this language, Kopp positions TFA as an extension of this movement. "One Day" has become a popular slogan in TFA and is listed as their vision: "Our Vision: One day, all children in this nation will have the opportunity to attain an excellent education" (TFA: Our Organization, 2014). CMs frequently referenced "One Day" as TFA's mission in their surveys and interviews.

The back cover of her book positions "One Day" as "Wendy's dream":

From her dorm room at Princeton University, twenty-one-year-old college senior Wendy Kopp decided to launch a movement to improve public education in America ...

Teach For America has become a stunning success. Since 1990, more than 9,000 individuals have joined its ranks, impacting the lives of well over one million children. And Teach For America alumni have carried their insight and commitment onward, assuming leadership roles from within every professional sector—from policy to law, business to education—in the fight for change.

One Day, All Children tells the inspirational story of one young woman's tenacious grasp on a seemingly impossible dream. It reveals the struggles of an organization created by and for young idealists. But more importantly it provides the blueprint for a new civil rights movement—a movement that demands educational access and opportunity for all American children. Wendy's dream is that one day, all children across the nation will have the opportunity to receive an excellent education. People are listening. (Kopp, 2003, back cover)

The metanarrative in this description contrasts with the metanarrative of the Civil Rights Movement. It is problematic to on one hand describe TFA this way while simultaneously trying to claim the title "new civil rights movement." TFA alumni Dr. Sondel and Dr. Kretchmar (2013) explained, "Though TFA consistently uses the language of the civil rights movement in its promotion and recruitment efforts, the organization stands in stark contrast to this justice-based rhetoric." It is inaccurate and problematic for TFA to appropriate the legacy, language, and authority of the 1960s Civil Rights Movement. TFA is not the new Civil Rights Movement.

The Civil Rights Movement was characterized by a "deep, reflective and locally driven approach" (Crawford-Garrett, 2013, p. 3) and was "majority-led by the oppressed group" (Rogers, 2013). It included a discussed history and process of development, grassroots organizing, mass direct action, community-wide protests, leading figures whose political identities often reflected the identities of the oppressed population they marched with, and a clear identification of oppression—indicating the existence of oppressors and oppressive forces (Garrow, 1978; Haley & X, 1964; Hanigan, 1984; Levy, 1998; Rogers, 2013; Washington, 1986).

In contrast, the narrative on Kopp's cover gives an ahistorical, colorblind account of meritocratic, underdog, heroic success. It tells a story of the movement to improve public education in America as beginning from Kopp's Princeton dorm room. It emphasizes the role of this twenty-one-year-old college senior, this "inspirational story of one young woman's tenacious grasp on a seemingly impossible dream," without acknowledging the decades of people who have labored before her for the cause of educational equity, without recognizing the people she's serving who—like anyone else—have and continue to want good for their own communities, without recognizing that this dream for justice existed long before her and continues, sometimes even existing in conflict with TFA's theory of change. Most people see a need for improvements in public education: in a 2014 poll of 1,800 individuals with children or grandchildren between the ages of 3 and 18, only 3% of respondents thought "the school system is fine as is," and 92% of respondents thought education is "the civil rights issue of our time" (Schoen, 2014, pp. 9–15). TFA's CEO Villanueva Beard's (2014) dismissal of TFA's dissenters as merely "folks [who] say the education system is 'fine' as it is" is a straw man argument. Structural educational equity can be the critical civil rights issue of this generation without TFA being the "New Civil Rights Movement."

Kopp's cover description also identifies TFA as "an organization created by and for young idealists," which contrasts with the Civil Rights Movement's identity of being created by and for the oppressed group. The front cover of *One Day, All Children* pictures the founding idealist, a white female Princeton graduate with a significant amount of power and privilege. TFA itself is an organization composed mostly of individuals whose racial and socioeconomic identities do not reflect those of their students (Lapayese et al., 2014; TFA: Who We Look For, 2014). When people now think back to the leaders of the Civil Rights Movement, leaders include allies of various other racial identities, but the most prominent leaders shared the particular identity of the people they led—the identity for which they were being politically and systemically persecuted (Barnett, 1993; Brown, 2002; Hanigan, 1984; Levy, 1998; Kim, 1999). The leaders of the Civil Rights Movement were working alongside the people who marched with them as much as they were working for them. The Civil Rights Movement included young idealists, but it was not created by and for young idealists.

As Noam Chomsky notes, it can be problematic for liberal intellectuals to "portray themselves and perceive themselves as challenging power, as courageous, as standing up for truth and justice. They are basically the guardians of the faith. They set the limits. They tell us how far we can go. They say, 'Look how courageous I am.' But do not go one millimeter beyond that. At least for the educated sectors, they are the most dangerous in supporting power" (cited in Hedges, 2010, p. 36).

The metanarrative of "One Day" and TFA as the "New Civil Rights Movement" positions TFA as equal stakeholders in this struggle, with as much to gain or lose as the people they are serving. While solidarity in the movement might be an aspiration, this language does not accurately describe current reality. For example, in addition to any differences in identity, CMs have the power to opt into and to quickly leave their schools in favor of another opportunity if they so choose—there are even recruiting events which will help them to do so. Most of the students and communities CMs serve do not have this privilege. Additionally, as CM Dionne and TFA alumnus and self-identified "critical friend" to the organization Dr. Royal describe, there is a difference in how CMs and students are impacted by TFA. TFA's narrative can focus on and benefit CMs, sometimes more than it does students and their communities, all while claiming they are "for the students":

> I think the messaging from TFA—and I've gotten this from multiple people—is not to have people stay in the classroom with kids, but to have people take this experience and to join whatever they do with this in their lives, which I think in some ways is really important. But I also think that that's not really having a focus on students. That's a focus on the CMs … Then when we're done with the program, we focus on CMs and the emphasis is less and less on the actual students. (Dionne)

> In too many instances, Teach For America does more for those who join it than for the students and communities it hopes to serve. If you do choose to Teach For America, please make sure your work improves more than just your life. (Royal, 2013)

Various CMs expressed cynicism with the TFA-endorsed narrative of "One Day" and questioned TFA's mission and effects as the "New Civil Rights Movement." Jane identified a disconnect between TFA's stated mission and TFA's actions and effects. Similarly, Aiden described CMs as disinvesting from TFA and becoming disillusioned with TFA's claim to "One Day." Maggie described TFA as an iron-fisted business that has built its brand and capitalizes on the premise of "One Day."

> Their whole mission "One day every child will whatever," I mean, that's great, but they're not doing that. (Jane)

> There are a lot of CMs who are giving up or surrendering on the mission. "One Day" has become an inside joke for people, where they chuckle at that principle. I think those ideas are very much eroded. At least within the Philadelphia corps culture, there's very little buy-in in terms of those corps values. Very little belief in them. (Aiden)

It goes back to the fear piece. TFA doesn't want to hear those things. Because if they hear those things, it shuts down on their main message. They don't want to hear it, because their whole brand is based on the "One day." "One day we're going to eradicate the problem of educational inequality" … I was in the Air Force, and [TFA staff] are trying to run [TFA] like an iron-fisted organization. TFA kind of can be an iron-fisted organization … it's like being in the military. In a lot of ways, more so than I realized … There is no "One Day" here. This is all business. (Maggie)

CMs highlighted problems with TFA appropriating the language of the Civil Rights Movement. TFA alumnus and staff member Stevona Rogers (2013) summarized ways TFA is not like and should not compare itself to the Civil Rights Movement:

I often find myself in meeting after meeting about students, families, community members, and teachers, and I am always perplexed about why the folks we are planning for are not in the room. Who are we to plan anything without the input of the folks we serve? While our efforts may be well-intentioned, this supports the notion that we are working on and not with communities. Now imagine a church, basement, classroom, or living room full of the people being served sharing their input about how the fate of their community should be handled. This is what the Civil Rights Movement was all about. We cannot continue to have conversations devoid of the people impacted by our decisions. When we master this concept we will be well on our way … The Civil Right Movement was majority-led by the oppressed group. While I'll never dismiss the power of having white allies, I believe until our organization truly reflects all the communities we serve we should dare not compare.

TFA says it is "embracing change" in a way that has potential to shift their work to a more local, egalitarian approach: Co-CEO Kramer stated, "We commit to aligning our placements with local demands, not national plans" (Villanueva Beard & Kramer, 2014); TFA's website explicitly supports "the importance of diversity" and states TFA is working to "increase our diversity and inclusiveness" (TFA: Who We Look For, 2014); recruitment efforts are shifting to encourage older and more experienced people to join TFA (Damast, 2012); and new training and development programs for CMs are being piloted in 2014 and 2015 (Villanueva Beard & Kramer, 2014). There are ways TFA is adapting and seeking to improve.

It is inaccurate and problematic to compare CMs to the leaders of the 1960s Civil Rights Movement or to position TFA as a new Civil Rights Movement. Jane stated, "When I think about the Civil Rights Movement, it was a fight for racial equality … TFA is only [addressing] half the battle. The other half is in the white privilege realm." Claiming TFA as the "New Civil

Rights Movement" discourages CMs from honestly naming their social location. Many CMs in this study acknowledged that they did not share the racial and socioeconomic identities of most of their students. CMs often expressed uncertainty about their social location and how it connected to the broader narratives of oppression and racial reconciliation. CMs can seek to build on the work of civil rights leaders, but this requires partnering with those who work for systemic change and acknowledging CMs' roles as both partner advocates and benefitting participants in the systems that oppress the students they serve.

Conclusion

Language matters because it communicates and shapes ideology; language indicates place, position, and power (Royal, 2012b). CMs found thematic problems with the "TFA script" in its application to both CMs and students. Points of critique included:

- The claim to absolutes found in "Nothing Elusive," "We Don't Back Down," and "No Excuses." CMs observed that their experiences were not this straightforward; CMs resisted this distortion of lived experiences. In an attempt to highlight the urgency of TFA's work, such slogans risk oversimplifying the struggle for educational equity and justice, allowing at best only oversimplified responses to historic inequity.
- The claim to the meritocracy as captured in "Work Hard, Get Smart" and "No Excuses." CMs grappled with the tension of what is and what should be; they resisted reducing historically and socially rooted struggles to issues of individual effort.
- The doublespeak and mislabeling in definitions of "more" and the appropriation of the Civil Rights language and narrative. CMs challenged positioning "more" in education as leaving the classroom and TFA as the new Civil Rights Movement. The claims to "more" and TFA as the new Civil Rights Movement are inaccurate and deceptive; there are euphemized falsehoods embedded in these grand narratives.
- Removing the struggle for educational equity from the landscape and history of race, class, and power as reflected by "Nothing Elusive," "Closing the Achievement Gap," "Work Hard, Get Smart," "No Excuses," and "New Civil Rights Movement." CMs expressed uncertainty over their participation in TFA highlighting the need of poor students of

color without asking how this need came to be. TFA speaks in the language of natural phenomenon and disenfranchisement and fails to recognize the intent, agents, mechanisms, and beneficiaries of created systems of oppression.

- Promoting a single story through slogans such as "Nothing Elusive," "Work Hard, Get Smart," "No Excuses," and "Data-Driven." Select examples of success in TFA are being presented as the norm in order to legitimate a specific theory of change. The anecdotes and data accompanying these slogans do not have to be fabricated to promote a false narrative. But select anecdotes and data can be championed and presented as a comprehensive narrative in a way that misrepresents reality. This metanarrative overlooks the important questions of what knowledge gets collected and prioritized, how phenomena are interpreted, and who has right to authorship.
- The narrative of "Nothing Elusive," "Closing the Achievement Gap," "Work Hard, Get Smart," and "No Excuses" positions as wholly individual what is, at its root, systemic. Education inequity is socially constructed and also needs to be spoken of and addressed as such.
- The effects of the script. CMs thought the TFA script inhibited needed dialogues, did not support their growth as helping professionals, and contributed to negative stereotypes about their students.

There is a gap between the TFA-endorsed narratives and what CMs experienced. Many CMs like Marie thought that TFA needed to change its messaging; CMs called for a more nuanced narrative which includes context, shared responsibility, and an acknowledgment of their lived experiences. Marie linked CMs' dissatisfaction to issues of conflicting narratives and theories of change. Marie believed TFA needed to "really look at the root" of CM dissatisfaction and respond accordingly; she stated, "They need different messaging, different expectations, and different responses to actual dissatisfaction." Still other CMs believed TFA's narrative and structure were so detached from reality as to render it ineffective, and they challenged the existence of TFA:

> If TFA works—because it's been around so long—if TFA works, then our education system would be fine right now. If it worked in line with their vision, and like all that shit happened, TFA wouldn't exist anymore. But it doesn't work … and putting five TFA teachers in a high-needs school and then leaving them to the dogs, it's not effective. It's not a broad enough approach. I don't really think they're the people to do the job. TFA may not fully understand the problem of schools … TFA fuels itself,

it's a self-fueling nonprofit. What is it—one of the richest nonprofits in the country? And what do we do? TFA's not the solution. (Jane)

CMs' counternarratives underscore the question of whether TFA's current discourse and approach are suited to addressing educational inequity. The challenges to public education have structural roots and existed long before TFA (Payne, 2008). TFA needs to reframe their conversations, approach, methods, and how they engage in this pressing work; how to respond to the complexity of what CMs and their students experience; and how to address the particular dynamics of politics and power which foundationally reinforce educational inequity.

Note

1. I recently learned about the origins of the phrase "drinking the Kool-Aid." "Drinking the Kool-Aid" is based on the collective misremembering of the 1978 massacre of over 900 people in a settlement in Jonestown, Guyana. Early news reports depicted the deaths as cult followers committing collective suicide by drinking cyanide-laced Kool-Aid. However, the deaths were not part of a mass-suicide, but a mass-murder: people were detained in the settlement against their will, senior citizens and children were targeted first and forced to drink the cyanide, and a Congressmen, news reporters, and concerned family members of the victims were also killed while investigating the allegations of human rights abuse. "Drinking the Kool-Aid" is based on the false premise of the initial news reports and became adopted into mainstream language to mean blindly following an ideology (Richardson, 2014). Though the phrase is problematic, several CMs used it in its colloquial definition as they described TFA's messaging. I was conflicted about including CMs' usage of this phrase, as I did not want to perpetuate false narratives, euphemize or trivialize murder, or denigrate the victims of Jonestown. I include CMs' descriptions of "Kool-Aid" and focus on what they explain "TFA Kool-Aid" to mean to them.

· 3 ·

UNEXPECTED LIFE CHANGES
TEACHING IN TFA

Counseling, Medical Prescriptions, Weight Changes, Increased Alcohol Consumption, Strained Relationships, Fatigue

"It's all related. Especially at the beginning of this year. I had problems with sleeping, my heart was constantly racing, I was having panic attacks like crazy, I did have to seek out counseling first year and second year, they did put me on anti-depressants, which I've recently gone off because I didn't like the way they made me feel. It's everything. It's all connected. You feel like you're not doing enough, and you work harder and harder. You work until you can't work anymore, and then you can't sleep because you feel guilty that you're not working. And it's this whole vicious cycle. It was ridiculous."

—Lola

While in TFA, CMs experienced a range of unexpected life changes not captured by the TFA-endorsed metanarrative. Contrary to the TFA narratives of "Nothing Elusive" and "Work Hard, Get Smart," CMs found the work of addressing educational inequity in their classrooms to be elusive and at times incomprehensible; CMs worked hard and still experienced both significant failures and unexpected negative life changes. These life changes include: needing professional counseling, needing prescription medications, major weight changes, increased alcohol consumption and dependency, strained relationships, and physical fatigue. CMs struggled to be present in their lived realities or to make sense of what they were experiencing.

TFA's "No Excuses" slogan and ideology interprets narratives that are out-side of or contrary to TFA's narrative as excuses. However, these life changes were not "excuses." Emerging patterns of alcohol dependency and needs for prescription medication are not calls to collectively try harder, ignore the needs of CMs, or press further into problematic aspects of TFA's narrative. CMs' negative life changes were often unacknowledged by TFA's narrative, even though these life changes were real parts of CMs' experiences. CMs' experiences call for a re-examination of TFA's narrative.

Of the CMs in this study, 25 of 26 reported at least one negative life change that was directly connected to their experience in TFA; many cited multiple negative life changes. The following graph is a visual representation of the 26 CMs' self-reported life changes:

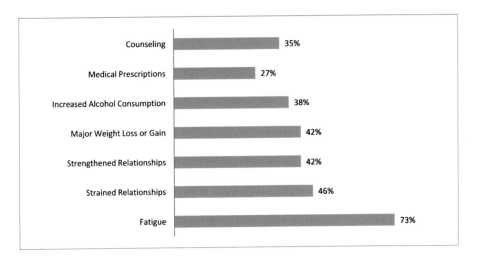

Figure 3.1. Life Changes Teaching as a TFA Greater Philadelphia Corps Member (% of CMs Who Have Experienced Change).

This data was made available to CMs in subsequent interviews and at the 2013 TFA/GSE Capstone Conference. Many CMs expressed that this data was reflective of what they experienced or witnessed among colleagues in the corps:

I was one of the people who attended your TFA/GSE Capstone presentation in May, and honestly, I was not that surprised because those were all trends I knew about to some degree or was kind of aware of the kind of stress that people were under … so it was not that surprising to me. The numbers matched up with what anecdotal evidence I have seen and heard in my time in the corps. It's heavy and it's hard to talk about … Given the level of strain people are under, I'm not at all surprised these numbers reflect that. (Aiden)

I certainly have a lot of friends who have experienced extreme anxiety, endured some degree of alcoholism, I don't know of anyone receiving therapy, but I wouldn't be surprised at all if people are. And I certainly have my fair share of friends who have broken into tears over this as well. (Bennett)

This is life-affirming—I'm not alone! … But there's all these people in TFA who don't talk about it … Like, you're not allowed to have these conversations [in TFA]. So I appreciate that you're opening these conversations and bringing these connections together, because I don't really get this [space] otherwise for me to process how this might be impacting me or impacting my students. (Dionne)

Marie was one of the few CMs in this study who had formal teacher preparation before joining TFA, but she said she still "really struggled." She experienced strained relationships during her first year and began seeing a therapist before the start of her second year, and expressed understanding over how other CMs were also struggling:

I feel like I handled TFA pretty well. I had a pretty clear expectation going in; there actually wasn't anything that was shocking to me. I had 4 years of teacher preparation, I knew it was going to be incredibly challenging. I majored in psychology education at the University of Delaware. I was interested in teaching secondary history. I kind of went into it with right expectations which kind of helped me. I definitely started drinking more from work-related stress, started counseling to talk about work, and some other things. Even having all the coursework beforehand and going in with the right expectations, I still feel like I really struggled—emotionally and mentally, especially in the first two years … I went into it with the right expectations and I was still overwhelmed. But at least I didn't have to deal with the shock part of it, whereas a lot of people did have to deal with it. (Marie)

After Jane reviewed this data, she paused to reflect on the fact that this is reflective of a sample of CMs who *stayed* in the corps. Jane shook her head as she thought about ways TFA does not consider the well-being of those active in the corps or acknowledge those who have left:

At our last All-Corps Saturday, they had a section with the mid-year survey results, and someone asked how many CMs have left, and [the TFA staff] said, "I can't tell you that yet." But it's a lot. It's a lot; 25% is the dropout rate right now, I think. It's really high. I think Philly actually has one of the highest dropout rates. I'd guess around 38 have left this year [from my corps year].

This chapter focuses primarily on the description of specific life changes experienced by these 26 TFAGP CMs; subsequent chapters provide further analysis of thematic causes, processes, effects, and underlying ideologies. These subheadings focus in greater detail on the experiences of CMs' life changes by category.

Counseling and Medical Prescriptions

"I snapped. I snapped at the end of last year. It would have never happened if I didn't have this job. I snapped, I did … It's totally a result of the work environment."

—Jane

Over half of the CMs in this study expressed a newfound need to seek professional counseling while in TFA. Thirty-five percent of CMs began therapy and cited anxiety, stress, depression, and trauma as the most common reasons for seeking out professional support. To address her newly emergent anxiety and depression as a CM, Adrian found support and counseling resources through her church community:

> The primary reason [I started counseling] was to learn how to deal with my anxiety and depression. The resources were readily available through my church community. During my first year of teaching I had almost no time for myself. I was exhausted and I suffered from anxiety. My second year I had more time but slumped into more of a depression. During college I worked around the clock too, however, my activities were much less draining than teaching a room full of students—both emotionally and physically. (Adrian)

An additional 19% of CMs considered seeing a counselor but did not pursue this option because of various constraints. When asked, "Have you sought out professional counseling since you've started teaching? Why or why not?", some explained:

> No—sounds stupid but honestly I don't know where I would find the time. I have considered going to a therapist. I have talked to the social workers/psychologists at my school. (Leigh)

> No. I would have if they had been more accessible, more affordable (my school's health plan doesn't cover mental health), and if I had more time. (Aiden)

> No. I don't know where to access them, and I don't have time to pursue this outlet. (Taylor)

I was thinking about it (my instructional coach at school also said she recommends counseling to most teachers she coaches) but I didn't have the time to look into it very much. I definitely would have, though, if time had not been an issue. (Mark)

Lack of time was cited as the most common barrier to pursuing counseling. Kate could not find time to take care of her physical health, and questioned when she would have time to even consider therapy sessions—"I don't even have time to go the doctor when I need to, so I HIGHLY doubt I would have the time to go to regular sessions."

Even those who prioritized counseling faced scheduling difficulties. For example, Josh sought out a therapist after joining TFA and described therapy as "extremely helpful for me," but he had trouble finding a counselor with evening hours compatible with his work schedule. Many CMs identified a need for emotional support in TFA, but described lacking the time, energy, financial means, knowledge, or support to obtain the help they needed.

Many CMs wanted TFA to provide greater behavioral health support to CMs. CMs were struggling while in TFA and critiqued TFA's lack of resources related to behavioral health and TFA's lack of acknowledgment of behavioral health struggles. Maggie thought TFA needed a dean of culture to advocate for CMs as CMs work alongside their students; Maggie stated that there was a needed position for someone whose "job is not to make sure you're doing 110%; their job is honest to goodness take a pulse and be that advocate [for CMs]." Similarly, Lola thought TFA needed to offer CMs counselor services, a help line, or a support person for CMs: "If you can't sleep, or if you're having panic attacks, someone who is just understanding and will listen to you."

Twenty-seven percent of CMs began taking prescription medications in TFA—this group only includes those who previously had not taken prescription medication. For example, Kate had taken anti-anxiety and anti-depression medication prior to the corps, so she was not included in the 27% statistic.

These 27% of CMs identified newfound work-related panic, stress, anxiety, depression, and trauma as the reasons for needing prescription medications to cope. This 27% does not include those who began taking medications for any physical health problems, such as acid reflux medication tied to a binge drinking problem developed during TFA. This 27% does not include those who had panic attacks but did not begin taking medication. For example, Mark, Nicole, and Maggie chose not see a counselor or take medications even though they each suffered multiple panic attacks:

Last year I had a number of panic attacks for the first time in my life. Last year, when I thought about all of the work I had to do in such a short amount of time, I would start to tense up and pass out. It happened 3–4 times from September 'to October '2011—my first two months of teaching. This never happened to me before—even through law school. (Nicole)

I only suffer from acute panic attacks because I'm afraid that I'll be labeled a fraud and fake and be dismissed as a result! (Maggie)

Of those who did begin taking prescription medication, Lola said of her experience:

I've had several panic attacks. I went to the hospital and got prescriptions. I got Xanax and Zoloft but I never took Xanax because I was scared I'd become addicted to it. I took Zoloft for 3 months but stopped because I felt not myself, very numbed, like I had no emotions. That could be part of why I didn't feel ashamed anymore [after taking the medication]—because I had no feelings at all! Then I got mad. I'd never felt like this but for TFA. I've never had to take antidepressants before, never been depressed before, never felt this bad about myself, never felt like this much of a failure until I joined TFA.

Increased Alcohol Consumption

"It is ridiculous that this intense amount of alcoholism is present and permeating the organization."

—Dionne

While in TFA, 38% of CMs experienced an increase in the frequency and change in the nature of their alcohol consumption. The 38% includes CMs who began drinking in TFA in a way that was previously unprecedented in their lives:

My alcohol intake has definitely increased. I have never thrown up while drinking before joining TFA. I have drank to the point that I threw up twice since joining TFA. I drink far more since I started teaching. (Dionne)

I feel like I "need" a drink during the week after work in a way I never felt before. (Devon)

Increased consumption, for sure. The advice I received my first day at work from a fellow teacher was "drink a lot of alcohol." (Reagan)

Oh dear! This is embarrassing. I have taken to drinking at least one full glass of wine every night while I lesson plan and create PowerPoints. I have noticed that I crave that glass in ways that I never have before. (Maggie)

Like Maggie, Bernadette and Leigh also described a change in the nature of their drinking patterns. Maggie described it as a craving. Bernadette identified a change in why she was drinking: "I was drinking alone more and really drinking more to force myself to relax, reflect, forget than to just to be social." Similarly, Leigh recounted, "In college I would drink for fun, now I drink to relieve stress or unwind after a hard day or week. Common response you hear—'I've had a tough day' equates to 'I need a drink.'"

Sofia directly linked her experience in TFA to alcohol dependency. When asked on the initial survey if she experienced a change in her relationship to alcohol, Sofia responded, "YESSSSSSS. Huge increase in consumption of alcohol. Black outs/brown outs every weekend. I just had this conversation with my physician and other TFA friends. I really believe being a teacher has led me to have an alcohol dependency."

A petite female, Sofia began drinking regularly and consuming at least 5–6 drinks each time she went out. In a follow-up interview, Sofia described how she realized her relationship to alcohol had changed in a problematic way during a break from teaching. Her doctor also helped to identify her habits as binge drinking:

My drinking level has increased dramatically since I joined TFA. I noticed that when I was in California for spring break, I was drinking more than anyone else there. They all seemed to have healthy work-life balances, whereas I was drinking more than 5–6 drinks to feel anything. It was blatant to me when I was hanging out with people who weren't working in my region [TFAGP] …

Recently I'm having issues where I'm having acid reflux problems, and I consulted my physician on this. She asked me, "How much have you been drinking?" And I responded, "Your standard 5–6 drinks" She told me, "That's actually binge drinking." Then we talked about the fact that I'm a TFA teacher. (Sofia)

In addition to health professionals identifying alcohol dependency, several family members or friends outside of TFA expressed concern to some CMs about their new drinking patterns. For example, Robin's nightly tequila shots worried her girlfriend:

The beginning of my second year, I was drinking every night, and I wasn't drinking to black or brown out. But I would have 4 shots of tequila. I have never blacked out, but my girlfriend was concerned that I was developing bad patterns because I was having tequila shots every day … In hindsight, I think this may have been related to stress.

Maggie, age 46 and the oldest CM in this study, initially thought alcohol dependency might be common in the relatively young corps because TFA recruits recent college graduates. But when she joined TFA, she realized her relationship to alcohol was also changing:

> I guess I knew that there was a lot more alcohol [in TFA], but I kind of just attributed it to the things college-aged kids do.

> I can only speak for myself. I was shocked by how quickly I got into the habit of drinking wine in the evening while I'm lesson planning, or just during the course of my week, and doing so in a way I never did, never, ever, before going into TFA.

> I worked twenty hours in my kids' schools for seven years as the support person, and I never—I would drink socially once a week or weekend, and that was it. So [realizing] that was like, "Whoa, Houston, this is kind of big," where you look forward to [drinking], and you do it, and it becomes a habit. So that was a bit shocking to me. (Maggie)

This 38% does not include those like Drake, Kate, and Elliott whose alcohol intake remained the same or decreased. Several CMs like Drake explained that their demanding work schedule translated to less time to drink socially— "I drink less now than I did in college, mostly because I don't have the time to do so anymore." Kate described a change in craving alcohol in TFA, but she did not think this constituted a significant life change because her purpose in drinking was not to get drunk: "I can't say that I didn't like alcohol before, but now I crave a beer or wine when I get home. I don't drink to get drunk." Elliott experienced an increase in the frequency of his alcohol consumption, but he was not included in the 38% because his drinking leveled out after the first semester:

> I drank more in my first semester teaching than I ever did in college. However, since then, I drink less than I did in college. I may get drunk once a month … I drink alcohol probably once a weekend. I simply don't have time for that—I work a lot on weekends, and I'd rather be working than nursing a hangover. I also don't feel the need—I love my job, even though it does cause considerable stress.

Dione commented on ways she saw TFA culture and programming supporting the intense drinking she witnessed in the corps. Alcoholism was normalized and treated like another necessary cost to "closing the achievement gap," or a way of coping with the stressors of "closing the achievement gap." Dione shared one example of this condoned normalization and described a mandatory, corps-wide TFA training in which a literacy specialist on TFA staff and a CM performed a skit using the vocabulary word "drunk" to demonstrate the use of a vocabulary graphic organizer. This skit acknowledged the prevalence of alcoholism without acknowledging the problematic reality that there are CMs becoming heavily dependent on alcohol to cope with their TFA experience. Dionne concluded,

> It is ridiculous that this intense amount of alcoholism is present and permeating the organization ... The culture of TFA does support this, this high level of drinking. It's very much normalized. (Dionne)

Major Weight Loss or Gain

"I lost about 20 pounds my second year of teaching due to stress and depression."
—Adrian

Forty-two percent of CMs experienced major weight loss or gain in TFA. CMs noted that their weight fluctuations were symptomatic of deeper causes such as stress, limited time to eat or exercise, and a work-affected lifestyle that precluded self-care.

Adrian stated that she lost 20 pounds from stress and depression in TFA. Josh reported losing 20 pounds in his first year. Kate said she did not have the time or desire to eat and as a result dropped to her pre-adolescent weight; from one year in TFA she "lost about 5–10 pounds (less than I've weighed probably since like 5th grade) because I don't have the time or desire to eat." Jane lost 10 pounds her first year teaching and described her weight loss in the context of not having time to "keep up with life" and take care of herself:

> I work about 80+ hours a week and my free time is spent keeping up with the life I've been ignoring (bills, talking with family members, maintaining a relationship, chores). I've lost about 10 pounds since I've started teaching. (Jane)

Lola lost 15 pounds in one year from stress:

> What is free time? When not at work, I'm still working. Sometime I get Saturdays off. My life is depressing and not fun. I don't get enough sleep. I don't take care of myself (showers, makeup, eating, exercise). I have lost about 15 pounds because I don't have time to eat and I'm walking around all day. (Lola)

Robin also experienced major weight fluctuation in TFA, as one of multiple responses to the stress:

> I barely have any free time now. My physiological reaction to stress and my mental attempts to combat stress … I've never had an eating disorder before, but my weight has fluctuated within around 30 pounds. From first year in TFA I became 15 pounds underweight and weighed less than I did in high school, and now I'm 20 pounds over what I started out as. I've been fluctuating a lot and it's been going up and down. I also got really sick my first year. (Robin)

In considering the impacts of their work-related stress, CMs found that they were suffering as both individuals and in their roles as teachers. Sofia summarized this concern expressed by other CMs as well:

> Physically I gained weight. I gained weight both my first and second year. Physically as well, my energy levels are very, very low when I'm stressed out. I have no energy, and I'm not as an effective teacher when I'm this stressed out. (Sofia)

Relationship Changes

"I don't plan to rebuild relationships until this summer. I honestly don't feel I can rebuild friendships in a genuine way until this experience ends."
—Nicole

In facing the stress of their work, some CMs found an opportunity to connect with others in ways that strengthened their relationships. Some felt bonded through facing, sharing, or discussing their struggles. Forty-two percent of CMs experienced strengthened relationships with significant others, friends, family, roommates, coworkers, corps members, or students:

> I do an after-school club that allows me to interact with students in a different way that replenishes my energy to teach. I have deeper relationships with children, especially my students. They are the people I get the most life-giving energy from. I didn't know how important having children around me was until I started TFA. (Dionne)

> I am very lucky in that I have many friends (TFA and non-TFA), coworkers, and family members who support me and whom I can confide in. I broke up with my girlfriend of one and a half years, but that was also due to long distance. I've made many valuable and lasting friendships [in TFA]. (Josh)

> My relationships with my girlfriend and close friends have grown stronger through the experience. [Though] I am opposed to a lot of what's happening in education

reform right now—and I even have very mixed feelings about being a TFA corps member. (Alex)

For many, the stress of teaching in TFA resulted in strains on their relationships. 46% of CMs experienced strained relationships with family, friends, and significant others:

My relationship, at the beginning of teaching and through institute, was really strained and there were many times it seemed like it wouldn't work out because he believed I was a workaholic who would never focus on anything but work. (Kate)

Strained relationships: Unfortunately, I have made plans a number of times with friends and simply canceled them. I was too tired at night from teaching or too stressed with the amount of work due. Luckily, my friends are fairly understanding, but they do not call nearly as much as they used to. I don't plan to rebuild relationships until this summer. I honestly don't feel I can rebuild friendships in a genuine way until this experience ends. (Nicole)

I feel guilty that I'm neglecting my relationships. My mom has had several interventions with me where she tells me, "I'm worried about you. I don't even recognize you anymore." Same with my grandparents. I ignore those who are closest to me because I just don't have time for the other things. (Lola)

I was in a pretty abusive relationship and I know had I not had such a stressful job, I would have not gotten into it or I would have gotten out of it a lot faster. Work was a huge factor in why I stayed in it for so long. It was kind of like, well, I'm already really stressed out at my job so I can't also deal with anything outside of that. Which is a really terrible reason to stay in a relationship. (Marie)

I got engaged after only teaching for a few weeks and some of the biggest arguments we've gotten into as a couple are because I can't manage my stress and I lash out out of stress. Sometimes I feel like teaching is so stressful, I can't handle any stressors outside the workplace. (Jane)

Kate, Nicole, and Lola explained that their time-intensive workloads were often incompatible with maintaining relationships outside of teaching. Nicole, Marie, and Jane explicitly identified work stress as a cause for strain in their relationships.

Fatigue & Changes in Sleep

"I felt like I had almost killed myself. It felt like if I had worked any harder, I would die."
—Robin

In TFA, Leigh described experiencing "fatigue—a constant tiredness that I never experienced before." The majority of CMs described regularly working themselves to the point of extreme exhaustion and deterioration of their physical health. Seventy-three percent of CMs surveyed described feeling fatigued, some to the point of needing to see a doctor:

> I was pretty fatigued my first year. I used to fall asleep during my preps and struggle to keep awake on my drive to school. (Adrian)

> I fainted regularly during the school day. (Lola)

> I am always fatigued; I can almost always feel the stress present in my neck and shoulders. (Jane)

> I have never been to the doctor for fatigue before teaching. I have gone twice since teaching. (Dionne)

> I kept social pace and met TFA/PENN/school commitments with fidelity but am just exhausted. Any free time is allocated for sleep. Daily/weekly routine is dramatically different. Just about every moment is consumed with—if not actually doing something for school—talking and thinking about the children, and what's happening next. (Bernadette)

Linked to fatigue, 85% of CMs also experienced negative changes in their sleep patterns—either not having enough time to sleep, having difficulties falling or staying asleep, or having nightmares. Some CMs did not experience negative changes in their sleep pattern, and Marie was the only one to experience a positive change in her sleep patterns, explaining, "I actually sleep better now, probably because I am so exhausted!"

Ariel's response characterizes the response of the 85% who experienced negative changes in sleep patterns: "I sleep a lot less, and often have teaching-related nightmares." Stephen, Jordan, Aiden, Mark, and Josh each experienced a decrease in quantity and quality of sleep in TFA:

> I have difficulty falling to sleep. I'm ALWAYS tired. (Stephen)

> Poor quality of sleep, sleep much less. (Jordan)

> Decrease in quantity of sleep. I generally am able to fall asleep fairly well, but I have started having nights where it takes me more than an hour to fall asleep, which I never had before. (Aiden)

> At the beginning of the year, I had a hard time falling asleep. Even after I fell asleep, I would wake up several times throughout the night, kind of like mini panic attacks. (Mark)

I fall asleep less easily, sleep less on the whole, and sometimes have lower-quality sleep. I do not remember my dreams, but I am often anxious when falling asleep or waking up. (Josh)

Reagan, Jane, and Elliott also experienced a decrease in quantity and quality of sleep in TFA; they found themselves staying up in an effort to keep up with their workloads, waking up through the night thinking about their teacher preparation work, or waking up in the morning thinking about work. Elliott identified teaching as "an 18-hour-a-day occupation of my mind":

Less sleep, less quality. No nightmares but a lot of anxiety when I wake up thinking of everything I have to do. (Reagan)

I either fall asleep quickly and can stay asleep or it takes me a long time to put the stresses of teaching aside and relax. I often wake up every two hours wondering about each step of the teaching cycle (Guided Practice, Independent Practice, Exit Ticket, etc.). (Jane)

At the very beginning, I would dream about school. Now, I basically have dreamless sleep ... However, when I wake up, my mind is immediately on school. It's basically an 18-hour-a-day occupation of my mind. (Elliott)

In addition to decreased quantity and quality of sleep, many CMs also had frequent nightmares about traumatic memories or feared scenarios:

After witnessing a shooting this year, I had persistent nightmares about guns and gun violence. Frequent dreams about being forced to deal with unmanageable school situations ... Sleep patterns are worse—issues with sleeping, and feeling over tired more often. (Leigh)

Nightmares are a huge thing. I was getting 4–5 hours of sleep every night. I would wake up with nightmares of not being prepared. The everyday deadline was so new and stressful. And there could be physical violence in my room if I wasn't prepared. (Robin)

I never used to dream, and I have anxiety dreams now. My dreams often relate to my students not coming with me. I don't know what we're getting to or running from. I am tired almost constantly. (Taylor)

I actually don't think I've had any recurring dreams or nightmares related to school, but my dreams are definitely infiltrated by thoughts of school or skewed scenarios involving the children (i.e., my students in a context outside of the school). (Bernadette)

Hard to fall asleep. I dream about school and work so it's not restful or relaxing. Only about 5–6 hours of sleep per night. (Lola)

My first year: I fell asleep really late last year. I was always falling asleep with my computer on my lap. I would stay up, thinking about the next day. My dreams focused on teaching a lot. This year: I fall asleep by 10, or 10:30. I sleep much more soundly, because I'm not as nervous about how things are going to go the next day. (Nicole)

Many nights I dream about teaching or about my students, some positive, some negative. (Kate)

My first year, I couldn't sleep when my behavior management was at its worst. Last week I was a wreck due to the added stress of fundraising, lost sleep, my kids noticed, gained weight, etc. ... I tend to have nightmares related to school when this stress/cortisol levels rise. (Sofia)

Bennett interpreted the frequency of nightmares as a combination of work stress and the demographic of TFA as individuals who are "passionate" about their mission:

I think everyone has some kind of nightmare at some point. I think that's part of the initiation process ... we've all had anxiety going to school teaching ... I think it's indicative of a group of people who are as passionate as we are. We wear our hearts on our sleeves to some gradient, and if you hold it on the inside it's going to come out in some way, shape, or form. (Bennett)

Is This TFA, Philadelphia, or First-Year Teaching?

"Is this TFA or first year of teaching? I think it's a bit of both."

—Jane

Bennett, Aiden, Jane, Lola, Maggie, Marie, and Elliott each contextualized some of the changes they observed. CMs noted that their experiences as a group were possibly different from CMs in other cities and questioned what of their struggles were directly connected to working in TFA, the public education system in Philadelphia, or public education generally.

Aiden and Bennett questioned what of these changes were tied to TFA versus changes tied to the education landscape in Philadelphia:

How do you separate what's happening in Philadelphia with what's happening in TFA nationally? It's impossible to extrapolate without looking closely at other regions. (Aiden)

I would argue that Philly is probably one of the worst in the country. I know that statistically speaking, TFA Philly approval ratings are lower than most of the others in the country. We're not the lowest, but we're one of the lowest. On the CM level, TFA Philly is very, very low … And there's Philadelphia itself, which is experiencing one of the worst education crises, the closing of all the different schools like in New Orleans where charter networks have taken over, and it is a big blow to people who are committed to closing the achievement gap. (Bennett)

Jane, Lola, and Maggie questioned what of these changes were tied to TFA versus changes tied to first-year teaching, urban education, teacher preparation, or their schools:

> I lost 20 pounds this year. I fainted regularly during the school day … I don't know if this is my school problem or if this is a TFA problem. I did reach out to TFA because all of the CMs at our school were having difficulties … All crazy things like fatigue, sleep deprivation, estranged relationships, etc. I did reach out, as did everyone in my corps. (Lola)

> I think we've been in a leadership vacuum for a few years now. There's just been a real big shuffle and we have major turnovers and inconsistency … and they don't know what to do with themselves. They don't know how to come up with a statement of purpose when they're just going off of knee-jerk reactions … It's the hardest stuff; they don't want to talk about it, and that's not just TFA—it's the schools that we're in, the administration, the teaching teams … that's the stuff they don't want to address because that's the stuff you can't control. All that's time and money. (Maggie)

Marie and Elliott thought these changes were not all caused by TFA and that these experiences were not exclusive to CMs:

> I don't think that this experience is unique to TFA CMs, I think it's an urban education problem and a teacher prep problem. (Marie)

> The conditions this year are separate from TFA to an extent. Personally, I don't blame TFA. I think TFA's influence is limited. I think they make the situation worse. They don't create the entire situation. (Elliott)

Research bolsters Maggie's statement that there are major challenges to teacher preparation and retention in hard-to-staff, poor, urban schools (Ingersoll, 2001; Prince, 2003; Shernoff et al., 2011). But even if TFA did not create this problem, in seeking to address historic inequities, TFA is responsible for how it defines, approaches, and influences change. It is questionable why TFA promotes a reform narrative to other educators, students, and communities without acknowledging the narrative's impact on its own CMs.

Conclusion

"What's not ok with this, it's just like how with our kids we need to be sensitive to their needs, you know, they matter, they're human beings. CMs have needs. Take care of them … [TFA] is ignoring the needs of our CMs! It's coming from a place of ignorance a lot of times."

—Elliott

Teaching in TFA was not what many CMs had expected. From increased alcohol consumption to strained relationships to fatigue, CMs experienced a range of life changes not captured by the TFA-endorsed metanarrative.

A recurring theme emerged in this study: many CMs felt they lacked the time, energy, or necessary supports from TFA to take care of themselves on a fundamental level. Aiden stated, "CMs just need more support than they're receiving." Some CMs felt misled by TFA in what support they could expect as CMs. Drake stated of TFA: "My main issue is that the support they advertise is not the support we get."

CMs theoretically agreed with the importance of self-care, but most described being unable to practically engage in self-care. Sofia, Jane, Robin, Elliott, Aiden, Dionne, Maggie, Lola, and Bennett each acknowledged the importance of self-care for themselves as individuals and in their role as teachers. Jane stated, "I'm not going to be my best teacher—I'm not going to be a good teacher—if I don't take care of myself." Bennett explained, "Obviously teaching was my number one priority and I did my damndest to get as good as I could. But … my saving grace was my ability to separate from work when I needed to." CMs experienced that they are better teachers when they take care of themselves, though they frequently experienced internal and external pressure to devote all their resources to teaching. The pressing injustices they witnessed combined with limited resources and a lack of support meant CMs often sacrificed their own health in some way for their work. Maggie summarized:

> [CMs] don't have time to take care of themselves. I do know the ones who have their heads above water are the ones who are actively exercising and taking care of themselves. But that's not the case for everybody. Not everyone is engaging in that practice and making that a priority. I'll be the first to say, if I were to be more consistent with that, I'd probably be in a better emotional state right now. But I'm not.

CMs had little framework to understand and interpret their negative life changes. CMs' negative life changes were largely unacknowledged—or when acknowledged, these negative experiences were misinterpreted—by TFA as an organization. Often, these life changes were addressed privately if at all and were interpreted by TFA and CMs as CMs' personal failures. Many CMs were borrowing against themselves to survive their TFA commitments. It is unsustainable and problematic for a group of helping professionals to be experiencing extreme negative life changes from their work, and then additionally problematic that these struggles are interpreted as CMs' personal excuses or ways CMs are failing students, or interpreted as a need for these CMs to work harder. It is precisely because some of these CMs were working so hard to live up to the TFA narrative that some of these negative life changes emerged (see Chapter 4, 5, and 7).

Emerging patterns of alcohol dependency and needs for prescription medication are not invitations to collectively try harder or press further into the narrative that exacts these costs and encourages these dehumanizing behaviors. It calls for a re-examination of the narrative. Ignoring CMs' humanity is a misguided and an ineffective means of addressing students' dehumanization in the education system.

These patterns of negative life changes are problematic for CMs both as people, regardless of their professional positions, and as helping professionals who are given significant responsibility to teach and extend care to their students. It is difficult for CMs to extend the best care possible to students when many struggle to care for themselves on a fundamental level. To illustrate, a recent exploratory study of 27 teachers and their 523 third graders found that the more depressive symptoms teachers had, the less progress in math their struggling students made during the school year; teachers' mental health affected the classroom learning environment and students' academic growth (Doyle, 2015; McLean & McDonald Connor, 2015). Though researchers have yet to pinpoint the cause,[1] teachers are shown to have higher rates of depression than the general population (Doyle, 2015).

TFA did not create educational inequity, but in seeking to address historic inequities, TFA is responsible for how it defines, approaches, and influences change. The extent of TFA's responsibility to care for its CMs can be debated, but TFA does have at least partial responsibility for the well-being of its CMs.[2] CMs struggled to be present in the realities they faced while teaching in TFA. CMs experienced negative life changes while in TFA, and they reported engaging in behaviors to help them cope with or avoid the painful challenges they faced. Beyond TFA's required responsibilities, if TFA wants to "invest in leaders [and] help these leaders increase their impact and deepen their understanding of what it takes to eliminate educational inequity" (TFA: Our Mission, 2014), then TFA needs to support CMs in their struggle to be present and respond constructively to the realities they experience. Aiden summarized, "CMs don't get the support they would need to drive the highest level of success."

Dionne questioned, "How come this experience is only useful to a CM after their two years of service? But while they're in TFA, and working in schools, and in graduate school, why are we not focusing on CMs then, and their health then?" As Elliott stated, people in professional helper positions still have needs, and they also need to be cared for. An institution focused on helping others must also listen to the needs of its own helping professionals. Additionally, it is questionable why TFA promotes a reform narrative to other educators, students, and communities without acknowledging the narrative's negative impacts on its own CMs.

Prescribing an untrue narrative has damaging effects on individuals and systems. Untrue narratives misstate the challenges at hand, skew what resources are needed to address these challenges, and set unrealistic expectations of what can be accomplished through the prescribed method. Burning through people has individual and systemic repercussions. Individually, CMs are valuable as people and as new teachers. Systemically, burning through people wastes the precious resources of CMs, promotes teacher burnout and attrition, contributes to the transience and instability of what is already often an unstable environment, and can cause harm where the intentions were to help.

Notes

1. According to the coauthor of the study, McLean, at this point, it is unclear whether the stress of teaching may leave teachers more vulnerable to depression, or the type of person who becomes a teacher also tends to be more sensitive emotionally, or both.

2. Originally, I approached my thesis as a working paper: researching to better understand the problematic phenomenon I was witnessing and with intentions of presenting findings and recommendations to TFA. As such, my early work included a focus on immediate actionable steps for the institution to better support its CMs. In Philadelphia, I spoke with both of my MTLDs about these observations, e-mailed recommendations to the TFA staff, and also presented my findings at the TFA and Penn Graduate School of Education Master's Capstone Conference. Both CMs and staff affiliated with the TFA/Penn partnership were in attendance. By invitation of TFA Hawai'i, I presented my research findings and recommendations to their regional chair, director of development and external

partnerships, managing director of external affairs, and managing director of teacher leadership development. I prefaced that I had limited localized knowledge of their corps, but provided my questions and findings to inform them of potential places of investigation and improvement. As a group of leaders in the institution, they were open, critically reflective, and constructively focused; they gave me hope for what positive growth could look like in TFA. In addition to copies of my paper and surveys, I also provided a summary of immediate, practical next steps for the TFA office to better support CMs (see Appendix D: Recommendations to TFA Staff).

· 4 ·

THE REALITY OF TRAUMA IN TFA

Trauma is defined by the American Psychological Association (APA) as an emotional response to a terrible event. People respond to trauma differently: some will have no ill effects, others may experience an immediate and acute effect, and others may not show signs of stress until after the event (Trauma, 2013). Trauma is inherently difficult to talk about, and how a person experiences and responds to trauma can change over time.

Many CMs experienced trauma in TFA. Ariel described herself as "stressed, traumatized, over-worked" in TFA; this was a common response among CMs. John, Aiden, Jane, Maggie, and Marie commented on the pervasiveness of trauma in TFA. John stated, "I thought TFA had a culture of people who were in over their heads … I was surprised by how many people seemed shell shocked."

Robin identified and described her experience with trauma:

Your perspective gets so skewed because you're under water. It becomes so hard to understand reality. It feels like you're high. I'm not sure if this is reality, or that is reality. That's my understanding of the situation. I didn't know why I was crying, but for like 3 weeks I began crying at the beginning of the 2nd year. I don't know if that resurfaced because of trauma, and I felt like I had almost killed myself. It felt like if I had worked any harder, I would die.

From their time in therapy with professional psychiatrists and psychologists, their personal reflection, and their independent research on the topic, CMs identified helplessness, primary trauma, Post-Traumatic Stress Disorder (PTSD), secondary trauma, and vicarious traumatization as part of their experiences in TFA.

I approach writing this chapter with caution, because interpreting trauma narratives is complicated work. People have trauma stories in TFA, and it is an act of interpretation to understand the meaning of these stories individually or collectively.

Three points to consider before continuing with this chapter: firstly, the nature of this discussion highlights pain and trauma, but I am not suggesting that these are students' only or defining characteristics. I do not intend these portraits to support deficit views about students. Secondly, CMs and students as individuals and as groups might have very different experiences of any mentioned events; their experiences are connected, but also distinct. Both sets of experiences and perspectives are significant, and in this book, I focus primarily on CMs' experiences. Thirdly, I am not a professional counselor. As a layperson, I want to convey CMs' stories honestly and communicate some of the trends they shared from their counseling sessions, but I do not want to claim greater authority on mental health issues than I have. To address this concern, Philadelphia-based family therapist Susanne Flood and social worker Nathan Lee reviewed this section and provided guidance and feedback.

Helplessness

Trauma is characterized by a debilitating sense of helplessness and loss of control (Gil, 1996). CMs regularly faced obstacles they did not feel equipped to address and were held to standards they were unable to attain, causing them to experience new depths of helplessness while in TFA. Jordan described struggling with "feelings of failure and despair." CMs described feeling powerless, insufficient, unable to help themselves or their students, unable to accomplish what they had initially set out to accomplish, unable to impact significant changes. Feeling helpless was traumatic for many CMs.

Jane, John, and Maggie described the connection between helplessness and trauma. Jane described the burdens of expectations she could not meet in spite of her best efforts, of facing systemic injustice and constantly feeling helpless to make any significant change:

As far as primary trauma goes, just failing every day when for a really long time when the stakes are really high. It's really hard. My first year teaching, I would wake up at 3 o'clock in the morning every day worrying about guided practice. Every day! And it seems like something small, but again, the pressure you put on yourself and the pressure that's being put on you, it seems like the biggest deal in the world. (Jane)

John described how CMs faced "constant obstacles" and "crisis after crisis after crisis" with limited support. CMs' resulting feelings of helplessness contributed to the pervasiveness of "shell shock" in TFA:

We're talking about constant obstacles, every single thing you want to accomplish after every single day … it's just crisis after crisis after crisis, particularly if TFA is not going to support you … many people seemed shell shocked. (John)

Maggie described CMs as overwhelmed, disoriented, unsure of how to cope with the environment of scarcity, and unsure of whether they had power to make any meaningful changes. The normalized expectations for achievement in TFA were so high that they were unattainable:

Feeling insufficient … that's really hard to handle … The whole, "What the hell am I doing?" Every first year teacher struggles with things to some different degree, to fundamentally not know the curriculum—that's going to be a bit overwhelming. And it's going to call into question your ability to do this job, over and over and over again. And on top of that, you're dealing with the lack of support from your school, the lack of supplies, the lack of space, the lack of time … all the deficits. And then you set yourself up for, someone comes in supposedly knows what they're doing and tells you you don't know what you're doing. You're going to be so low, your sense of self, your sense of ability. It's hard to recover from that. (Maggie)

Environmental instability contributed to CMs' feelings of helplessness. CMs described being moved between schools or classes, or having students leave their schools midyear with no explanation. Bennett shared, "I knew a child that I've spent hours and hours mentoring that the next day never showed up to school, never showed up again … We've seen it. And I'm sure this is not unusual for other teachers out there." Leigh described the instability of being assigned to teach chemistry class in her first year though she was not certified as a science teacher. John was part of forced transfers and also taught outside of his subject:

I've worked in 5 different schools over 2 years. It was part of a forced transfer by the district, where the district basically says you're the last person in this school and we have a budget cut or resource allocation problem, so we're going to move you. So I was moved quite a bit. On the first day of my placement, I was trained to teach history, and I was teaching math. It was chaos. It was a shit show. (John)

Dionne described the constant fluctuation and instability of poverty:

> Our kids are used to constant fluctuation. In general, poverty and the structure of a lot of resources available to their community are stretched. It's way more difficult, if not impossible, to see things through. Because they're not adequately funded, or people leave, and there's turnover of staff … in poverty a lot of times, things are not consistent. (Dionne)

Environmental instability makes it difficult for people to invest deeply in work or relationships. It is difficult to establish stable, trusting, teaching relationships when both teachers and students are frequently and abruptly being moved. It is difficult to claim agency in a situation that is in constant flux.

CMs joined TFA with expectations of what they could accomplish and many had come from positions of power. It was traumatizing for many CMs to feel powerless and helpless.

Primary Trauma

Many CMs experienced traumatic situations firsthand, including though not limited to breaking up physical altercations and witnessing verbal and physical violence.

CMs were confronted with a significant number and range of traumatic experiences in their work. Lola started seeing a counselor and taking anti-depressants and anti-anxiety medication after joining TFA; when asked if she experienced trauma in TFA, Lola gave examples of trauma from her past week alone:

> Just in the last week, I can count numerous instances … there were 2 fights this week, and I was in the middle of both of them. My 10th grade girls, they got into a lot of fights in October, during my breakdown they were getting in fights, and that made my breakdown additionally hard because I love these girls, and I've gotten really close with them for 2 years, and to see them get in a fight and to see them hurt each other really hurt me … There are 2 cliques all in my 6th period class. As they're leaving they get into this huge fight in the hallway, their boyfriends get involved and it turns into a 15 person fight—and I was right there, because it was my room. And it was really hard for me, I was telling one of the girls to come into my room and calm down, and get away from the situation to stay safe, and she literally comes in my face and is like, "Get the fuck away from me, I don't give a fuck about you, leave me the fuck alone." And I'm like, wow, that really hurt my feelings, because I thought you were, I loved you, and you were my student … to be cursed out really hurt my feelings. They all got suspended, but three [others] didn't. So on Friday a girl left my room and she got jumped by another student, and she was getting the crap beaten out of her like

right in front of me. If I had just been at my door, if I had known that was coming, I could have stopped it, so I felt really guilty that I wasn't there to prevent her from getting jumped. I guess those are two instances of primary trauma. That stuff occurs—stuff like that happens every week though. (Lola)

Lola described the verbal and physical violence as traumatic, exacerbated by both the care she felt for her students and her feeling helpless to prevent or address the conflict. Lola encountered aspects of a foreign structure and culture, and she did not have the tools to understand what was happening. Even though she was officially in the position of authority, her offers of help were rejected as irrelevant. She felt ineffectual and powerless, and still responsible for the outcomes.

Other CMs also cited violence as a source of trauma. Marie and Dionne both described traumatic loss of students; Marie's student to a shooting and Dionne's student to suicide. Leigh cited students' arrests and fights as the most life-draining experiences in her work. Leigh also described the trauma of witnessing a shooting and subsequently experiencing persistent nightmares about guns and gun violence. Bennett described a stabbing on school grounds and other traumatic situations he experienced in TFA:

> I've certainly gotten screamed at, I had a parent stab another parent that bled out on the steps of our school before, I knew a child that I've spent hours and hours mentoring that the next day never showed up to school, never showed up again ... We've seen it. And I'm sure this is not unusual for other teachers out there. You don't get examples of the types of trauma you're going to experience with TFA when you sign up, but you are told that it's really hard. (Bennett)

CMs experienced a range of behavioral and emotional responses to difficult events. Many CMs who described experiencing trauma from witnessing violence as new teachers specifically noted that they had not experienced violence when they were students; these CMs stated that as students they had attended either private schools or public schools in wealthier neighborhoods. Experiencing violence within schools was new to them, and this impacted their experience of trauma. Trauma is characterized by unexpected and non-normative events that overwhelm a person's perceived ability to cope (Gil, 1996), and some CMs explained that shock contributed to their experience of trauma. Marie stated, "We wasted a lot of time in our two years just dealing with shock. And that time could have been spent otherwise. And so much of it was just, 'Wow, what is happening?'" CMs' accounts of trauma raise more questions than answers about how an individual's background impacts how a person might experience trauma, and how to support helping professionals to recognize and cope with shock and trauma.

Post-Traumatic Stress Disorder (PTSD)

Two CMs raised concerns about PTSD in their interviews. PTSD is defined by the APA as an anxiety problem that develops in some people after extremely traumatic events, such as combat, crime, an accident, or natural disaster. People with PTSD may relive the event via intrusive memories, flashbacks, and nightmares; avoid anything that reminds them of the trauma; and have anxious feelings they didn't have before that are so intense their lives are disrupted (PTSD, 2013). Since people have different responses to trauma, not everyone who experiences trauma develops PTSD.

Jane and Sofia shared stories about their firsthand and secondhand experience with PTSD. Jane identified and described her experience with PTSD from being a CM, connecting it to her nightmares, major weight loss, resulting fights with her former fiancé, and various other challenges. Sofia described negative changes she experienced and changes her friend in TFAGP experienced their first year before he dropped out of TFA. Feeling helpless to change their own or their students' realities can create trauma which then creates PTSD among some CMs:

> [Rob] did not feel like he was supported, going back to that fear of failure. He's very Type A and wants everything to go right, and he was overwhelmed by his feeling of failure. He quit in the fall of our first year, and after he left the region and went back to his home, he saw a physician and was referred to a counselor, and the counselor told him he had PTSD and his hair fell out—he was definitely affected physically by his corps experience. (Sofia)

Both Jane and Sofia stated that they thought TFA did not acknowledge CMs' experiences with either trauma generally or PTSD specifically, among active CMs or CMs who quit TFA.

Secondary Trauma, Compassion Fatigue (CF), and Vicarious Traumatization

Newer research is shedding light on a condition with similar effects to PTSD, known as secondary trauma. The difference in these conditions is the exposure to trauma: PTSD involves direct exposure, and secondary trauma involves indirect exposure (Figley, 1995).

Seven CMs explicitly identified some form of secondary trauma as part of their TFA experience. Secondary trauma, also named compassion fatigue (CF), may be experienced by people who engage empathically with another person who has been traumatized. CF is defined as "the natural consequent behaviors and emotions resulting from knowing about a traumatizing event experienced by a significant other" and "the stress resulting from helping or wanting to help a traumatized or suffering person" (Figley, 1995, p. 7). CF is thus more common among professional helpers: nurses, social workers, therapists, teachers, and others who are called to frequently empathize with someone else who is experiencing trauma firsthand. CF is defined by "a state of exhaustion and dysfunction—biologically, psychologically, and socially—as a result of prolonged exposure to compassion stress" (Figley, 1995, p. 253). CF reactions may include avoidance of the trauma, and a range of distressing emotions including horror, fear, rage, grief, dread, depression, anxiety, and shame (Figley, 1995, pp. 53, 85, 155).

Aiden, Robin, Bennett, Lola, and Jane each commented on the commonness of CF in TFA, CMs' predispositions to experiencing CF, and the environmental contributors to CF among CMs. Aiden independently read research on CF to better understand what he and his friends in TFA were experiencing. From his readings, personal reflections, and conversations with TFA friends, Aiden thought CF was a common struggle among CMs and educators teaching in low-income public schools:

> I've read research on compassion fatigue and think it's an endemic problem in education and some low-income public schools. I've felt it myself, I've talked with TFA friends about it, and they have verified it for me as well. A lot of people in the corps are experiencing this, absolutely. I think it would be harder to find CMs who do not suffer from compassion fatigue [than those who do]. (Aiden)

Robin and Bennett thought many CMs were "Type A people who care about children" and "very empathetic individuals" in a way that made CMs predisposed to experiencing CF:

> I think it all makes sense if you look at who TFA recruits—Type A people who care about children. You're already on edge and seeking perfection, and you're absorbing a lot of emotional baggage of kids with whom you're empathizing with and care about. My caricature of a TFA person is an emotionally sensitive person but Type A. I'm predisposed to pick up on things. (Robin)

Most of us are very empathetic individuals who feel for students every single day. And we take on their burdens very, very significantly, but that only gives us motivation to show up stronger than I was before. I think a lot of us have lived with burden for a very long time. That's very normal for us. (Bennett)

In addition to many CMs' predispositions towards empathy, Jane, Bennett, and Lola described work environments that regularly exposed them to traumatic situations. Jane described struggles in her school environment that "happen all the time." She described seeing her students' resilience to survive and learn in an environment that she could not imagine learning in herself. Jane began crying as she described the challenges her students faced in her school, challenges that she felt helpless to address:

And as far as secondary trauma goes, the school environment that we work in, I can't imagine learning in ... I'm going to start crying, I'm sorry. It's so weird. I was teaching my 6th graders, and I had to stop teaching for 5 minutes because the fight next door was so loud that they couldn't hear, and I stepped back and I thought, how do you learn? How do you move on from that? In a place where that happens all the time? I didn't grow up in that type of environment, so I don't really know. But these kids are so resilient. And nobody understands that unless you see it. And I just think the kids we teach are so incredible. And it's not just the outside factors that they come in with, it's the school. Coping with it is unreal. (Jane)

Bennett and Lola gave examples of their traumatic experiences and described their need to not take everything to heart. Bennett explained, "I can't take everything to heart, because that will get you killed." Lola described violence in her school and stated "stuff like that happens every week," and described it as fatiguing. She identified her need to move on because the trauma became overwhelming for her:

That stuff occurs, stuff like that happens every week though ... Philadelphia is a traumatic city. All that bad stuff gets fatiguing. Students will come up to me and tell me things like, "Oh, I've been gone because my dad died," or "My sister was murdered" or "My brother got in an accident." It's just like every day something bad happens. I want a day where nothing bad happens. You can't let that affect you. You're like, "Here's your makeup work." You can't really address that; you have to move on. It's draining. (Lola)

CMs' roles in these traumatic situations were blurred and confusing. Like Lola, most CMs came from backgrounds in which traumatic situations were addressed by parents, pastors, counselors, or social institutions. In this new environment with extremely limited resources and greater instability, many

CMs struggled with how to be supportive of their students. Often, the needs they witnessed surpassed their capacity to meet those needs; additionally, the needs were outside of their job descriptions as teachers. CMs described taking on the responsibilities of a social worker or counselor during and outside of school hours. As teachers in low-wealth communities, CMs faced a double bind: trying to teach while their students were emotionally overwhelmed was ineffective, but if they tried to address those emotional needs, they were no longer teaching the necessary material.

Marie and Dionne shared about how they were affected by some of the student tragedies in their schools. Both CMs began their fourth years teaching in fall 2014 and shared these stories in the middle of their third year teaching. Both began seeing counselors in part to help grieve and cope with these experiences. Marie described two tragedies in her school and how they impacted her:

> I feel like at this point [in my third year], I feel very differently [about trauma] than I did my first or second year. My first year, I had a student who was essentially gang-raped by two students at our school and three other students who did not go to our school. And there was a huge fallout because of that. It wasn't handled in a way it should have been. That was kind of traumatic to me, because I was in my very first part of teaching. It wasn't that I was experiencing trauma, but I felt such a sadness for my inability to do anything. And just the fact that something so awful could happen. And it didn't feel like much happened after. It wasn't necessarily the event that caused the trauma, but the lack of reaction. And that made me have the effects of trauma. For when my student was killed, one of my first thoughts was, "Well, this is part of the job." Like this is almost to be expected. That reaction was very different to the way I reacted to the first one, where I was outraged and asked, "How could this happen?" Whereas for the second one, I was like, "Well, that's to be expected." I feel like that's almost a different kind of reaction to the trauma. Like going to the funeral, and seeing how my former students were reacting to it. Even his best friend who had to go and pick him up off the sidewalk. In the end, he was the one who was with him when he died. He could be really having an outrageous reaction, and he just seemed like so ... over it. We were talking about it and asking how he could be so calm—either he's in denial or he's just so used to losing people that this is just expected for him. Both of those are also reactions to trauma, it's just a different kind of reaction. (Marie)

Marie described different reactions to both traumatic situations. With her student's rape, Marie described "such a sadness for my inability to do anything" and grappling with the "fact that something so awful could happen." With her students' murder her third year, she described her shift in reaction from "How could this happen?" to "Well, that's to be expected." Marie observed her students' responses to losing their classmate and friend. She noted how work-ing in her school changed her orientation to secondary trauma. In her first and second year, she experienced significant shock; in her third year, she was able to empathize with students more than she could her first or second year.

Dionne also experienced secondary trauma from student tragedies, stat-ing "I feel like sometimes we as teachers experience or are impacted by the trauma that our kids go through." Sessions with her therapist helped Dionne to identify her experiences with vicarious traumatization, a condition linked to CF. Vicarious trauma focuses more on the cognitive effects of trauma and the change in the professional helper's inner experience, whereas CF focuses more on the trauma symptoms (Pearlman & Saakvitne, 1995, p. 151). Dionne described several traumatizing experiences:

> At my last therapy session my therapist and I discussed "vicarious traumatization." I feel like sometimes we as teachers experience or are impacted by the trauma that our kids are going through … I think there is not a lot of access to certain resources. For example, I have a student who has experienced abuse and who in first grade attempted suicide. She doesn't feel comfortable speaking with the counselor at school or outside of school. She'll talk to me. So, as a teacher I have to balance, ok, what do I need for myself, like time for myself, and then what is best for kids. Because I don't want to say no when she's not talking to anyone else and comes in and says, "Can I come in with you at lunch?" It's really hard for me to say no, even if I have something else to do, because I feel this responsibility towards kids. I think that has been weighing on me.

> Students come up to me, and you just worry about them. A girl came up to me before break about how her sister had accused her dad of abusing her. And this was right before spring break. And you're nervous about what's going on when they're not with you. Recently with my students' passing, he was struggling with mental illness. Processing that, I need summer break, but at the same time, I'm so worried about what's going to go on this summer. I had a group of three girls come up to me, one of them is the girl who asks me to come to lunch, and they asked me, "Who gets picked for summer school? We want to come to summer school." Because they don't feel safe at home, or it's uncomfortable at home, and they want to be in school for an escape. Knowing that is difficult, because that balance of being a great teacher you need to be empathetic in my opinion, but there has to be a balance of how far that empathy goes, and how much responsibility you're taking.

> Especially with my student passing, I was very close with him. I've been processing, and literally on Monday, I was like, I don't know if I want to be a teacher any more. It wasn't like I don't want to be in my school or my classroom. I don't know if I want to teach anymore because I don't want to lose another student. I think that respon-sibility piece, managing empathy … You just can't take on that much responsibility.

But I should—and I do—feel responsible for my students. Because I was close with him, it's easier to grieve … I've been so sensitive around [his] death that it's been hard for me to say no to kids when they're asking for something. But I need a break, more so now than ever before. I need a break from speaking with kids, and I need to feel very planned and certain, because a lot of other things feel so uncertain. But I honestly don't think that that would necessarily have come if I wasn't in therapy, and if I wasn't explicitly discussing my needs and my job.

Actually this year has been the roughest in terms of, I know so much more about my kids because we're closer, and I think they feel more comfortable. I'm pretty sure my past students, they were going through things, but I didn't know as much. The better and more space you make kids feel, the more you're going to find out about their lives. (Dionne)

Dionne described complex experiences with vicarious traumatization; entwined with her experience of trauma, she grieved her students' struggles, grieved her student's suicide, struggled with her limits, and struggled to manage her empathy. She found that the closer she became with her students, the more she learned about the painful parts of their lives and the more she was impacted by the trauma they faced.

War Language & Imagery

Various CMs used war language and imagery to describe their experiences in TFA; John described the war-like challenges as invigorating, while Maggie and Bennett linked the war-language to trauma.

John described the challenges he faced in TFA with war language and compared CMs' mentalities to those of soldiers. He viewed fighting for public education as fighting a war, and he described feeling invigorated for what he viewed as volunteering for the draft by joining TFA. John was the only CM in this study to not cite any negative life changes from his experience in TFA, and he explained:

We thought of ourselves as soldiers. People don't like it when you compare fighting for public education to a war. But I think those in the cohort in the district believed that. I know war has negative connotations, but for me it was invigorating. You hear stories about people who volunteered for the draft. I felt like one of those people. There are very few jobs that give you that rush of intensity right off the bat. Teaching at a school is not the same as walking into a corporate office. It's loud, there's chaos, depending on where you're working there's a possibility of physical injury. For me that's invigorating. (John)

Maggie and Bennett used war comparisons to describe their experiences in TFA, but they framed it as traumatic situations that needed to be addressed rather than invigorating. Maggie had previously served in the Air Force and identified parallels in her experiences in the military and in TFA: "I sort of equate the whole experience to being in a mass unit, like in the militia ... It's like being in the military." Maggie linked various CMs' struggles with trauma to the challenges they faced and what she identified as TFA's "iron-fisted" military culture. Bennett grew up in Philadelphia, and compared his fellow CMs to "comrades in arms" and serving in TFA to being "on the frontlines of a really big war." He acknowledged trauma as something that "you can't let get to you":

> All of us [CMs] seem constantly on the lookout for our "comrades in arms" who appear to be struggling ... I know my city. I'm here serving my city. There's sort of a war mentality, to be honest, when you go in. A lot of times when you're teaching and any situations come up, well, you are on the frontlines of a really big war, one that, unfortunately, for many in the school district, we're losing. At institute it's like basic training. And at the start of every single day, go to your fleet of yellow buses and you have your standard-issue lunchbox and your basic training, and you go to your buses to schools throughout the city, you fight your battles and do the best you can, come back, reorganize, and go back out and do it again. I sort of have that mentality some time. You can't let trauma get to you. (Bennett)

Though TFA is not in a military war, it is alarming to note that various CMs compared their experiences in TFA to being in the military, often in the context of discussing trauma in TFA. Research details how similarly people are affected by being at war and being in high-poverty, high-crime neighborhoods (Garbarino, 1995; Garbarino, 2000). CMs' usage of war language speaks to the perceived intensity of many of their experiences, and it raises questions of how being in high-poverty schools affects CMs.

Isolation, Avoidance Behaviors, & Tipping Points

CMs described different effects of their experiences with trauma, including, though not limited to, isolation, avoidance behaviors, and tipping points. Experiencing trauma can be isolating; Psychology professor Dr. Qualls stated, "A piece of the trauma reaction that is so devastating is the intense privacy of it" (Graham, 2013). Many CMs described isolating experiences in TFA; Bernadette, Robin, and Jordan each explicitly mentioned feeling isolated in

TFA. Further, Bernadette noted that she sometimes felt isolated even with colleagues she thought would understand her experiences: "There are times when I feel very isolated, even from colleagues that I know can empathize."

Bennett and Aiden commented on the commonness of isolation in TFA. Bennett described personally feeling a strong bond to Philadelphia because he is from the area, and he recognized that other CMs might feel alone and isolated without the supportive community he had in Philadelphia. Aiden thought CMs did not have resources or space to cope with their isolation:

> I get a real sense of isolation from so many people ... they feel like when they come, and come to ACS or something like that where they're supposed to be recharged they oftentimes end up just walking away feeling that much more alone and unable to engage in the meaningful dialogue that needs to happen. (Aiden)

Avoidance behaviors are another common effect of trauma; people who experience trauma are drawn to avoidance behaviors to cope with and survive trauma (Graham, 2013). Many CMs were drawn to avoidance behaviors, as identified by their doctors and counselors. As described in Chapter 3, 25 CMs in this study experienced negative life changes in TFA; many explicitly cited their new behavioral changes as responses to their work stress. For example, 38% of CMs experienced an unprecedented increase in their alcohol consumption in TFA. Binge drinking was identified by CMs' doctors and counselors as an avoidance behavior among various individual CMs. CMs described "needing" and "craving" alcohol to provide a break from their work stress and trauma.

Trauma is also characterized by its way of pushing people past their tipping points; Stanford psychiatry professor Dolores Gallagher-Thompson describes this process: "stress can accumulate during caregiving and reach a tipping point where someone's ability to cope is overwhelmed" (Graham, 2013). Some CMs passed a tipping point in their experience with trauma. For example, Jane stated that she "snapped" at the end of her first year teaching due to the stress of her work environment. Robin described her experience with trauma and stated, "I felt like I had almost killed myself. It felt like if I had worked any harder, I would die." Lola fainted in her classroom from exhaustion, started taking medications for the first time in her life, and was hospitalized for panic attacks; she explained that these changes were direct effects of the overwhelming trauma she experienced in TFA: "I couldn't deal with it anymore and I just crashed." Marie believed she stayed in an abusive relationship in part because of work stress:

I stayed in an abusive relationship because of the stress of my first year teaching. I knew it was a bad relationship, but I didn't feel strong enough emotionally to end it (and to be alone) because of work stress. Also, I have spent my entire life trying to become a teacher, so it is a huge part of my identity and I didn't want to let my work suffer because of personal problems. Once I began to feel more in control at work (somewhere around April or May of my first year), I ended the relationship. Now, I feel so much stronger and I am confident that is a mistake I will only make once.

CMs described a range of additional challenges they faced as their ability to cope with stress and trauma was overwhelmed; many described reaching their respective tipping points in TFA.

Limited Space in TFA

CMs described limited space in TFA to discuss trauma or process their experiences; deterrents included the demands of work, the corps culture, conflicts with TFA staff, and TFA programming and messaging.

Maggie explained that the work demands in TFA limited CMs' ability to slow down or process their experiences:

> There's no finesse to it at all. You do triage … You don't have really time to think, you don't have time to reflect, you just have to do, do, produce, produce, and get through the day. There's just very little room for slowing down and taking the time to not feel overwhelmed or feel deficient … You have a mission and you do that mission to the Nth degree until your last dying breath. I feel like that's the TFA model … [but] listen, you need to know your limits. (Maggie)

Additionally, some CMs described ways CMs contributed to TFA as an unsafe space to process their experiences. For example, Josh described TFA as full of "one-upmanship and martyrdom." Marie described TFA as "judgey" and thought CMs perpetuated this culture.

Dionne, Lola, Maggie, and other CMs described ways they thought TFA staff deterred CMs from raising concerns related to mental health. For example, Dionne reached out to TFA staff about her depression and did not receive a response:

> When I told my MTLD I was diagnosed with depression … I did not receive an e-mail back. I was vulnerable and took a risk, but I was ignored. That vulnerability, that was another emotion of rejection I had to deal with on top of the myriad of other emotions I have to deal with. With everything else going on, sometimes it's

just easier to ignore it; to not take that risk. I wasn't being perceived as a human; my needs as a person weren't being considered … There's all these people in TFA who don't talk about it. I send an e-mail to TFA about mental health and, "Oh, we're not going to respond to it." People shutting down that communication makes it even more difficult. These "Excellence," "No Excuses" model type things, make it even more difficult to deal with. Like, you're not allowed to have these conversations. (Dionne)

Similarly, Lola brought up her emotional health concerns with TFA and felt like she was repeatedly ignored. She described TFA as unsupportive and indifferent to her struggles:

Why would I put myself out there and tell [TFA] my story? Why would I? It's so emotionally raw, and it hurts to keep opening that up and keep telling that story and have it be met with nothing. Like, why would I go through that emotional trauma to not only be met with lack of support, but a blatant indifference to my situation? (Lola)

Maggie thought staff did not acknowledge CMs' mental health concerns because to do so would mean going against the TFA narrative. Maggie described CMs' efforts to initiate conversations and explained, "they [TFA staff] keep shutting it down because it goes against the TFA narrative." CMs described the "TFA script" similarly, calling TFA's narrative and messaging unresponsive, pre-written, unsupportive, ineffective, and not human (further explored in Chapter 2). In addition to feeling like their concerns or needs were ignored, other CMs described feeling shamed in TFA for expressing their concerns or needs (further explored in Chapter 8). CMs identified their interactions with staff as limiting their ability to process their experiences while in TFA.

Dionne thought that for CMs to name their experiences honestly in TFA would be "counter-cultural" and require vulnerability and risk. Though Dionne thought space to process was critical to CMs' development as individuals and as educators, she thought it was easier for CMs to internalize TFA's dominant narrative than to identify or grapple with what they experienced. Honestly naming their experiences included the risk of being marginalized by the dominant culture and narrative of TFA:

It's counter-cultural to [name your own experiences]. I also think that we internalize [TFA's] message, too. By naming the difficult pieces of it, it's easier to grapple with in many ways, but there's also a risk because there's a culture around you that doesn't seem to support that narrative, you might be on your own, and that might be another thing to deal with. (Dionne)

Some CMs like Marie thought TFA's lack of acknowledgment of trauma exacerbated CMs' experience of trauma:

> I don't know how to fix the TFA problem, but I feel like a lot of these TFA teachers go into their positions with very little understanding of what it's going to feel like and look like or how they can get help when they're struggling ... I don't know that TFA approached trauma or secondary trauma. That wasn't even a conversation. I don't ever recall them having conversations with us about how to keep ourselves healthy. Eventually we would go into our Penn classes and people would start complaining about all of this happened, and this happened, and this happened. And that was a therapy session in and of itself because everybody just needed to unload. But that wasn't TFA doing that, it was professors recognizing that we weren't at that time in a space to learn new material; we were in a space to get something off of our chests. And I don't think that TFA really—at least not in a way that was effective— addressed trauma. Or even mentioned it ... It didn't even feel like it was on their radar. I think it was more, "We're focused on student achievement and so should you." You know? There wasn't that additional piece of, "But you have to make sure you're healthy first. (Marie)

CMs' experiences raise questions about TFA's role and responsibility in helping its members engage with and process their trauma. TFA describes itself as a "group of leaders," and it promises "intensive training, support and career development that helps these leaders increase their impact" (TFA: Our Mission, 2014). TFA blurs the lines between a community and an employer. Many CMs hoped for and expected the support of a community upon joining TFA and expressed disappointment over the lack of support from TFA. Drake stated, "My main issue is that the support they advertise is not the support we get." Lola said of CMs' struggles and negative life changes, "TFA can't advertise this, can't put this in their message, because no one would do it." Many CMs felt like they were viewed and treated as if they were expendable in TFA's mission.

Finding Space to Process & Cope

CMs described requiring strategies, mechanisms, and space to cope with their trauma, stress, anxiety, depression, and work-related challenges. Jane described the challenges her students and fellow teachers faced in their school and stated, "Coping with it is unreal." Dionne explained, "To sustain this profession, we need to be able to cope with a lot of the stressors and the complexity of the educational system."

CMs shared positive ways of coping they found helpful, including talking with friends and family, finding affirming colleagues, finding a supportive faith community, seeing a counselor, starting long-distance running, joining a kickball or softball league, or generally making time for self-care. Sofia, Jane, Robin, Elliott, Aiden, Dionne, Maggie, Lola, and Bennett each stated that though it is difficult to make time for anything outside of their work, they are better teachers when they also take care of themselves. Bennett explained, "You have to understand yourself on a holistic level and understand that you're a better teacher when you're taking time to work out, or whatever it is that people do."

The majority of CMs identified talking with friends, family, fellow CMs, or counselors as especially helpful to processing difficult experiences. Dionne summarized, "Talking about why it's difficult is helpful in overcoming the difficulty. It's the same thing with therapy, where you go in and talk with somebody, and that makes it easier." Over half of CMs in this study expressed a newfound need for professional counseling while in TFA. Devon described seeking therapy because "I didn't feel like I could cope sufficiently by myself." Many who began seeing a counselor described therapy as a space to be honest and process their complicated experiences; CMs stated that therapy helped to normalize their responses to trauma and helped with their healing processes. Normalizing the response to trauma is important to combat feelings of isolation and to encourage individuals to seek help when they need it (Graham, 2013). Josh described therapy, talking through his experiences, and working on strategies to cope as "extremely helpful." Dionne and Marie described therapy as important to helping them cope with the loss of their students. Various CMs explained that therapy was one option to help process and cope with work-related challenges such as trauma. Therapy also helped CMs to explore and respond to their limits.

Conclusion

CMs described a range of experiences with both direct and indirect exposure to trauma. As people who self-identified as high-achieving, Type A individuals who cared deeply about their students, CMs struggled to cope with trauma and their feelings of helplessness. Many CMs who experienced trauma described lacking adequate space, support, or resources to process and respond to their experiences with trauma in TFA. Though CMs entered into their classrooms in the role of helping professional, many expressed requiring support for themselves as well. As Jane asked, "I love my kids, but what about me?"

CMs described requiring tools to understand and respond to new conflicts, resources to cope in a healthy way, and a culture that promoted self-care. Many CMs identified a need for TFA to acknowledge the reality of trauma among CMs; they viewed acknowledging trauma as an important part of caring for CMs as people and as teachers.

· 5 ·

TFA'S CULTURE OF GUILT
AND SHAME

"If my students don't do well, it's my fault. If I am not teaching the way TFA wants me to, I am widening the achievement gap … Of course it's important, but you know, I'm not fucking perfect."

—Jane

"… the emphasis is that you're failing children. I don't know how you couldn't feel shame over that. You wouldn't get into TFA if you didn't feel shame over failing children."

—Marie

"We're doing the best we can. You're one human being."

—Bennett

CMs frequently described their TFA experiences with the words guilt and shame.[1] Guilt and shame are both feelings associated with negative evaluation (Lewis, 1974); as such, guilt and shame are considered "self-conscious" and "moral emotions" (Tangney & Stuewig, 2004; Tracy & Robins, 2004). Colloquially the words guilt and shame are often used interchangeably, but therapists draw a distinction that helps to nuance the experience of causing harm to someone. Guilt and shame are connected but distinct emotional responses. Guilt is defined as a feeling of responsibility and remorse for causing harm to someone; guilt relates to others. Shame is defined as a painful feeling from our interpretation of who we are for causing harm; shame relates to and interprets ourselves (Burgo, 2013). Simply put, guilt is feeling badly for something you do, and shame is feeling badly for who you are; guilt is behaviorally linked, and shame is identity linked. Guilt can help promote empathy, practical responsibility, and growth when it is connected to actual harm caused by the person feeling guilt, while shame limits empathy and practical responsibility, and it impedes constructive change.

Individually and systemically, what are CMs responsible for and what can they hope to accomplish in TFA? As teachers who are also tasked with "closing the achievement gap" (TFA: Achievement Gap, 2014), CMs straddle and blur the line between responsibility for individual and systemic change. CMs experienced guilt from the narrative of what they were responsible for and shame for how they were interpreted in light of that perceived responsibility. CMs blamed themselves and were blamed by TFA for a wide range of perceived individual and systemic failures.

Marie described the basic guilt and shame narrative that many CMs experienced. In an effort to promote CMs' agency and responsibilities, TFA overstated CMs' agency and blamed and shamed CMs for what were interpreted as failures:

> [TFA] made the mission over-simplified. And in trying to teach teachers that "You are the driving force in your classroom," it also made it seem like "You are to blame for everything. If you ever mess up ever, then you're a terrible person." And that's clearly just not true. And I think having that message so heavily and turning CMs against each other made it like, "I'm better than you" and "This is why you're a bad person." And I don't think that's healthy for anyone involved. (Marie)

Many CMs echoed Marie's description: CMs recognized that they were not matching up to their own or TFA's expectations, even though they were doing everything they could, some pushing themselves to the point of requiring self-medication and prescription medication. An event would occur, and whether or not CMs had the capacity to control that event, they internalized TFA's message that as aspiring highly effective teachers, CMs were "ultimately responsible for what happens in their classroom" (Farr, 2010, p. 185). CMs received this message, and it generalized into "You are to blame for everything." Believing their actions were the "root cause" of all student outcomes caused CMs to feel significant guilt. CMs felt like they were causing harm to others, particularly to the people they intended to serve, which resulted in more guilt. Then, CMs were interpreted as "terrible people" for these perceived failures, which globalized these thoughts into shortcomings of their person as a whole and caused CMs to feel significant shame.

The following chart illustrates the basic flow of CMs' experience of guilt and shame in TFA. An event occurs; then a problem is identified and CMs are held responsible for the problem, which results in CM guilt; and then CMs are interpreted as "selfish," "terrible," or "bad people" for the perceived failure, which results in CM shame:

Figure 5.1. Guilt and Shame Chart.

The event may be situated in reality, but the interpretations of the problem and interpretation of CMs are designated narratives. TFA and CMs both assigned blame to CMs in a way that promoted a corps culture of guilt and shame.

The Backdrop for CMs' Guilt & Shame

CMs' identities as idealists and young professionals, the context of the American meritocracy narrative, and the culture of TFA contributed to CMs' narratives of guilt and shame.

As self-identified empathetic, idealistic, high-achieving, Type A, dedicated individuals, CMs were already inclined towards an over-inflated sense of agency and responsibility. Additionally, though CMs had a range of previous job experiences, most were new to the field of professional teaching. Inexperienced professionals generally tend to blame themselves for everything in their work environments because they do not have an accurate sense of what they are responsible for or what they can control (Cherniss, 1995, p. 19).

Dominant American culture's emphasis on the meritocracy narrative also contributes to CMs' guilt and shame narratives. The American Dream, ideological emblem of the meritocracy narrative, holds that all Americans have equal opportunity, regardless of their economic status at birth, gender, or race; it encourages individualism and self-reliance (Urahn et al., 2012). Though aspirational, the meritocracy narrative is not accurately descriptive of the current social reality (Coates, 2014a; Thomas et al., 2014; Ture & Hamilton, 1992). In this narrative construct, when people struggle, systemic factors might be paid cursory acknowledgment, but it is often ultimately interpreted as a lack of individual effort. In this ideological context, the effects of educational inequity may be briefly acknowledged, but the individual CM is ultimately held accountable for the challenges he or she encounters.

TFA research emphasized CM control and encouraged CMs to be highly effective teachers by seeking root causes in their own actions (Farr, 2010, p. 185). This narrative has its strengths of acknowledging CMs' individual agency, responsibility, and effects. However, this narrative of responsibility was often over-extended and contributed to unproductive guilt and shame narratives. CMs experienced a range of situations that they had limited control over. In the urgency to address injustice, TFA's "No Excuses" culture over-inflated individual responsibility in a way that interpreted struggles as excuses, failure, and personal shortcomings.

CMs' Individual and Systemic Responsibilities

CMs described feeling like they were responsible for everything and therefore at fault for every individual and systemic problem, regardless of whether or not they had the capacity to control the situation. CMs were given the immediate responsibility of individual teachers for individual students, but were told they were to impact a system. Aligned to the TFA directive that "highly effective teachers first seek root causes in their own actions" (Farr, 2010, p. 185), many CMs bore an overextended sense of responsibility and felt guilt for not doing enough for their students and the cause of educational equity.

CMs emphasized their belief in the importance of expanding educational opportunity for their students and took their perceived responsibilities seriously; CMs felt a significant level of personal responsibility to their students, many to the point of feeling that students' lives were depending on them. CMs described their perceived responsibility to "save children." Reagan stated that TFA messaged, "If I don't save the lives of all my children from poverty, I have failed." Similarly, Jane stated, "I felt the pressure to do so just because that's what TFA told me I had to do, because if I didn't, you know, children's lives were at stake." Aiden felt "a sense of guilt in knowing that lives are counting on us as CMs." Both CMs and TFA faulted CMs for a range of perceived individual and systemic failures.

Individual Responsibilities

According to TFA, highly effective teachers are "ultimately responsible for what happens in their classroom" (Farr, 2010, p. 185), and many CMs wrestled with this message:

> I do feel that TFA messages that everything that happens in my classroom is my fault. I realize logically that this is not the case, but it has caused distress for me. (Ariel)

> I feel like I'm not doing a good job or my kids are failing because of me. I take a lot of responsibility for actions in my classroom. (Lola)

> [TFA messages that] if things are not going well it is your fault. Your classroom is your locus of control no matter what is going on around it. (Adrian)

> [TFA messages that] everything in my class is my fault. On a more general scale, "everything is my fault." I disagree. (Kate)

> It seems like people succeed in a vacuum and fail in one, too … TFA puts a lot of emphasis on teacher actions. It's harmful to our well-being when we must then assume that it's completely our fault when our students are not succeeding. (Stephen)

> I am definitely still in the mindset that if something happens in my classroom, then it's my fault. First year that's 100% of what I believed, but now I realize that the reality of the situation—you do have to understand that other things affect my classroom outside of my classroom and outside of myself. If my school has shitty culture, there's going to be things going on that I can't really help prevent. I don't teach in a vacuum and I don't teach on an island. I teach in a school. (Jane)

CMs struggled with TFA's messages that classrooms are isolated spaces and CMs are responsible for everything that happens in their classroom. On one hand, CMs wanted to create a constructive learning environment and believed they were responsible for students' outcomes (learning and otherwise). However, after they began teaching, CMs realized that in reality they did not have as much control as they expected or as much control as was narrated by TFA. As Stephen and Jane explained, CMs can do their best to create a safe and constructive learning environment, but their classrooms are not isolated from life and structures outside of the classroom. Maggie stated that she struggled with her lack of control: "I have no control over so many uncontrollable factors in my students' lives, in my professional life, in the insane machinations of the Philadelphia public/charter school system." (Maggie)

On an individual level, CMs wanted to take responsibility for everything that happened in their classrooms, but they found they had limited control over the external factors that impacted their classrooms. CMs described challenges that included, though were not limited to, their own exhaustion and limitations, broader school instability, violence outside of their classrooms that still affected students coming into class, behavioral health issues, and students' experiences with immediate hunger or urban poverty. Aiden summarized:

> Personally, I still fully believe my kids can achieve at the highest level, but I've come to far more deeply understand how rooted and entrenched many of the forces are that do hold my kids where they are, and how critical school systems and structures are that I have limited influence over … it takes a lot of work to accept your locus of control and do the best that you can do given the context and situation of what you're given.

Systemic Responsibilities

CMs experienced blurred lines between their individual and systemic responsibilities and impacts. CMs felt responsible to affect systemic change and address the "achievement gap" during their TFA commitment; struggles in their classroom were interpreted as CMs somehow actively exacerbating systemic educational inequity. Jane stated that TFA messaged, "If my students don't do well, it's my fault. If I am not teaching the way TFA wants me to, I am widening the achievement gap … My school on my formal evaluation rates me as highly effective, but according to TFA I am ineffective and I am widening the achievement gap." Like Jane, many CMs thought that they were individually responsible for enacting systemic change within their classrooms. Reagan described feeling responsible in TFA to save her individual students from poverty. CMs struggled with the narrative that they were responsible for systemic injustice and felt they did not have the capacity to individually address systemic injustice in their classrooms. They could do their best to serve and work alongside their students, and they witnessed some of the manifestations of systemic injustice in individuals' lives, but they did not have the capacity in their classrooms to enact immediate, broad systemic change. Nicole stated that she understood that TFA needed to make grand claims and talk in the language of impacting systemic change for recruitment and fundraising purposes, but she thought this narrative was inaccurate. Nicole also stated that TFA made her feel guilty for not believing that she was addressing structural inequity during her year of teaching:

I just wish they were a little bit more humble about it. A little bit more like, "We're trying our best and we realize that we're a part of the solution." But TFA doesn't want to do that. They want to say they're actually shifting inequality in the city. And it's just crazy to me. It's just crazy … I believe that for real change to occur for our students, there needs to be massive structural changes. We would need to overcome [the limits of] capitalism, racism, classism, etc … I do not believe that my year of teaching is really "changing the trajectory" for my students. I think that's really naive and I am made to feel guilty for not buying it. (Nicole)

CMs' responsibilities and capacities were overstated on both an individual and systemic level. CMs grappled with the extent to which they were responsible for students' lives and for enacting systemic change in TFA. This narrative contributed to CMs' feeling guilty for failing their students and failing to achieve TFA's mission of impacting systemic change.

The Storm Fallacy: Illustrating a Narrative Problem of Blurring Individual and Systemic Responsibilities

CMs' roles were vaguely defined while they served in TFA and this exacerbated the blame narrative. TFA often treats educational inequity like a natural disaster that requires individual relief work and assigns CMs to serve individual students, but it simultaneously tasks CMs with enacting systemic changes. This narrative misstates the problem at hand, overextends CMs' capacities, and blames CMs for a wide range of perceived individual and systemic failures.

TFA, like other idealistic helping organizations, often positions the problem of systemic inequity as an individual-level struggle while still speaking in the language of systemic change. To illustrate, Nicole compared TFA's approach to her previous experiences serving in City Year. City Year is an 11-month commitment and places its mentors into Philadelphia's most underserved schools to "help close the gap between what students need to succeed and what schools are designed to provide" (City Year: Our Approach, 2014). City Year cites the Starfish Story as a "founding story" for the organization, and City Year's mentees are called Starfish:

A young girl was walking along a beach upon which thousands of starfish had been washed up during a terrible storm. When she came to each starfish, she would pick it up, and throw it back into the ocean. People watched her with amusement. She had been doing this for some time when a man approached her and said, "Little girl, why are you doing this? Look at this beach! You can't save all these starfish. You can't begin to make a difference!" The girl seemed crushed, suddenly deflated. But after a few moments, she bent down, picked up another starfish, and hurled it as far as she could into the ocean. Then she looked up at the man and replied, "Well, I made a difference to that one!" The old man looked at the girl inquisitively and thought about what she had done and said. Inspired, he joined the little girl in throwing starfish back into the sea. Soon others joined, and all the starfish were saved. (City Year: Starfish Story, 2014)

TFA often takes a Starfish Story approach, but still speaks in the language of systemic change. Place aside for a moment that this narrative also positions students as starfish with no agency and CMs as young idealists who change the world with their idealism (see Chapter 7), the Starfish narrative positions the problem of educational inequity as "a terrible storm." TFA narrates educational inequity in America as "the achievement gap" (TFA: Achievement Gap, 2014) and presents a historical problem as if it were a natural phenomenon. TFA speaks in absolutes, reinforces the meritocracy narrative, and removes the struggle for educational equity from the landscape and history of race, class, and power (see Chapter 2). Natural disaster language is different than man-made disaster language; natural disaster responses are different than man-made disaster responses. Positioning educational inequity as a decontextualized, out-of-nowhere natural disaster actually precludes a need for systemic change. This problem, as it is narrated, requires only relief work. Scaling up relief work is not enacting systemic change for problems that are socially constructed. The relief work is incredibly valuable, but it is not enacting systemic change, because in this story there is no system that requires changing. This is not an accurate depiction of addressing systemic injustice.

To make a change to the Starfish Story to better parallel the problem at hand, educational inequity in Philadelphia is more akin to a terrible ongoing oil spill than a terrible storm. Educational inequity was created through a system; it did not just happen. An oil spill does not only require a young girl picking up individual starfish; even a group of inspired helping individuals picking up starfish would be inadequate to address the entire problem of the oil spill. All the starfish will not be "saved" through individual aid. People need to take responsibility for and address the dripping oil rig. Relief work is still incredibly important and needed, and people who are addressing the oil rig are not doing "more" needed work (see Chapter 2). Both forms of work are needed to effectively address and take responsibility for the oil spill.

There is a need both for people to work alongside individuals and people to address the system which continues to disadvantage groups of individuals. These people can work together and they are both working towards good, but it is important to understand the distinctions of these responsibilities. Increasing the number of people who are picking up starfish is an inadequate means of "saving" all the starfish from the oil spill; similarly, increasing individual educational access is valuable work but does not address the systemic-level cause of inequity. People who are committing for at least two years to "pick up" starfish cannot in good conscience be shamed for failing to pick up all the starfish or possibly worse, blamed for the oil spill. This narrative is inaccurate and not only causes harm to the helpers, but also skews the problem of systemic injustice and minimizes the need for actual systemic change. The man-made problems of structural oppression, institutional racism, and historic inequity require committed people to address the negative effects of these systems on individuals, and it also requires committed people to address the systemic problem.

The Diagnosis: Lack of Effort and Caring, Failing Children

On an individual level, CMs wanted to be effective teachers and already felt inadequate and guilty without TFA's reinforcement of their perceived failures:

> I felt guilt over not being a better teacher because I wanted to be a better teacher for my students, and I wanted to make growth for them. (Marie)

> [I feel] guilt and shame for not being the teacher I want to be. Just feeling like I'm not effective enough in the classroom, not effective enough in presenting content, not effective enough in getting students invested in the material. (Aiden)

> [I feel I am] being an inadequate teacher for my students. I feel more comfortable talking about education reform in general than I do talking about my actual teaching. (Alex)

> [I feel] guilt about student achievement, not having as great of a relationship with my students as others. (Devon)

> I feel guilty about not being as supportive to students as possible. (Nicole)

CMs wanted to be successful teachers who served their students well, and they already faulted themselves for their perceived shortcomings. When they did not live up to the expectations of enacting individual and systemic change, CMs were interpreted as not trying hard enough, not caring enough, and failing children.

CMs frequently narrated their own failures in the language of fault and guilt from not working hard enough. When asked what challenges of their job were difficult to process, CMs responded:

> My feelings that I am not doing all that I could be in my classroom [and] my guilt and mixed emotions when I feel like I am not doing everything I can. (Drake)

> It's most difficult to talk about failures that may result from a lack of motivation or stamina on my part. (Josh)

In addition to this self-interpreted fault and guilt, CMs were also interpreted negatively by TFA's narrative and staff. When asked what messages they perceived from TFA, Aiden, Adrian, Alex, Ariel, Bernadette, Drake, Jane, Josh, Kate, Lola, Mark, Stephen, and Taylor stated that if they or their students did not meet TFA's standards, it was because they were not trying hard enough. CMs' perceived failures were reduced and misinterpreted as resulting from inadequate effort. Additionally, CMs felt judged, unsupported, and like they were not allowed to disagree with this messaging:

> We're failing in some way ... if my students or I are not meeting TFA standards, we are "not trying hard enough," though I feel it has also been messaged that we're not allowed to disagree with these ideas. (Stephen)

> If my students aren't achieving, then I'm not trying hard enough but I still won't get assistance from TFA, just judgment. (Taylor)

CMs' perceived failures were also interpreted as resulting from their lack of caring. Aiden, Jane, Reagan, Nicole, Lola, Dionne, John, and Marie stated that when they disagreed or deviated from TFA's message of what they were responsible for achieving, they were interpreted as not caring enough about their students or educational inequity. Nicole explained that when she disagreed with TFA's messaging that CMs were enacting systemic change, she was "made to feel guilty" by TFA and interpreted as not caring about her students. Lola stated that TFA narrates the problem as her lack of effort and caring, which then contributed to her feeling guilty and "like complete shit":

> It's all your fault. You're not working hard enough. You are not measuring student success enough. You're not doing a good job and if you cared about your students

you would do more. Your successes aren't really a success. They all make me feel like complete shit ... I didn't sign up for that. It's very dismissive. I feel like I give 110% and when I go with legitimate concerns to TFA, I'm not taken seriously. They just tell me to work harder. I hate the way TFA makes me feel. I don't feel inspired or motivated, I feel guilty. (Lola)

CMs commonly felt like they were never doing enough for their students, and this contributed to CMs' guilt. Lola explained that she felt TFA preyed on CMs' idealism and built a culture of guilt to drive achievement:

I think one of the things with TFA is that it purposely recruits people who are very idealistic and people who really want to help and people who really want to do a good thing, and then I think TFA preys on that a little bit. They'll make you feel like you're not doing enough, ever. Everything I do is not enough. It's always like that, trying to attain more. And guilt that I can't achieve success. (Lola)

Marie explained that TFA emphasized that CMs were failing children and that this contributed to CMs' shame:

I think trying to teach teachers that you're in control comes from a good place and to be a successful teacher you have to truly believe those things in some ways, but I don't think it's healthy to tell first-year teachers who you *know* are going to be terrible teachers—very few people can turn out to be amazing teachers their first year. I don't think it's fair to say that, "If your kids aren't making growth, you are at fault." And the emphasis is that *you're failing children*. I don't know how you couldn't feel shame over that. You wouldn't get into TFA if you didn't feel shame over failing children. I don't think that's productive and I don't think that's healthy. (Marie)

TFA's message that CMs were failing children because they were not working hard enough or because they did not care enough about their students or social justice created a heavy burden for CMs, particularly because many CMs identified as passionate and caring people. Within this interpretive narrative of what success is and the formula for how it is achieved, CMs felt guilty for not working hard enough or caring enough about their students. Further, CMs felt shame over what kind of lazy, selfish, inadequate, uncaring, terrible people they were to be failing children.

Getting Actively Blamed & Shamed by TFA

CMs described experiences in which they felt that TFA interpreted, blamed, and shamed them for failing students and TFA's mission. From smaller actions like not bringing a pencil to a meeting to struggling to meet TFA's standards to larger decisions like leaving TFA, TFA interpreted a range of CMs' actions as negative reflections of CMs as people. CMs were asked whether they were taking their work seriously, had their motives and character questioned, were labeled selfish or uncaring, and their perceived failures were connected to their personal identities.

John and Dionne both gave examples of TFA staff making major assumptions about their character and motivations based on limited knowledge of a minor action, such as taking a phone call during an assembly and not bringing a pencil to a meeting. Dionne stated, "A person higher-up than my MTLD in TFA asked me, 'Are you taking this seriously?' because I didn't have a pencil in our meeting." John shared a similar story in which he left a mandatory TFA assembly to take a phone call about his second job and was interpreted negatively. From taking this phone call, John was told he disappointed TFA's regional director and she questioned his motives, his move to Philadelphia, and his reasons for joining TFA:

> During one of the assemblies where somebody for the cohort was talking, I stepped out to take a phone call. It was a phone call for me to arrange my utilities and apartment situation and all that stuff. Utilities for me—cable and internet—were particularly important at the time because that's how I was supporting myself, without a placement yet. I started consulting at the tail end from graduating from college … TFA sent me on only one interview. I had no income other than how I was supporting myself. I didn't really think anything of it until someone stopped me when I was on the phone in the hallway and basically interrogated me about why I was on the phone. Then later on I get another e-mail from the regional director or whoever, that she felt I had "massively disappointed her" and she wanted to meet with me and sit down and discuss it. We had a face to face meeting and she told me, "I feel like you disrespected me, blah blah blah." She had the nerve to say, "Why are you in this, what is it that you care about with this work." I just felt like, honestly I didn't know what to say. It wasn't my first rodeo in terms of being in a professional environment. For me and most people, stepping out of a meeting to take a phone call without being disruptive is just normal professional practice. But when she was meeting with me, she questioned my move to Philadelphia, and I just didn't know how to respond. I couldn't believe that she'd make the jump from taking a phone call to, "Oh, you must not be doing this for the right reasons." (John)

In addition to negative interpretations of minor actions, many CMs articulated feeling like they were actively shamed in TFA for struggling, not showing adequate growth with their students, or for other perceived failures. Maggie described this as part of TFA's fear-based model for success. She thought that

CMs were not allowed to show weakness and were pushed to overcommit to TFA: "It goes back to that fear model ... You really aren't allowed to show weakness. You have a mission and you do that mission to the Nth degree until your last dying breath. I feel like that's the TFA model."

According to Maggie, CMs who "showed weakness" were interpreted negatively. Similarly, Aiden described another incident: a "friend who's a CM told me that TFA made her feel like a bad person for not being successful enough." Elliott also described an interaction in which TFA shamed his friend and fellow CM for struggling:

> One of the people who I hung out with yesterday is a second year CM, Sophie*, and the staff member said, and this is paraphrased, "I think you need to stop putting your selfish needs before the needs of the community you're serving." There's two ways to look at that. One, not ok. On a personal level, it's not ok. Sophie works very hard, she stays 'til 8 pm tutoring ... Those are the messages that are coming from up top [in TFA] ... What's not ok with this, it's just like how with our kids we need to be sensitive to their needs, you know, they matter, they're human beings. CMs have needs. Take care of them. That woman, when she said that to Sophie, and all these women and men who are serving TFA, I've heard this message from multiple people ... The fact that Sophie's MTLD is questioning her allegiance to the cause, it just kind of makes her feel shitty, and bad, not valued, and unsupported. (Elliott)

Elliott cited multiple examples in which CMs' struggles or unfavorable classroom outcomes were by default interpreted as a lack of the CMs' effort or caring. When CMs struggled or when their students were not making adequate progress, TFA staff and the TFA-endorsed narrative questioned CMs' character or their "allegiance to the cause."

Even as a Sue Lehmann nominee and therefore someone TFA recognized as positively impacting her students' academic growth, Adrian stated that she was shamed and pinned as "the sole problem" for any problems in her classroom: "At TFA at least, if there is a problem with investment in the classroom the teacher is pinned as the sole problem. I am also shamed during my first two years if my students are not making appreciable progress." (Adrian)

Lola described feeling shamed by TFA for struggling. When she and the CMs at her placement school reached out to TFA, Lola described TFAGP leadership faulting her for the environmental problems she was struggling with and told her to "hold up a mirror":

> I lost 20 pounds this year. I fainted regularly during the school day ... I did reach out to TFA because all of the CMs at our school were having difficulties ... All crazy

things like fatigue, sleep deprivation, estranged relationships, etc. I did reach out, as did everyone in my corps … Our MTLD, Veronica* (TFA's Director of Teacher Leadership Development), and Karla* (TFA's Vice President of Teacher Leadership Development), they're higher-up, and they came up to listen to our complaints, we went on for an hour or two hours, just saying everything that was wrong at our school and how we felt, how we were literally going crazy and couldn't stand it anymore, and how it was such a negative, unhealthy environment—and an abusive environment. And then instead of supporting us or saying, "How can we help you?" they said—I'll never forget this—"You need to hold up a mirror and realizing what are you doing in your classroom that contributes to this environment." They said, "You need to hold up a mirror."

They were saying, metaphorically you need to see what you're doing wrong. See what I'm doing wrong. And I went, "I'm not doing anything wrong. I'm doing everything I can." My first year I wouldn't have had the empowerment to stand up for myself like that. I said, "I'm not doing anything wrong, I'm not going to hold up a mirror because it's not me." Instead of saying, "Wow, this is a really bad school and I'm sorry you're being abused," they were like, "You need to hold up a mirror and see what you're doing wrong." It was like victim blaming, almost. I'm not doing anything wrong. Stop saying that.

… And Veronica goes, "Oh, things are messed up in every school. No school is perfect." She didn't want to hear what was going wrong and just kind of brushed off my concerns. My legitimate concerns, not wanting to hear them because, "all schools are messed up and you signed up for this" kind of attitude. I didn't sign up for that … It could be like, "hold up a mirror" or "think about your commitment" or they just have these five lines that they say over and over to the point where they're not even real people. They're robots reciting a script. (Lola)

Maggie, Lola, Nicole, and others also expressed feeling shamed for disagreeing with TFA, even if they were trying to advocate for their needs or their students' needs. For example, Lola's school cut down their history department to only offer one history class through the high school, which Lola felt was wrong and unfair for students. She described working within the school to advocate for students, but that ultimately her efforts were unsuccessful. She reached out to TFA, but instead of being offered support or encouragement, Lola said she was called "selfish" and interpreted as not thinking about her students:

I told TFA that I cannot teach at a school that only offers civics. This is doing a disservice to our students. And instead of TFA being supportive and say, "How can we help you?" or "Change the curriculum at this school" or "We'll find you a better placement" or "Help your students because they need more than civics," they were very like, "Your quitting is not what's best for the students. You're being selfish by thinking about yourself and you should really think about your students and what they need." They need history! (Lola)

When CMs who were pushed past their limits decided to leave TFA prior to the completion of their two-year commitment, they were interpreted negatively. Jane shared a placement school with other CMs and provided an example of TFA shaming one of these CMs, Elle*, who dropped out of TFA:

> Dayna*, my MTLD, she's really the worst. Do you know Elle? Our MTLD told Elle, "Well, when you sign up for the military, you made a commitment and you finished that. Why can't you do that with this?" ... Come on! She fucking risked her life two times, and you're going to compare TFA to that? Like, no. As shitty as TFA is, as much PTSD as it's given me, as much trauma, Elle fucking got deployed two times. And you're trying to compare? To have the audacity to say that this is like the military. Elle can say it all she wants, because she's experienced both, but to be in a position at a desk job and saying that to a first-year CM who's placed in a subject that she has no background knowledge in, how *dare* Dayna. I think it's disgusting. I have a real problem with that. I can't. I can't. (Jane)

Elle was part of the TFAGP 2013 corps so she was not part of the 26 CMs surveyed and interviewed. However, she confirmed Jane's descriptions and forwarded her correspondence with TFA staff (see Appendix E: Elle's E-mail). Elle claimed full responsibility for what she described as her shortcomings in her classroom and left TFA after her first semester teaching.

Arbitrary & Subjective Judgment

Constructive feedback is important to growth. However, CMs stated that TFA's evaluations often felt arbitrary, subjective, and more centered on negative judgment and control than growth. Additionally, CMs questioned what they were being evaluated on and the authority of their evaluators.

Jane described one of her evaluations and questioned how TFA's evaluations of her relationships with students could be accurate with an observation lasting thirty minutes and talking with a sample size of five students:

> I got feedback on a lesson [from my MTLD], she was approximately in my classroom for 30 minutes, I believe we were learning about the Articles of Confederation, and somehow, maybe talking to about 5 kids in my classroom, she said that only 55% of my kids say that I reach out to their personal interests and engage with them on a personal level. And I got mad. She said the same thing to Lola. And Lola is running

student council, and goes to all the football games, and knows a lot about her kids. And I do too. And 55%, I only know 55%? I *don't* think that that's appropriate. And I don't think that that's fair. (Jane)

Lola also described her evaluation and questioned her MTLD's judgments:

My MTLD was like, "You don't have strong relationships with your students," and I was like, "How do you know that? You came in here twice in the entire year, how do you know I don't have good relationships with my students? Every single one of them would say they have a good relationship with me. (Lola)

Like Jane and Lola, other CMs questioned what factors they were being evaluated on, how the numbers were derived, and the accuracy of this data. Elliott questioned TFA's authority to make these judgments, explaining "You're not coming home with me, you're not listening to the phone conversations I'm making with parents, and you're not seeing the extent of my efforts." Parallel to the fact that new CMs have limited knowledge of their students, TFA evaluators have limited knowledge of CMs. In highly relational work, it is difficult to provide valid and constructive feedback without deeper knowledge of the individual you are intending to support.

As a 46-year-old with three children not much younger than the average CM in their early- to mid-twenties, Maggie described feeling particularly frustrated with TFA's way of evaluating CMs. Maggie described ways TFA could bully CMs with negative feedback; she explained, "It's about control." Maggie described different situations in which she sat with both first- and second-year CMs who internalized TFA's subjective evaluation of them and felt inadequate and ashamed. For example,

[TFA] was like, "You're going to fail. You're going to fail." Everything out of their mouth was, "You're going to fail. And these are the numbers." And it's so subjective, the observation. I was appalled. I was so appalled … I see the new CMs sitting in a lot of shame and, "Oh, I'm no good," and just feeling just awful. One guy told me from his meeting with his TFA MTLD, "She said I'm not rigorous enough." I'm like, "Honey, you've been very rigorous. You're fine. Just breathe. It's going to be ok." He internalized somebody's subjective view on some unforeseen metric. What rubric is this? [CMs] just internalize things because these are pretty high-functioning people. (Maggie)

CMs also questioned their evaluators' levels of experience to make these judgments. Also parallel to the fact that many CMs are new to the work of teaching, many TFA evaluators had limited experience teaching and were new to the work of supporting teachers. Elliott and John stated that many TFA evaluators and staff were young, had very limited classroom experience, and were new to supporting CMs. Elliott explained that when he worked to support CMs during the summer after his second year, the people who supported new CMs were all "my age or younger … And I look around and I'm like, 'Oh my goodness. The oldest person here is 26.'" John stated,

> TFA needs people who have taught for more than two years. The people who are pulled in to support new CMs had taught for 2, maybe 3 years. TFA's not bringing much to the table. Especially considering the fact that so many CMs leave after their second year. The vast majority do … to me it seems like a pretty big oversight to not have people who have been in the trenches for more than two years. (John)

Relationships require trust, and CMs described feeling highly skeptical and distrustful of their evaluators. Being 26 or younger is not inherently bad and it does not inherently preclude trust from working relationships—in fact, Elliott described admiring the individuals on summer staff who supported new CMs. Rather than a problem with individuals, CMs' experiences point to a systemic problem of relying heavily and primarily on young idealists with less experience. In their critique of detached, arbitrary, and subjective evaluations and in their resistance towards their inexperienced evaluators, CMs experienced some of what their students face in Philadelphia's public school system with its current structural instability and high teacher-attrition rates. CMs also acknowledged that, parallel to the large class sizes of many of their schools, their evaluators were held responsible for an estimated 40 CMs, which made it difficult to provide tailored or significant support to CMs.

Behavioral Health Struggles & the Limits of CMs' Agency

When it comes to students' behavioral health, what is an ethical narrative of CM responsibility?

CMs often shouldered significant responsibility for all situations they encountered. Bernadette stated, "I think I internalize the reality of my students' situations much more than I or others realize." This internalized belief has strengths of recognizing CMs' theoretical agency, but it also has very real and often ignored limitations. Ariel explained that TFA messaged that everything is her fault in a way that sometimes helped her fix the problem, but it also made her internalize some actions that she had little control over:

For example, when a student misbehaves in my classroom, I instantly think, "What did I do?" This does help me take steps to fix the problem, but it also puts undue pressure on me to internalize the actions of others. (Ariel)

Internalizing other peoples' actions has limitations; there are root causes to other peoples' actions that exist outside of CMs. CMs' descriptions of their experiences with students' behavioral health struggles underscore CMs' limits. Ariel described feeling helpless and unsure how to respond to instances of child abuse that affected her students and her classroom:

The first aspect of my job which is the most difficult to talk about is the various instances throughout the year when I have had to report child abuse, hear about child abuse, or handle the after-effects of child abuse (students being removed from home, etc.). In these cases, I feel powerless and more emotionally invested than I am accustomed to being. (Ariel)

Dionne and Marie both described their feelings of responsibility, guilt, and shame over students' reports of child abuse and tragic student suicides. Dionne lost a student she was close with to suicide, and she described feeling guilt and being unsure whether she did enough or if she had been too hard on him. She questioned how to recognize particular students' mental illnesses while still pushing them towards academic growth, particularly in the context of TFA's "No Excuses" culture:

Especially with Will* passing, I feel like his mom and I still tried to hold him to certain standards, and I feel like we did our best to have an empathetic aspect to it, but there is a bit of guilt around being so hard on him and holding him to certain expectations every day. He still needs to do his work. He's bipolar and ODD. How do you recognize the limits of students around mental illness or special education for certain kids, but also holding them to a certain standard and pushing them. How do you balance that? … Especially with my student passing, I was very close with him. I've been processing, and literally on Monday, I was like, I don't know if I want to be a teacher any more. It wasn't like I don't want to be in my school or my classroom. I don't know if I want to teach anymore because I don't want to lose another student. (Dionne)

After Will's death, Dionne described feeling especially worried about her other students and their well-being. Dionne described personally needing the upcoming summer break, but she also felt fear for students who had discussed family abuse accusations with her, or students who needed school to be a safe space away from home. TFA provided no training or support for CMs encountering students with mental illness or particular behavioral health needs. From time in therapy and personal reflection, Dionne described the balance between how much responsibility a teacher can realistically take on: "That balance of being a great teacher, you need to be empathetic in my opinion, but there has to be a balance of how far that empathy goes, and how much responsibility you're taking."

Marie also felt responsible and guilty for her students' death, which she directly connected to TFA's culture and emphasis on CM control. She described feeling significant guilt and shame in TFA, and she rejected TFA's narrative of control in relation to her student's death:

> As for my shame, that I've had to deal with. And I've gone to therapy, and a lot of it has been, yes, you can say all day long that you're the one in control, but really you didn't control the fact that a few weeks ago—was it last week? One of my kids shot himself in the head. My former student was playing Russian Roulette, and shot himself in the head and he died. And I can't take that on me. It was an interesting experience to see it beyond TFA, because my first reaction was, "What did I do wrong?" And I was like, that's not a normal reaction. Or that's not healthy. A lot of the people I talked to were like, "Why didn't we teach this? Or talk to him about this?" But you can't feel guilt or shame that are truly outside of your control. It feels like in TFA that realm doesn't exist though. (Marie)

It is understandable for Dionne and Marie to feel grief, trauma, and a range of complex emotions. And they both asked questions of how they could better support their students. But it is deeply sad and problematic for TFA to foster a culture that encourages CMs to take full responsibility and internalize others' actions to the extent of faulting themselves for students' suicides. Other CMs described feeling guilt or shame for violence outside of their classrooms, including fights or shootings. These occurrences are tragic, and they require redress. But it is inaccurate, unproductive, and highly problematic to narrate these tragedies as individual teachers' faults.

CMs' Limits: "I'm Doing Everything I Can"

CMs' experiences raise questions about CMs' responsibilities and limits. What can CMs control and what should they be held accountable for during their TFA commitment? How can TFA develop a narrative of responsibility and encourage people to work hard and care well without blaming CMs for some of the real challenges that are out of their control?

TFA messages that "highly effective teachers bring to all their efforts a relentless persistence, a determination to do whatever it takes to navigate and overcome seemingly insurmountable challenges to fulfill their students' potential" (Farr, 2010, p. 209). Lola thought TFA shamed CMs with convoluted messaging that, "If you're tired, it's because you're not doing enough." Many of these CMs described feeling pressure to "work relentlessly" for their students in a way that required they work and sacrifice beyond their limits. Despite their efforts, CMs described that emotionally, spiritually, intellectually, and physically, they reached their limits and were unable to work harder, care more, or "rescue" their students from systemic injustice.

In TFA, 27% of CMs began taking prescription medications in TFA to cope with their newfound work-related panic, stress, anxiety, depression, and trauma; 38% of CMs increased their alcohol consumption in TFA to an extent that was previously unprecedented in their lives; 85% of CMs experienced negative changes in their sleep patterns and 73% of CMs described feeling fatigued, some to the point of needing to see a doctor. These are not behavioral changes of people who are not trying hard enough or not caring enough. However, these CMs described feeling like they were still not working hard enough, caring enough, or doing enough for their students and educational equity. Further, these CMs were still assigned negative value judgments and shamed for what was interpreted as failure in the narrative of overextended responsibility and agency.

After periods of disillusionment and struggle, many CMs described cognitively resisting the narratives that bolstered feelings of guilt and shame. When confronted with the narrative falsehood that she was to blame for a broader school environment that caused her students and herself harm, Lola asserted, "I'm not doing anything wrong. I'm doing everything I can." Jane explained that CMs were doing all that they could do and that she was also doing her best given her situational context. She described initially feeling guilty and shamed in TFA for failing to live up to TFA standards, but then asserted that she has limits:

Sometimes I felt, my first year in particular, guilty for not wanting to work until midnight because number one, I just didn't feel like that was humanly possible, I didn't think it was healthy ... but I felt the pressure to do so just because that's what TFA told me I had to do, because if I didn't, you know, children's lives were at stake.

You feel like you are a shitty teacher that is not doing their job, when in reality, you're doing all that you can do, and there's a chance that you might be doing it better than other people. But in the realm of this organization, it's never enough ... My school on

my formal evaluation rates me as highly effective, but according to TFA I am ineffective and I am widening the achievement gap, when all I'm trying to do is do the best
I can with the resources I've been given, which I've found on my own ...

Every time that I've critiqued TFA or thought about critiquing TFA, it's been thrown
back in my face. Like, "Oh, I'm not living up to their standards, I feel bad ... Oh, I'm
not doing everything I can do ... Oh, I haven't updated my exit ticket in two days ...
Oh my gosh, I'm the worst. I'm the worst teacher ever because I'm not showing
them their progress in data." Of course it's important, but you know, I'm not fucking
perfect. (Jane)

In response to the guilt and shame in TFA, Bennett summarized that as individuals, many CMs were doing the best that they could as a single person:

I see that guilt and shame are probably rampant in schools where they ... feel like
they're not doing enough, but at the end of the day, we're already doing so much. The
best cure for guilt and shame is that you have nothing to feel sorry for ... As long as
you're working harder to be better the next day, you have nothing to feel shameful
for. We're doing the best we can. You're one human being. (Bennett)

Negative Effects of Guilt & Shame Narratives: Individual & Systemic

The narrative that promotes a pervasive culture of guilt and shame among CMs
is both flawed and unproductive. Can one person change a system from within
the system? TFA's narrative overextends the responsibilities of CMs during
their TFA commitment in a way that positions CMs to feel guilt and shame.
Most CMs were not struggling because they were not trying hard enough or
not caring enough, or because they wanted to "fail children." They were struggling because the individual-level work of teaching in Philadelphia's public
school system is complex and challenging. Many CMs felt guilty because they
felt they were not doing enough for their students, and additionally guilty for
not addressing systemic inequity while they were focusing on individual-level
work. Further, CMs were negatively interpreted as terrible people for these
perceived failures, resulting in shame.

CMs disagreed with how TFA interpreted and narrated their failures and
personhoods. For example, John described how failures can be growth opportunities, but in TFA he thought they were used to control and shame people:
"Failure and data are not supposed to be things you slap people around with,
which is what they were in TFA. It's not about control. It's about feedback
and it's about getting better."

Additionally, similar to how CMs do not have full knowledge of their students' lives, TFA has limited knowledge of CMs' lives. CMs pointed out that TFA had limited grounds, experience, or authority to make some of these guilt- and shame-laden judgments:

> You're in my room once a month, maybe once every two, three weeks, which is fine. But you're not coming home with me, you're not listening to the phone conversations I'm making with parents, and you're not seeing the extent of my efforts, and for you to say that to me, it's just not ok. (Elliott)

There are narrative and interpretive flaws that have negative effects on individual CMs and on TFA's mission of enacting positive systemic change.

The Negative Effects of Guilt & Shame on Individual CMs

Individually, CMs are valuable as people and as new teachers. CMs were negatively impacted by guilt and shame narratives. These narratives damaged CMs' way of relating to themselves, to TFA, and to their work; rather than promote growth, these narratives contributed to CMs' feelings of helplessness and resistance to TFA.

The overemphasis on CMs' responsibilities and agency discouraged self-care; CMs commonly described that guilt and shame prevented them from engaging in self-care. Marie stated, "In my first year, I had no free time. If I took time to do something non-work related (even on weekends), I would feel guilty." Self-care is important for CMs both as people and as teachers. Lola explained, "TFA needs to change their message; instead of 'in the service of students,' it needs to be, 'self-care.' What are you doing that you're ok. Because if you're not ok, you're not going to be a good teacher. It's not even about being a good teacher, you need to be ok. And I don't think they emphasize that enough." Lola highlighted that CMs also are people with needs; it is damaging to treat CMs as superhuman individuals and push them past their limits.

Further, CMs needed to engage in self-care to support their challenging work as teachers. Sofia, Jane, Robin, Elliott, Aiden, Dionne, Maggie, Lola, and Bennett each acknowledged the importance of self-care for themselves as teachers; they experienced that they are better teachers when they also work to take care of themselves. Overstating CMs' responsibilities and shaming CMs for having needs or struggling is not conducive to building a healthy culture of teacher self-care. Jane stated, "TFA needs to change the way that they support teachers." Mark explained that TFA's message was applied in ways that dehumanized CMs:

> The main message has been that nothing is too _____ that should cause you to give up. Some of my friends are in absolutely ridiculous schools ... but TFA has basically told them to suck it up. I agree that we shouldn't whine and be picky with our placements, but I think that in some situations TFA should understand that we are human and should be treated as such. (Mark)

Guilt and shame narratives caused harm to CMs who extended themselves far past their limits. Robin stated, "The feelings of guilt and failure ... I would wake up in the morning and not want to go to school, felt like something bad would happen and did not know what it was, and I would start crying." CMs reported significant negative life changes that they directly connected to their work in TFA (see Chapter 3). These narratives caused CMs harm and resulted in CMs feeling helpless, disillusioned with TFA, or disinvested in their work. Shame narratives caused CMs to feel helpless—they felt isolated, blamed, inadequate, and like they were the sole reason for their and their students' struggles.

CMs commonly described their experiences as isolating. Shame contributes to isolation. Positioning struggles in TFA as private, personal, shameful failures is isolating. Robin stated, "[I] definitely feel alone/isolated." Drake explained that theoretically he could talk with people about his difficult experiences, "but in this case I keep it to myself and feel guilty." Mark felt disconnected from his friends and struggled to "articulate what is stressful about teaching in the inner-city to my non-teacher friends. They provide support as best as they can and sympathize, but they don't fully understand why I was as stressed or upset by things as I was during my first months of teaching." Similarly, Jordan described a significant other who tried to be supportive but "doesn't understand firsthand what I'm going through. I feel pretty isolated." Bernadette stated, "There are times when I feel very isolated, even from colleagues that I know can empathize." Shame isolates people from potential avenues of support.

The shame narrative also contributed to CMs' feelings of helplessness by blaming CMs for failures they had limited control over and by situating the failure in CMs as people. Shame self-centers people in a way that impedes growth (Burgo, 2013). Shame situates failure in a person; it narrates that this person has failed—period. In this way, shame narratives do not help CMs recognize specifics of what needs to change or what can change, because they are to blame as people. Many CMs described their shame of feeling like they were inadequate teachers and failing students. Jane explained her experience with shame in TFA and described how shame was encouraged by the narrative of personal responsibility and how this sets CMs up to feel perpetually inadequate:

> [In TFA, I felt] shame. Honestly, more so than guilt, shame. Because TFA makes it such a personal experience, and they make your identity in the classroom so personal, and I think those are really strong things, but I felt shameful so many times. It's the first time I've failed and the stakes are so high that that failure is the greatest failure I've ever felt ... that moral weight is unreal. You feel like you are part of the enemy. You feel like you are a shitty teacher that is not doing their job, when in reality, you're doing all that you can do ... in the realm of this organization, it's never enough. It's feeling perpetually inadequate ... when the stakes are so high, that feeling of inadequacy takes on such an emotional and deep meaning that it's unbearable sometimes. (Jane)

Shame is a marker of private failure and does not encourage growth. Lola described her experience with shame in TFA:

> [My experience with TFA] leans more towards shame. There's times I feel guilty, and times I feel shameful, but ... especially my first year, it was *shame*. I felt inadequate, I felt like I wasn't doing a good job, like my students weren't learning because *I* was their teacher. (Lola)

Shame narratives did not help Lola become a better teacher; they simply faulted her for being inadequate. Lola did not feel inspired or learn how to become a better teacher from the shame narrative; rather than learning about what she could do differently, shame narratives implicated and blamed her as a person. Shame narratives are not constructive; they focus more on personal blame than on particular changes that are needed and can be implemented. Shame self-centers people in a detrimental way and locates the problem in an individual's identity and character in a way that makes it difficult if not impossible to address any external problem. If the problem truly is that CMs are uncaring, lazy, terrible people, what is the antidote to being a terrible person? Shame narratives create a damaging circle of inaccurate and unproductive interpretations. CMs were better able to address challenges when they were able to recognize that some of the challenges existed outside of themselves. For example, in her second encounter with tragic student loss, Marie felt distance from TFA's narrative and experienced less shame, which enabled her to better empathize with and support her students. Blaming herself for student suicide was detrimental and actually prevented her from claiming what agency she had in response to this tragedy.

Shame narratives also damage CMs' relationship to TFA. CMs experienced shame narratives as coercive, and these narratives alienated CMs from TFA, curtailed important conversations, made CMs feel dismissive of TFA, and broke trust between CMs and TFA. It is coercive of TFA to interpret CMs' perceived failures as resulting from CMs not caring enough about children. Such tactics discourage needed honest dialogues; Elliott explained that MTLDs questioning CMs' allegiance discourages needed conversations because it builds a fear of being attacked as a person:

> I think there is a place for honest conversation and dialogue. However, what I do hear—messages like what MTLD's are saying—it does call that into question, doesn't it? Because you're afraid that somebody's going to jump at your throat. (Elliott)

In this way, shame narratives promote withdrawal from needed conversations or prompt CMs to respond defensively and dismiss TFA. Many CMs described distancing themselves from TFA's narratives and began distancing themselves from the organization. Shame narratives blame CMs and do not acknowledge ways CMs require support, thereby alienating struggling CMs. Dionne explained that after being negatively interpreted and ignored when she reached out for help, she withdrew from engaging with TFA: "Now I understand the culture more, and I wouldn't say anything. I know they don't really care. If you've been shut down or your opinion hasn't been listened to, I feel like I'm not likely to share those things." Similarly, Lola distanced herself from TFA and explained that TFA's narrative and interpretation of her made her angry because it was untrue and caused her significant harm to believe it:

> I think TFA is maybe even worse now than it was my first year. But the thing is I stopped caring about it as much. I don't take it as personally. I do find myself getting very defensive sometimes … [I had] several panic attacks. I went to the hospital and got prescriptions. I got Xanex and Zoloft but I never took Xanex because I was scared I'd become addicted to it. I took Zoloft for 3 months but stopped because I felt not myself, very numbed, like I had no emotions. That could be part of why I didn't feel ashamed anymore—because I had no feelings at all! Then I got mad. Never felt like this but for TFA. I've never had to take antidepressants before, never been depressed before, never felt this bad about myself, never felt like this much of a failure until I joined TFA. And not only is it that, I feel guilty that I'm neglecting my relationships. My mom has had several interventions with me where she tells me, "I'm worried about you. I don't even recognize you anymore." Same with my grandparents. I ignore those who are closest to me because I just don't have time for the other things.

Why would I put myself out there and tell [TFA] my story? Why would I? It's so emotionally raw, and it hurts to keep opening that up and keep telling that story and have
it be met with nothing. Like, why would I go through that emotional trauma to not
only be met with lack of support, but a blatant indifference to my situation ... [I had]
fainting spells, [was] hospitalized for panic attacks, it had a lot to do with shame and
just the pressure and I couldn't deal with it anymore and I just crashed. After that I
just got mad. I got mad that TFA didn't help me more. I got mad at our school. And
now I'm just mad. Maybe sometimes I still feel guilty, but I don't feel ashamed about
myself any more. I'm mad at TFA. (Lola)

Like Dionne and Lola, many CMs described withdrawing investment, dis-
engaging, and dissociating themselves from TFA. Similarly, John described
TFA's shame narratives as a form of negative reinforcement, which damaged
CMs' relationships to TFA:

[TFA] just motivated [CMs] through negative reinforcement, which is how I was
approached, which obviously didn't resonate with me very well. Maybe it works for
people who are used to being micromanaged. For other people, they were either non-
plussed or it really just made things worse for them. Maybe there's a small fraction of
the cohort that responded to that. From what I saw and heard though ... no. (John)

Elliott described CMs who became defensive and resistant to working with
TFA because of these shame-inducing interpretations. In response to his
friend being shamed and interpreted as not working hard enough or caring
enough, Elliott challenged TFA, "I have devoted my entire life and existence
and health and well-being to this pursuit. How dare you?" Shame narratives
break trust between CMs and TFA.

Additionally, if people learn through modeling, what are CMs taking
from TFA's guilt and shame narratives and possibly passing down to their students? A separate study could be conducted on students' experiences of TFA
narratives and methods.

The Negative Effects of Guilt & Shame on Systemic Change

There are several ways in which TFA's guilt and shame narratives actually
work against TFA's purported hope for enacting positive systemic change. The
guilt and shame narratives overextend CMs' responsibilities and agency in a
way that can inadvertently contribute to structural instability, worsen teacher
attrition rates, minimize the need for systemic change, burn out CMs who
want to help enact systemic change, and discourage CMs from constructively
challenging policies that were detrimental to CMs or students.

First, the guilt and shame narratives do not promote sustainable models for teaching in high-poverty schools. Guilt and shame narratives contribute to a culture of teacher burnout and exacerbate transience in an environment that already suffers from structural instability. TFA and "No Excuses" schools struggle with burnout and teacher attrition (Neufeld, 2014) and should not be treated as a "proven strategy ready to go to scale" (US Department of Education, 2009). Working-class schools already tend to have predominantly young teachers with limited experience compared to wealthier schools (Anyon, 1980; Finn, 1999), and nearly 20% of teachers at high-poverty schools leave every year, a rate 50% higher than wealthier schools (Seidel, 2014). The revolving door effect has enormous fiscal and student learning costs (Ingersoll, 2004; Murnane & Phillips, 1981; Rockoff, 2004). High teacher turnover rates also negatively impact schools' cultures and investment in professional development (National Commission on Teaching and America's Future, 2003). Overextending teacher responsibility and placing all blame or credit on individual teachers is an inaccurate depiction of a complex, systemic problem, and it further destabilizes teaching as a profession. Dionne summarized:

> The rhetoric of TFA [causes] guilt and shame … To sustain this profession, we need to be able to cope with a lot of the stressors and the complexity of the educational system, especially in an urban setting. And TFA does not provide any sustainable model for this to happen. (Dionne)

Additionally, guilt and shame narratives reinforce the misconception that educational inequity is a problem of individual access separate from a created systemic inequity. How a problem is positioned influences the type of solutions generated to address this problem. Individual and systemic responses are required to address what is manifesting as both an individual- and systemic-level struggle. Shaming CMs for not "closing the achievement gap" while they are doing individual-level work is unproductive and minimizes the need for actual systemic change.

Further, these narratives push CMs to burn out and disinvest from the work of addressing educational injustice. Shame narratives reinforce CMs' overextended sense of responsibility and deter CMs from responding to their limits. CMs described burning themselves out when they tried to take on heroic levels of responsibility (see Chapter 7). Lola stated, "TFA Philly is not living up to their commitment. They're not producing teachers who are ready for the type of environment that Philly has. Philly is a tough, tough district to work in." Many CMs joined TFA wanting to advocate for or help enact systemic change, and as a group, CMs have significant power and privilege which can be leveraged towards positive systemic change. Shame narratives contribute to CM burnout in a way that wastes CMs' capacities.

To be effective advocates on an individual or systemic level, CMs require space to grapple with and process their lived experiences. TFA's narratives deter critical action-reflection, shame CMs away from questioning dominant perspectives on knowledge, and push CMs to adopt false narratives that reduce complex struggles to issues of individual effort and caring. How can CMs advocate honestly or well if they are shamed away from honestly grappling with what they have experienced? It is important for CMs to allow the personal to illuminate the political (Lorde, 1984, p. 113), for CMs' lived experiences to help shape how they approach their future individual- or systems-level work.

Conclusion & TFA's Responsibilities

CMs' struggles with guilt and shame in TFA raise questions about TFA's responsibilities. In seeking to address educational inequity, TFA is responsible for its narrative and how it defines, approaches, and influences change. CMs blamed themselves and were blamed by TFA for a wide range of individual and systemic failures. Many CMs thought that they were individually responsible for enacting systemic change within their classrooms. CMs struggled with the narrative that they were responsible for systemic injustice and felt they did not have the capacity to individually address systemic injustice within their classrooms.

Since TFA is evaluating and holding CMs accountable to certain standards, it is important for TFA to clarify CMs' responsibilities while they are in TFA. CMs' responsibilities and capacities were overstated on both an individual and systemic level. CMs described feeling immense guilt over events they had limited control over, and they were shamed in TFA for perceived failures. This is detrimental to CMs as individual people and teachers, and it also has negative impacts on TFA's mission to enact positive systemic change.

CMs' experiences with guilt and shame raise questions about TFA's role in helping its members engage with and process challenging experiences. TFA blurs the line between employer and social impact community. CMs reported experiencing incredibly challenging situations in which they felt they had limited control, and they required support. How much of this support should come from TFA and how much should come from a broader support network of family, friends, faith community, etc.? Arguably, it is to TFA's benefit to care for and support rather than shame its CMs, but the extent of TFA's responsibility to provide care to its recruits is debatable.

Finally, it is unacceptable for TFA to promote a narrative that blames and shames individuals for behavioral health struggles or broad systemic failures. Shame narratives are counterproductive; they discourage and prevent important conversations. For CMs to become "highly effective teachers" or advocate honestly for educational equity, they must listen to their students, grapple with the contexts in which they are teaching, and seek to make sense of their experiences despite TFA's problematic narratives. How are CMs to work alongside their students or advocate honestly for educational equity without space to critically reflect on their lived experiences?

Note

1. This chapter explores CMs' experiences with guilt and shame in TFA. As I am not a professional counselor, Philadelphia-based family therapist Susanne Flood and licensed clinical psychologist Rachael Kerns-Wetherington reviewed this section and provided guidance and feedback.

· 6 ·

THE COMPLEX, POLITICIZED
PROCESS OF TFA AND
CM IDENTITY DEVELOPMENT

Rather than a fixed entity, identity is a changing construction and perfor-mance (Butler, 1990; Foucault, 1977; Rigole, 2011). Identity development is the ongoing process of narrowing the gap between actual identities and designated identities, what is and what can be (Connelly & Clandinin, 1999; Sfard & Prusak, 2005). The process of identity development is complex and politicized; power and knowledge are inter-related in a way that makes every relationship, every narrative, a negotiation of power (Foucault, 1977).

Within this landscape, CMs struggled to understand their intersecting, developing personal and professional identities as new TFA teachers. CMs experienced a conflict between the nature of identity development as a pro-cess and a pressing, immediate need for improvement as new teachers. Addi-tionally, many CMs felt ill-equipped to work through their questions about complex racial, class, cultural, and political dynamics experienced while teaching. These CMs felt they lacked the language, time, and support to engage meaningfully in understanding their own identities independently or in relationship to their students' identities.

The first two subsections in this chapter explore the general constraints teachers experience: Learning the Basic Professional Identity explores a range of teaching and extra-teaching challenges, and Teaching as Political and

Intellectual Work explores the power dynamics of teaching. The next three subsections explore particular identity development failures in the TFA context: CMs Struggling to Identify their Social Location & Prejudices explores the problematic deficits of CMs' personal identity development, CMs' Invisible Privileges explores the absence of discussions on privileged identities in TFA, and The Awkward Struggle of CMs Teaching Students to be Aware of Race and Class explores problematic deficits in CMs' identity development in its relationship to students. Race and class are not the only advantaging/disadvantaging systems at work in society, but since they are the systems TFA is purportedly addressing in trying to "close the achievement gap," I focus on the race and class dynamics in this chapter.

Learning the Basic Professional Identity

All professionals require time to develop and shift from student to practitioner. Professionals do not emerge from training as finished products; rather, professionals grow and change in response to the pressures of practice, and they continue to change throughout their careers (Blackburn & Fox, 1983; Cherniss, 1995).

Teaching is praxis work and involves the practical application of theory; as such, new teachers need to develop a range of skills and practices, including though not limited to: content and pedagogical knowledge, situationally relevant approaches to the content, a performing public self that the teacher can live with comfortably, learning from the effects of their practice, and using what they learn to inform their lesson planning and teaching (Ball & Cohen, 1999; Featherstone, 1993; Feiman-Nemser, 2003). The learning curve for new teachers is steep, particularly in the first three to four years (Feiman-Nemser, 2003). CMs face a double bind: they require time and reflection to grow into their professional identities as competent teachers, but they are immediately placed in charge of classrooms and need to steepen an already-steep learning curve in order to perform competently in their two-year teaching commitment.

Bennett, Aiden, Jane, Lola, Marie, Maggie, and other CMs identified the baseline struggle of being a first-year teacher in Philadelphia's public school system. CMs echoed research findings on common challenges to new teachers: the instability of high teacher and staff turnover rates, lack of resources and supports, excessive workloads, low salaries, limited career growth, limited understanding of how to respond effectively to disruptive student behavior, and limited teacher influence in decision-making, accountability policies, urban poverty, and teacher preparation (Ingersoll, 2001; Prince, 2003; Shern-off et al., 2011). Maggie stated,

> The whole, "What the hell am I doing?" Every first year teacher struggles with things to some different degree … and it's going to call into question your ability to do this job, over and over and over again. And on top of that, you're dealing with the lack of support from your school, the lack of supplies, the lack of space, the lack of time … all the deficits.

In their work settings, CMs encountered a wide range of obstacles, many of which were complicated and required more knowledge or resources than CMs possessed at the time. The challenges that fall within the scope of teacher responsibility are already enormous. In Philadelphia's transitioning educational landscape, where many publicly funded schools were over-crowded, limited in their resources, lacking in support staff, with few or no nurses, counselors, or social workers, CMs found that they regularly encountered challenges that do not fall traditionally in the scope of what teachers are trained to do. Where there were gaps in service, CMs struggled to learn and take on these responsibilities; this further complicated CMs' growth into their professional identities. For example, without additional staff to provide emotional support to students, CMs faced another double bind: trying to teach while their students were emotionally overwhelmed was ineffective, but if they tried to address those emotional needs, they were no longer teaching the necessary content. The responsibilities presented in CMs' work lives were beyond the scope of their professional training.

CMs experienced significant strain on their professional identity development and struggled to develop, perform, and function as new teaching professionals in Philadelphia's public schools. Elliott, Maggie, Lola, Aiden, Bennett, Jane, and Marie recognized that the challenges they faced were not entirely unique to CMs. Jane posited, "Is this TFA or first year of teaching? I think it's a bit of both." Marie stated, "I don't think that this experience is unique to TFA CMs, I think it's an urban education problem and a teacher prep problem."

Teaching as Political and Intellectual Work

In addition to developing content and pedagogical knowledge, CMs grappled with complicated power dynamics while learning to be teachers. CMs require time to develop pedagogy beyond the most rudimentary functions of a classroom; as Elliott explained, "I'm a third-year teacher now and only now am I beginning to explore beyond just running the classroom. I did a little bit my second year. And I don't think TFA is into that at all."

Teaching is an inherently political act and schools embody a struggle over what power relations, social practices, and privileged forms of knowledge ought to be transmitted to students (Anyon, 1980; Finn, 1999; Freire, 1970; Giroux, 1983). Schools are one space in which students make meaning of the world. Through classroom structures, practices, interactions, and pedagogies, all teachers communicate a hidden curriculum and influence students' relationships to work, economy, and authority (Anyon, 1980; Finn, 1999; Hidden Curriculum, 2014). Education is not a static product that involves only the transference of knowledge, and educational inequity is not only a matter of unequal access to this conceptualized education product. Through its overt and hidden curriculum, schooling introduces and legitimates particular forms of social life; schools support a specific vision of past, present, and future in a way that can reproduce inequity and oppressive dynamics (McLaren, 1989, pp. 160–161; Giroux, 1996, p. 150).

CMs expressed discomfort with TFA's hidden curriculum, which Elliott critiqued as "rote," "monotonous," and "dehumanizing, especially for marginalized students." CMs described TFA's "No Excuses" as a working-class pedagogy (see Chapter 2), and they questioned whether they were promoting educational access for poor students of color or inadvertently facilitating social reproduction. Additionally, CMs expressed concern about the limited and superficial conversations on race or class in TFA. TFA often positions education as a product and removes the struggle for educational equity from the landscape and history of power. For example, TFA-endorsed phrases such as "The Achievement Gap" and "No Excuses" focus on the depoliticized present in a way that, when scaled up, can inadvertently ignore some of the complex, historically rooted structural oppression and thereby overlook what might be required to address the injustice. Since the development of the public education system to its current state of class and racial segregation was a complex political and intentional movement, the revision and reform would also need to include political, intentional, structural changes.

Because schools are politicized spheres, and because education is inherently political, it is important for CMs to recognize their social location and develop an understanding of power. Every act of applied development— including what CMs are being trained to do as "leaders" addressing educational inequity—is an act of interpretation and a negotiation of power

(Foucault, 1977; Nakkula & Ravitch, 1998, p. xi; TFA: Our Mission, 2014). Whether CMs seek to do individual-level work and serve as transformative intellectuals through teaching or whether they seek to do systems-level work by influencing policy, both paths require a growing understanding of power, race, and class.

CMs Struggling to Identify Their Social Location & Prejudices

CMs' social locations are significant as they seek to engage in the inherently political work of teaching, and significant as they seek to address what is inherently a socially constructed inequity. CMs' interpretations and their hermeneutics (principles of interpretation) shape their individual interactions and their systems-level advocacy. All people have prejudices. Critical reflection is necessary to unpack some of the prejudice, understandings, and misunderstandings CMs will inevitably have in their interpretations of their students, themselves, and their work in TFA (Nakkula & Ravitch, 1998). While in TFA, many CMs were overwhelmed with their workloads, were confronted daily with complex and often cross-cultural experiences that they needed to respond to as teachers, and had little space to unpack their interpretations or critically consider how their own racial and class identities might influence their experiences.

CMs entered TFA with problematic interpretations about their students, themselves, and their work. Jane, Kate, Lola, Elliott, Dionne, and Marie also described that they and/or their peers held deeply rooted prejudices that shaped their interactions with their students and their work in TFA. For example, Jane described her own participation in believing and perpetuating stereotypes about her students, and explained how both the trainings and structure of TFA do not facilitate critical examination of these assumptions: "During institute, TFA really makes it easy to make assumptions about your kids. You assume someone's parent is in jail, you assume all these things … Not all children growing up in poverty are the same … The whole program really makes you make assumptions about the people you're going to be working with. And two, you're so overwhelmed, your first year, you may not have time to understand the people—the kids—that you're serving." Similarly, Kate and Lola shared comments about how their time in TFA contributed to problematic interpretations of their students and their students' abilities.

Lola confessed that this dynamic can be difficult to avoid in TFA: "I feel like I'm advancing negative stereotypes of African Americans … I feel like I've started to believe in them and their ability less—that's tough to admit." The TFA experience positions CMs to witness students' disenfranchisement without necessarily recognizing the intent, agent, mechanism, or beneficiaries of this system; CMs are to serve a disenfranchised, racialized "them" and CMs are given little education, support, or space to critically evaluate their interpretations.

CMs' beliefs shape how they see, understand, evaluate, and engage in their work as teachers or as advocates for educational equity. CMs' prejudices impacted their interactions with and relationship to students; this emerged in intra-corps discussions. For example, Elliott and Dionne explained that CMs often assumed the right to define their students' identities with "they can't" and "they don't" statements. Many CMs spoke for their students of color with statements such as, "they don't want to learn," "they have no discipline," "they can't sit silently," or "they don't have grit." These gross generalizations define students by what CMs perceive as students' lacks. All people have prejudices and CMs are no different; CMs held internalized prejudices which emerged in their interactions. Elliott described CMs' "they can't" and "they don't" statements as example expressions of "cultural and racial stereotypes that we've internalized." CMs require space to address and unpack the prejudices that underlie and shape their interactions.

TFA trainings inadvertently reinforced CMs' prejudices through encouraging CMs to consider their students' race and class without considering racism, classism, systems of power, or CMs' social location in these systems. This narrative implies that race begets racism rather than recognizing that racism has constructed race in America (Coates, 2014c). Jane, Lola, Dionne, Nicole, and Elliott expressed frustration over TFA's non-existent to superficial engagement with structural racism, white privilege, and the cultural and racial stereotypes that are held within TFA. Questions of race in TFA trainings were only about students' race and not about CMs' race; this reified whiteness as invisible and positioned students' race and class identities as the source of any problematic interactions. For example, Dionne explained how students' and their parents' race and class were introduced in the context of a problem, without considering how CMs' identities might contribute to the problems. Dionne expounded that TFA could initiate discussions on CMs' racial and class identities, but instead focused on only students' racial and class identities:

It's directly related to the "Excellence, No Excuses" model, like, "Institutional racism is not a reason for you to not succeed." And not in a, "Let's talk about this and work through it," but more like, "Let's ignore it—excellence, no excuses! I don't want to hear it!" They don't want to digest that. I think it's a lack of programming around this in general. In the DCA sessions we're only talking about racial remarks or very explicit or oppressive remarks around race from students to teachers, and we're not understanding how actions from teachers to students might be an issue …

If students' parents think you're a racist teacher or find something you did offensive, we just get really defensive instead of thinking, "Well, where is this parent coming from? What actions have I taken that make them react this way?" The way parents are framed in TFA, like they're not valued … even in DCA sessions,[1] that was another time race came up. We talk about the race of parents and the class of parents and not about how we could be impacting things and our place …

The race of the teacher is never discussed. And that's what TFA can control more so—that discussion and the interaction between teacher and students and how that plays out. But the only time I remember anyone raising this stuff about teachers is when students make comments, or students made offensive remarks around the teacher's identity. Like, this kid called the teacher a "white bitch" or where kids are initiating these quote-unquote oppressive terms. But that's very skewed and a very roundabout way of not discussing what that means. (Dionne)

Rather than considering or questioning why students or their parents might be wary of racism, Dionne thought TFA's programming encouraged CMs to be dismissive of these concerns and treat institutional racism as an excuse. Conversations on race in TFA focused on the perceived deficits, problems, or conflicts with students and communities of color in a way that reified whiteness as invisible, thereby ignoring the reality of group-based advantage (Lapayese et al., 2014). CMs were well-versed in discussing the "achievement gap" but were not prompted to discuss white privilege or systemic racism. At best, institutional racism was superficially acknowledged as a label or a catchphrase to check off, rather than presented as an immediately relevant topic that requires deep engagement. TFA positions CMs to witness students' disenfranchisement without necessarily recognizing the intent, agent, mechanism, or beneficiaries of this system; CMs are to serve a disenfranchised, racialized "them" in a way that makes it too easy for CMs to reinforce uninformed prejudices about students and their communities. It is difficult for people to acknowledge and address their prejudices, and it becomes increasingly difficult in an environment that focuses on students' race and class without considering systems of oppression or CMs' varying participations in these systems. CMs described forming problematic conclusions from their experiences focusing on students' disenfranchisement in TFA. For example, Kate stated,

> The most difficult thing for me to talk about is how teaching in this neighborhood is affecting my personal beliefs about hope and change in the community. I feel at times that I have become much more pessimistic about this community. (Kate)

CMs' Invisible Privileges

CMs often felt more comfortable identifying students' disenfranchisement or their own disadvantaged identities than they did identifying the existence of oppression or their own advantaged identities. CMs described how TFA provided trainings for CMs to discuss students' race and class, but TFA did not provide trainings for CMs to engage with white privilege or class privilege. There are differences between CMs and most students they serve: possibly the most common is that the majority of CMs have the choice and power to leave the public school system at any time, whereas most of their students do not. Dionne described that most CMs had the choice to leave their schools and relocate jobs or neighborhoods if they wanted:

> CMs have the option to leave. And CMs have the option to leave to be in a neighborhood surrounded by people that they would feel comfortable with. I don't think there's many CMs living in neighborhoods that are as dangerous as [those that] a lot of our kids live in. And there's this thing where we don't talk about how we feel about walking from school, or feel about how we're talking with parents who we might not understand where they're coming from. (Dionne)

CMs' privileges were treated as invisible, and many CMs seemed more comfortable discussing only their students' disenfranchised identities without discussing CMs' identities. Some CMs discussed their identities only when it overlapped with an oppressed identity, selectively magnifying aspects of their experience with past or present hardship for the purpose of minimizing their present privileges. CMs seemed more comfortable discussing students' disadvantage or CMs' past disadvantage without discussing present systems of advantage/disadvantage. Dionne expounded,

> People are sometimes only comfortable bringing identity up when they can relate to it directly. For example, a Jewish teacher was talking about the Holocaust and how that relates to slavery, and it's like, "I'm comfortable talking about my identity when it's the oppressed identity, but not talking about what it means to be privileged, to be

on the other side of things." I think that's also very difficult. In general we don't talk about that. TFA doesn't talk about identity and privilege. We only talk about it in the deficit model. Culture is looked at as a barrier, instead of thinking that we could ever learn something from our students about our own experiences or privilege from the experiences of our kids. (Dionne)

Speaking only of disadvantage out of the context of systems that advantage and disadvantage groups of people promotes deficit views about students and precludes CMs' need to concede privilege. Jane described how TFA acknowledged students' race and class, but did not engage with white privilege; she thought this was problematic and presented an inaccurate picture of systemic injustice:

I think that education is the battleground for the new civil rights movement but not just in low-income schools with students of color. The other side—the "privileged" schools or student populations—is just as much of a part of the battle. (Jane)

In the shared work of liberation from oppressive systems, it is important for CMs to identify their social location, inclusive of both disadvantaged and advantaged identities. Racial and class privileges should not be treated as invisible; this facilitates ignoring the reality of systemic oppression.

The Awkward Struggle of CMs Teaching Students to Be Aware of Race and Class

CMs were instructed to actively engage with students' racial and class identities, despite their at times overwhelming struggle to be competent first- and second-year teachers in Philadelphia's public school system, their limited understanding of their own racial and class identities, and their limited understanding of broader systems of oppression.

The 2012 CM class faced formal TFA evaluation metrics that included raising students' "critical consciousness." The 2012 CMs were the first to be evaluated in this system called "The Big 7," which included rating CMs' performance based on "[How many] students are racially aware, understand the socio-political context of their communities, and can articulate how they can positively impact their peers, families, communities, and this world" (TFA: The Big 7, 2014). Should CMs be tasked with teaching students about students' sociopolitical contexts, particularly when many CMs did not know how to discuss their own sociopolitical contexts? And if CMs should facilitate conversations about sociopolitical contexts with their students, what is an appropriate space for this and how should CMs engage?

Mandating CMs teach students about students' racial and class identities assumes CMs have the authority and knowledge to teach students about their identities, and it assumes that students need to be taught about being poor people of color. These are inaccurate and problematic assumptions. CMs have at least as much to learn from their students about systems of oppression as students have to learn from CMs. This TFA narrative positions CMs as speakers, but not listeners; it undermines the knowledge students already possess and the role of students' voices in their education. Paulo Freire (1970), Adrienne Rich (1976), Audre Lorde (1984), and Lisa Delpit (1988) observe that it is oppressed people who are often most acutely aware of the existence of oppression and disadvantaging systems, and people with privilege who are often least aware of, or least willing to acknowledge, its existence.

Maggie, Jane, Lola, and Dionne expressed disbelief and frustration over TFA's Big 7. Maggie described these metrics as extremely subjective and was incredulous about TFA's enforcing this rubric: "I was really shocked actually that they took the whole TAL Teaching as Leadership rubric and took that whole premise and put it on steroids and *ran* with it." As she observed new CMs learning about these evaluation metrics, Maggie described them as "terrified and overwhelmed." Many CMs did not know how to teach other people about their racial and class identities, and TFA did not provide this training.

Jane and Lola both believe in the importance of understanding systems of oppression; however, they problematized TFA's approach of teaching students to be "racially aware." Jane described a conflict between TFA's evaluation and what she thought she should be teaching her students during class. Jane questioned the purpose or validity of prompting her students in class to be "constantly racially aware that they're black. And low-income":

> I got feedback on a lesson, [my MTLD] was approximately in my classroom for 30 minutes, I believe we were learning about the Articles of Confederation, and somehow, maybe talking to about 5 kids in my classroom, she said … "55% of students are racially aware." We're learning about the Articles of Confederation right now. It has nothing to do with race at the moment and I don't want my kids to be sitting in class and being constantly racially aware that they're black. And low-income. (Jane)

Lola took issue with one, her position to engage parents on a topic she felt unfamiliar with, and two, a perceived disconnect between TFA's evaluation and her classroom work. Lola explained that she did not know what the label "sociopolitical context" meant, and she was not sure what knowledge, position, or authority she had to call parents and ask them about their sociopolitical contexts. Additionally, she thought TFA's classroom evaluations were detached from CMs' and students' work in the classroom:

> I have a big problem with their evaluation this year, the Big 7. Five out of the seven things have nothing to do with me as a classroom teacher. [According to TFA] I didn't reach out to my parents to talk about their "sociopolitical context." I don't even know what that means. My students' parents don't even know what that means. And what position or authority do I have to call and ask about that? It's ridiculous to me. A lot of the stuff they're evaluating us on has nothing to do with us in the classroom, it has to do with sociopolitical backgrounds, and all this stuff I do already, but I don't like the way they define it. There's this cognitive dissonance between what they're evaluating us on and what's going on in the classroom. (Lola)

Dionne had previous experience learning and teaching about identity development prior to TFA and contrasted the complexity of actual human identity development with TFA's approach of labeling and evaluating people with buzzwords. Dionne described how TFA used catchy phrases like "institutional racism" or "achievement gap" without giving CMs the space or resources to engage in-depth with what these phrases mean. She critiqued TFA's way of superficially labeling students' races and class without listening to students' experiences. Dionne also recognized the challenge of facilitating complex conversations about race and class, and she questioned how CMs were expected to teach students about students' identities when many CMs did not know their own social location:

> How are you supposed to teach someone about their identity when you haven't—and I'm not saying CMs necessarily haven't—but how is TFA telling you that you need to teach other people about their own identity, but never ask you or themselves to do that individually? With TFA, if you're not allowing me or helping me explore my own identity, how do you expect me to teach someone else that? ... I taught and facilitated two different courses in undergrad around identity and discussing identity. So I'm used to discussing identity. But even with that background, teaching and being so unprepared for teaching period, it's very hard to address those things. It's still, to this day, difficult to know how to do that. With my experience, if I'm struggling this much, for people who don't have the experience that I have in terms of talking about these subjects ... I mean, TFA hasn't given us that experience, so how are people going to be able to do that? (Dionne)

Dionne's description of a conversation with her students in her third year teaching highlights the time, training, and practice required to create a safe space and facilitate complex discussions on identity development; the importance of listening to students' experiences and voices; and the insights and perspectives students already have about race and class. Dionne taught middle school math and facilitated an African American History Club afterschool. In one of these meetings in 2013—prior to the wave of national mainstream media discussions on police violence against black men, the protests declaring "Black Lives Matter," and the growing national awareness of racial inequity in 2014 (Blow, 2014; Coates, 2014d; Demby, 2014; Hill, 2014; Martin, 2014; Mueller & Southall, 2014)—Dionne's middle school students expressed a clearer understanding of racial profiling, institutionalized racism, classism, and stereotypes than most CMs in this study were able to articulate. Dionne utilized events which are relevant to students to make space for students to name their experiences with systems of power, and she related to her students as co-partners in constructing meaning rather than treating students as receptacles of knowledge (Freire, 1970; Gutstein, 2006):

> In African American History Club I'm getting more and more comfortable discussing the history of things, but then also discussing how kids experience it today. As a white woman, it's harder, but this year's been the easiest because with time, you build relationships with students. As a teacher, you develop skills to make more space for students. For example, this year we're talking about people being labeled by their skin color and saying they committed a crime. If the police put us all in a room, who would they assume did it and why. So first, students excluded the women, and said, "They wouldn't think that the women did it." So me and the one girl who is in the group, we were excluded, and we went back and also, since I'm white, students said I'd be the first one excused. And then the other girl would be excused. And we're processing that as a group. And going into lighter skinned people, half the group is Latino, so they said, "You're light, they won't think it was you." And then one of the kids has braces and they said, "They're going to think you have money, and you don't need to steal because you have braces and braces cost money." And then next up was the darkest black boys. And then they're brothers, actually. The younger brother looks less threatening, and students thought they're probably going to assume it's the older darker brother. These students are 11, 12, 13. They went through and did that. They asked if there was a white man, then who would be excused first? They said I'd still be first, but then he'd be excused before the woman of color. They'd excuse the white people first.

> So really, I can have those conversations in smaller groups with certain content. In *American Promise*, the documentary, the dad spoke about how anything that would happen at the school he attended, they would just throw all the black kids out of class and assume they did it. That's where this conversation came from. In smaller groups this is easier. This is very much a creation of my past experience with African

American History, and with my experience with the group "The Hearts of Black Men" since I was in high school.

I have had more success this year than in previous years, and I have a very mixed school, which is abnormal in general. This year we're even more diverse because we moved locations. So this year we have less Latino students, more black students, more white students, and I have two Cambodian students this year. My school just has more explicit difference, and kids can see it, so conversation comes out more explicitly now. When there's a remark around Asian stereotypes we can talk about how that student is not representative of all Cambodian people. Being able to have those conversations. (Dionne)

In contrast to Dionne's middle school students, many CMs confessed honestly that they struggled to understand—much less talk about or teach others about—race, class, and systemic oppression. For example, Devon stated that prejudices and stereotypes were difficult to talk about in TFA. Kate stated that she did not share her honest thoughts in TFA, and she said that she was called racist in TFA for voicing her opinions: "Even with less drastic viewpoints I regularly feel attacked in classes and on more than one occasion I have been called a racist. TFA CMs and staff are generally some of the most close-minded people I have come across." Instead of co-constructing meaning with her peers, Kate stated that she did not think TFA was a safe space to engage in conversations, and she opted instead to keep a private blog. All people have prejudice, and it is especially important for helping professionals to have space to unpack their prejudice. It is an ethical responsibility for helping professionals to contextualize themselves and understand the beliefs that underlie and direct their work. TFA did not provide CMs the training or support required to facilitate difficult conversations on identity, race, class, power, or systems of oppression, and CMs struggled to teach students "critical consciousness" or "how to be racially aware." Additionally, TFA's pedagogy and evaluations for CMs to teach students about race and class positioned CMs as holders of knowledge and discouraged CMs from listening to and learning from their students' experiences and understandings of race and class in America.

Conclusion

Identity development is a process and requires time and critical reflection. CMs struggled to accelerate an already steep learning curve to function competently in their professional identities as new teachers in under-resourced schools. Additionally, teaching is an inherently political act, and CMs grappled with complicated power dynamics while learning to be teachers.

Educational inequity is a complex social construction, and creating a TFA fast track to educational leadership has as much potential to harm as it does to help. Elliott explained that he was "troubled" by TFA's system of placing young and relatively inexperienced CMs and alumni in positions of power, and concluded, "Right now we've got this fast track … I don't know if that's the best way." John summarized his concerns about TFA: "I think it's an issue of maturity for the institution, when it comes down to it." TFA set unrealistic expectations for CMs and made inaccurate, problematic assumptions about students, CMs, and identity development in its messaging and evaluation systems such as "The Big 7." CMs struggled to identify their own social location and were ill-equipped to facilitate meaningful conversations about race, class, or power with their students.

Whether CMs seek to do individual-level work and serve as transformative intellectuals through teaching or whether they seek to do systems-level work by influencing policy, both paths require a growing understanding of power, race, and class. TFA has a number of strengths, including though not limited to: acknowledging educational inequity in the U.S. as a problem that can and needs to be addressed; recruiting thousands of idealistic, high-achieving individuals to join TFA; and establishing itself as a powerful force in the dominant discourse on education and social change. TFA's website claims, "TFA CMs and alumni are helping lead an educational revolution in low-income communities across the country" (TFA: Our Mission, 2014). Educational inequity is a civil rights issue and it needs to be addressed; however, it is important for TFA and CMs to identify their social location in this "revolution" to help dismantle rather than reify systems of oppression.

Both CMs as individuals and TFA as an institution require time to listen, learn, contextualize themselves, and develop a stance of working alongside rather than for the students and communities they serve. What "help" CMs extend and how CMs extend "help" matters. In order to be an egalitarian movement working towards educational equity, TFA's epistemology needs to seek out rather than exclude perspectives of those directly affected by its claims. Both individuals and institutions—consciously or subconsciously—have a set of underlying ideological beliefs, which drive their actions. To address the particular dynamics of power which foundationally reinforce educational inequity, it is critical for TFA and CMs to make the unconscious conscious, recognize the politicized nature of schools and school reform, and listen to and learn from the students and communities they serve. TFA and CMs have at least as much to learn from their students and students' communities about systems of oppression as students and students' communities have to learn from TFA and CMs.

Note

1. DCA sessions refers to Teach For America's internal "Diversity, Community, and Achievement" trainings.

· 7 ·

TFA IDEALISM AND THE HERO TEACHER NARRATIVE

"Everybody in the teaching world knows that it's going to take more than two years for you to be an outstanding teacher. If you're an outstanding teacher in two years, then you're an outlier or you're really naive. [TFA is] setting people up to feel like failures. Like, they go in expecting to be Erin Gruwell and they are, you know, the 99.9 other percent of teachers."
—Marie

Idealism is a core identity marker for TFA on both an institutional and an individual level. The summary of Wendy Kopp's book *One Day, All Children …* identifies TFA as an "organization created by and for young idealists" (Kopp, 2003, back cover). CMs frequently described themselves and their peers as idealistic, noting specifically their identity as a group of empathetic, high-achieving, dedicated individuals. TFA successfully recruits many idealists to work towards its cause of addressing educational inequity.

Though idealism has its strengths, idealism becomes problematic in its tendency towards telling an oversimplified, incomplete, or exaggerated story. These stories are untrue in how they misstate challenges, what resources a person needs, and what a person can accomplish through the prescribed method.

The hero teacher narrative is an active expression of idealism in TFA, and CMs' counternarratives explicitly and implicitly point to shortcomings of the hero teacher narrative. This chapter explores the gap between the hero teacher narrative CMs expected and the actual, disillusioning reality that they experienced. The first subsection of this chapter provides an overview of idealism in TFA, and the second subsection provides a description of the hero teacher narrative as an expression of idealism. The next two subsections explore TFA's and CMs' perpetuation of the hero teacher narrative, both within and outside of TFA. Then I explore the damaging effects of the hero narrative on CMs, including experiencing cognitive dissonance, disillusionment, blame, and burnout. Finally, I discuss the damaging effects of the hero teacher narrative on systemic change, including the reinforcement of stereotypes and the problems of doublespeak and euphemisms.

Believing a narrative that is detached from reality set CMs up to be like Don Quixote tilting at windmills—Quixote is at best ineffectual and at worst causes harm to himself and the people around him. Performing the idealistic hero narrative can do harm to both CMs and the people they are intending to serve. Additionally, the hero teacher narrative minimizes the need for systemic change and calls for CMs to overcome the obstacles of structural oppression, institutional racism, and historic inequity through their individual hard work and caring. Scaling up idealism is insufficient to dismantle systemic, historically rooted inequity.

An Overview of Idealism

TFA's mission and messaging attracted idealists. Lola described, "TFA purposely recruits people who are very idealistic and people who really want to help and people who really want to do a good thing … The mission and the script is really what drew me in." Similarly, Robin stated, "Look at who TFA recruits—Type A people who care about children. You're already on edge and seeking perfection." Themes emerged from CMs' descriptions of themselves and their fellow CMs as idealists. Idealism was a broader umbrella for a combination of traits, namely empathy, high standards, and passionate personal commitment.

CMs identified themselves and their peers as empathetic people: "people who really want to help" (Lola), "Type A people who care about children" (Robin), and people "who wear our hearts on our sleeves to some gradient … Most of us are very empathetic individuals who feel for students every single day" (John). Dionne added that "[to be] a great teacher you need to be empathetic in my opinion."

CMs also held high standards for themselves; many self-identified as perfectionists with track records of achievement. For example, Robin described typical CMs as people "already on edge and seeking perfection," and Aiden stated that he had "a very clear vision of what my classroom should look like and I am a perfectionist by nature," and he had known that he has "succeeded at so many other things in [his] life." Maggie stated of her fellow CMs, "These are pretty high-functioning people. These people are smart. TFA hires people for a reason."

In addition to these high standards, many CMs had a passionate personal commitment to achieving these standards. John described CMs as a "passionate" group of people, and he thought many CMs entered TFA believing it was up to them to personally "fix" the system. CMs highlighted their past accomplishments and their present commitment to personally address educational inequity. TFA's website states, "We recruit committed recent college graduates and professionals from all majors and career backgrounds to teach for two years in urban and rural public schools" and to "close the achievement gap" (TFA: Achievement Gap, 2014).

Idealists can be summarized as "people who want to do a good thing" (Lola). Many CMs described joining TFA to achieve TFA's mission of "ensuring that kids growing up in poverty get an excellent education" (TFA: Our Mission, 2014). Maggie described her fellow CMs as "all bright, extremely empathic, idealistic people."

There are positive aspects to idealism, such as highlighting the potential for positive change, providing a rudimentary vision of what needs to be accomplished, and reminding individuals of their power and capacity. However, there are also ways that idealism can be insufficient or even cause harm to both the helpers and the people they are trying to help. Idealism can provide false expectations of what an individual can hope to accomplish, and it can contribute to disillusionment, blame, and burnout among helping professionals. Additionally, idealism can reinforce a narrative that is detached from reality and history in a way that limits the relevance and effectiveness of idealists' efforts to address structural inequity.

The Hero Teacher Narrative

There is a hero teacher narrative in TFA; it is an expression of idealism. Popular media stories, the "professional mystique," CMs' expectations, and TFA's culture helped to shape the hero teacher narrative in TFA. CMs explicitly referred to themselves or the expectations of themselves as: hero, superhero, savior, white knight, and martyr:

> And [CMs] went into it thinking, "Yeah, I'm going to make some growth, and I'm going to teach them change, and yeah, I'm going to be that girl from Freedom Writers! (Marie)

> A lot of people came into this thinking they were going to be a great white knight on a shining horse. (John)

> Another stereotype of CMs is CMs as white knight. Going into it and trying to save people. And I do feel like that's still true. I do feel like a lot of CMs feel like they're changing the world and their children *need* all the help they can get from the CM. (Nicole)

> It's interesting how TFA expects this super teacher, this hero, this savior. (Dionne)

> We need to be ... superheroes. (Maggie)

> I'm a martyr; I am devoting two years of my LIFE to this cause and I should be working 24/7/365 for my kids; I'm not important in this cause at this time in my life. (Devon)

In their hope to do good, many CMs held a romanticized view of their professional work and had unrealistic expectations of what they could accomplish, a phenomenon called "professional mystique" (Cherniss, 1995, p. 17). Popular stories in media contribute to the professional mystique. Stereotypes, narratives, images, and characters from movies, books, and television have been shown to influence professionals; example archetypes include "the competent physician, the dedicated teacher, the clever attorney" (Cherniss, 1995, p. 17; DeFleur, 1964). Some CMs referenced popular films and narratives about heroic teachers when describing the idealism and disillusionment in TFA.

The hero teacher narrative is common and can be found in movies such as *Blackboard Jungle* (1955), *To Sir With Love* (1967), *Conrack* (1974), *Stand and Deliver* (1988), *The Hobart Shakespearians* (2005), and *Freedom Writers* (2007). These movies are billed as "based on true events." The hero teacher narrative is straightforward: students need to be saved from their families, drugs, and violence, and the hero teacher "must win [students] over to a better life, all while doing battle with his idiot colleagues, the dull-witted administration, and the dangerously backward parents. He is a solitary hero. The Saint-teacher's task is urgent because he must figure out who can be saved before it's too late ... the bad teachers have already given up on all kids. That's their sin" (Ayers, 2001, pp. 201–202). The hero teacher narrative even appears in films highlighting

TFA CMs, for example, *Won't Back Down* (2012) presents a "handsome young TFA teacher who we learn is great because his classes are often line dancing while he sings songs about going to college" (Rubinstein, 2012b).

There are problems with Hollywood dramatized stories that are promoted as true stories: often the timeline is drastically accelerated, greater responsibility is placed on a single individual, and students' growth trajectories are exaggerated. For example, Jaime Escalante, the teacher whose experience served as the inspiration for *Stand and Deliver*, called the film "90 percent truth and 10 percent drama" (Lanier, 2010, p. 32). In the film, Escalante enters the troubled Garfield High School in Los Angeles, teaches basic math to poor Latino students, then those same students take Advanced Placement (AP) calculus with him the next year and pass the rigorous test. The department head and principal are depicted as dismissive or out of touch. A student named Angel, typifying the troubled youth with a "Fuck You" tattoo, initially struggles with math, but eventually earns the top score on the AP calculus exam.

In real life, the timeline was significantly slower, responsibility was not shouldered by only one educator, and students' growth trajectories were amazing, though there was no Angel student. Escalante did not teach calculus until his fifth year teaching; in his first attempt, five students completed the course, and two of them passed the AP exam. It took Escalante and other key supporters eight years to build the phenomenal math program that *Stand and Deliver* condenses into two years. Though Escalante was instrumental in the creation of this program, he had partners. Escalante's first principal resisted his efforts, but the next principal, Henry Gradillas, supported Escalante; with Gradillas, Escalante designed a pipeline of courses to prepare students for AP calculus, became department head, selected teachers for his feeder courses, and facilitated the development of algebra classes at neighboring middle schools. Together, they changed Garfield's math department (Lanier, 2010). Contrasting with the film's narrative, Escalante's actual narrative highlights that changes within and outside of the classroom are critical to students' success. Additionally, though his actual students achieved incredible academic results, Escalante emphasized in interviews that there was no real student like Angel who went from basic math in one year to AP calculus in the next (Lanier, 2010, p. 32). Additionally, Fernando Bocanegra, one of Escalante's actual students stated, "I think the wrong things were exaggerated, for example, the troublemaker in the class (Angel). There was really no one in our class who was like that." Bocanegra criticized what he viewed as the film's tendency to reinforce negative stereotypes and said his classmates were "college-bound students who didn't identify with the image of the cholo or barrio tough" (Valle, 1988).

Escalante had an arguably immeasurable impact on his students, the growth of AP courses to public schools instead of remaining a privilege of wealthier, elite private schools, and the discourse on what all students can accomplish given the necessary supports (Jesness, 2002, pp. 34–39). However, Escalante's successful program collapsed after he left. The AP calculus scores at Garfield peaked in 1987, Gradillas' last year at Garfield. After Gradillas left, Escalante stayed a few years more, and the rest of the hand-picked enrichment teachers left soon after. Garfield's AP calculus passing rate dropped below ten percent (Jesness, 2002; Lanier, 2010). This reality does not undercut the amazing accomplishments of Escalante, his partners, and his students; rather, it emphasizes both the individual effort and the structural changes needed to enact and sustain meaningful changes in the education system.

Aside from any factual differences or dramatic licenses of film narratives, another issue with these films is the collective telling of the single story, over and over again: the solo hero teacher comes in and with hard work and heart is able to overcome all odds and save his students from their lives of poverty. The narrative implicitly says that good teachers can and will dramatically improve all their students' lives, and those who fail to do so are incompetent, lazy, uncaring, or all of the above. The hero narrative puts all blame or all credit on teachers. Contrary to the hero narrative, many CMs—even those nominated for the prestigious Sue Lehmann Award—found that despite their best efforts, they were unable to achieve the hero teacher's results.

Additionally, the hero teacher narrative is limited because it designates as primarily individual what in reality is also systemic. Within the dominant narrative, it is unrealistic and unproductive to act like individual effort is the only factor to influence students' educational outcomes. Even if the results of Escalante the actual person or the film character are possible and achieved by the rare hero, this is not a sustainable, realistic, or scalable solution to a systemic problem. The hero narrative removes the need for others to be involved, for broader social responsibility for public education. The hero teacher narrative positions structural oppression, institutional racism, and historic inequity as obstacles to be overcome through personal, individual effort alone, and in doing so, it minimizes the need for systemic change. It is difficult to effectively work towards and advocate for educational equity without recognizing the roots and nature of educational inequity. Individual and systemic responses are required to address what is in nature both an individual and systemic struggle.

Collectively, these movies shape cultural consciousness around what it means to be a teacher and how to address educational inequity. Both the dramatized and actual versions of these movies are inspirational stories. Competent, compassionate, and hard-working people are needed. These are powerful narratives and they should be heard. However, this hero teacher narrative seems to be the only narrative that dominant discourse is familiar with, and it is not the only story.

TFA Perpetuating the Hero Narrative

The hero narrative is embedded into TFA's training materials, messaging, structure, and culture. Aiden stated,

> We're told legends of people who achieved unbelievable things in TFA in a very specific context. And those stories are passed on in a kind of lore. I certainly believe that they happened, but they're not at all the norm. And TFA talks like everyone should be that and can be that and the only difference between someone who is that and isn't that is effort. (Aiden)

Aurora Lora and Justin Meli are two of these legends in TFA. New CMs read a lengthy case study on Aurora Lora and her students as pre-work for Summer Institute. The preface of Ms. Lora's Story presents Lora's experience as part of the "TFA experience" and a "first-hand view of the achievement gap and a model for closing it" (Farr, 2009), and it holds up Ms. Lora as someone Aiden would describe as having "achieved unbelievable things in TFA." Though Ms. Lora and her students undoubtedly achieved great things, educator Gary Rubinstein analyzed Texas State Education Department testing data that suggests the dramatic growth claims made in Ms. Lora's Story were exaggerated (Rubinstein, 2012a). Additionally, Lora the person expressed disappointment that aspects of her story were omitted from TFA's account (Rubinstein, 2012a). Similar to the movie narratives, Ms. Lora's Story both reinforces the hero teacher narrative and is presented as a true story though it may take dramatic license.

In addition to case studies, CMs watched videos of model CMs as part of their training. Justin Meli was featured as an example of success in videos such as "Instruction with Investment in Mind Video Justin Meli and 3rd Grade Class" (Farr, 2011). Lola observed that these model classrooms depict ideal students as compliant, "raising their hands and repeating a kind of script," and "sounding very Teach For America."

John and Marie described the influence of TFA's videos on CMs' expectations. John stated that TFA did not adequately prepare CMs for the challenges they were going to face: "I don't think TFA really prepares its cohorts for that. At TFA, it's all sunshine and rainbows." Similarly, Marie observed that TFA's videos featuring only very successful teachers perpetuated the hero teacher narrative in a way that left CMs unprepared to cope with reality:

> They went into [their classrooms] thinking, "Yeah, I'm going to make some growth, and I'm going to teach them change, and yeah, I'm going to be that girl from Freedom Writers!" And we were shown time after time [in TFA] these videos of people who were doing just that. And it was just watching these really successful people and you're like, "Yeah, I'm going to go in and go do that." Kind of like, "I don't really know what that means, but that's good." That is really hurting the community as a whole. We wasted a lot of time in our two years just dealing with shock. (Marie)

In addition to TFA's training materials and messaging, the hero narrative was also reinforced through the structure of TFA: the pedagogy CMs are instructed in, how CMs are evaluated and interpreted by their MTLD, the style of ACS trainings, the people who are highlighted or brought in to speak to CMs, the questions TFA asks CMs, and what is affirmed with prestigious awards like the Sue Lehmann Award. For example, the hero narrative was incorporated into the CM rating system. Maggie thought the TAL rubric and rating system promoted unrealistic standards and set CMs up to feel like failures:

> I was really shocked actually that they took the whole TAL *Teaching as Leadership* rubric and took that whole premise and put it on steroids and ran with it. At the beginning of this year, I have never seen more terrified brand new CMs. I thought we were pretty overwhelmed when we were brand new ... Nothing, nothing can compare to the faces I would see on these kids ... they were just shocked by the amount of negativity, about the rating system. It was Institute, like—"You're not being, you're not pushing rigor, you're not going to show enough tremendous growth." (Maggie)

The hero narrative was also communicated through trainings and mandatory surveys. TFA repeatedly asked CMs whether they thought the achievement gap could be closed, and Dionne thought this was a way to reinforce the idealistic hero narrative:

> You know how TFA's always like, "Do you think the achievement gap can be closed?" I feel they raise this question to have more people to answer yes to it ... they want you to say that the achievement gap can be closed, because they want you to have this idealistic view of the world. And that is a lot of pressure. (Dionne)

Many CMs identified the trend of entering TFA with expectations of being a kind of savior to students and then having these expectations affirmed through TFA's messaging and structure. Culturally and experientially, many CMs had limited understanding of what working in Philadelphia's public schools might be like prior to joining TFA. TFA's narrative emphasized ways CMs' past successes in other endeavors could and would translate into eliminating educational inequity in their new classroom environments.

When asked what messages they perceived from TFA, CMs highlighted the hero teacher narrative and their individual responsibilities as aspiring "highly effective teachers." CMs internalized TFA's message that they needed to be in control in all situations, that their performance alone determined their students' success or failure, that it was their responsibility to save their students through their relentless hard work and caring, and that if something went wrong they were failing children.

In CMs' required reading, TFA's Chief Knowledge Officer, Steven Farr, argues that, "Highly effective teachers first seek root causes [for student failures] in their own actions. Because they see themselves as ultimately responsible for what happens in their classroom, they begin with the assumption that their actions and inactions are the source of student learning and lack of learning" (2010, p. 185). CMs wanted to be highly effective teachers, and many then began "with the assumption that their actions and inactions are the source of student learning and lack of learning." CMs identified ways TFA-endorsed phrases (see Chapter 2) and trainings shaped their understanding of the problem at hand and their role in embodying a solution.

The Ms. Lora Story–type training materials and programming have strengths; in addition to introducing specific tactics that new teachers can adopt, these powerful narratives highlight the inspirational possibility of dramatic teacher and student growth. However, by mythologizing these accomplishments and presenting hero teacher narratives as the only reality, TFA tells an untrue story.

Prescribing an untrue story as a model for success is problematic. Everyone has stories that shape their expectations of new experiences; from embarking on a first date to beginning freshman year of college to starting a new job, stories guide people and help to inform what they need and what they can expect. The problem with untrue stories is that they leave people ill-equipped to face and operate in reality. Untrue stories can misstate challenges, what resources a person needs, what a person can accomplish, etc. Believing a narrative that is detached from reality sets CMs up to be like Don Quixote, who is at best ineffectual in his knight-errantry and at worst destructive towards himself and the people around him.

CMs grappled with TFA's idealistic narrative and the call for heroic individual responsibility. CMs believed that they were responsible for their classrooms and wanted to be effective teachers, but they did not know how to interpret the reality that their efforts often fell short of achieving hero teacher effects.

CMs Perpetuating the Hero Narrative

Within TFA, CMs perpetuated the hero narrative among TFA colleagues and helped to construct what some CMs described as a culture of judgmental, competitive martyrdom. Reagan stated that she preferred spending time with non-TFA coworkers and away from TFA functions, explaining "TFA events and even GSE ones are more judgmental." Marie and Josh also commented on the judgment-heavy, competitive culture among CMs. Marie said she thought CMs who did not comply with TFA's definition of how to "be a good teacher" would be interpreted negatively and judged as unsuccessful, not doing what's right for students, and not doing things for the right reasons:

> I don't feel like I was being honest with CMs at All-Corps Saturdays. I just didn't feel like I had a relationship with them. I don't feel like it was a safe space. Even after TFA when we graduated, and people asked if I was sad to be leaving TFA, and I said, "Not particularly," and they would ask, "Why?" And it was very judgey. A lot of that is the culture, and it's perpetuated by the CMs, like, "This is what I need to do to be a good teacher" and if you're outside of this realm, then you're not very successful, you're not doing what's right for kids, you're not doing things for the right reasons, like there are these big assumptions made about you. (Marie)

Unlike Reagan and Marie, Josh said that TFA events sometimes provided a space for him to process his experiences; he stated that he had many friends in TFA, including his roommates. However, he still felt CMs as a group often perpetuated a negative culture:

> Classes and ACS sessions can often turn pessimistic, heavy in gratuitous bitching, one-upmanship, and martyrdom … I'd like to think that I have a pretty healthy awareness of my strengths and weaknesses as a teacher, and I'm pretty willing to talk about any of them. For me, the thing that makes teaching hardest to talk about sometimes is the one-upmanship that people sometimes engage in. It seems like some people are primarily concerned with letting everyone else know how hard their jobs

are and how much they care about their students. I think conversations about teaching can be extremely valuable, but they are much less so when used as a means for self-aggrandizement. (Josh)

As Josh described, CMs' idealism and its accompanying characteristics—empathy, high standards, and personal commitment—could turn into competitive martyrdom. How much a person cared about their students and how much a person suffered in their jobs became a measuring stick by which CMs compared each other. While conversations about teaching can be valuable learning experiences, these conversations could turn towards "one-upmanship" and "self-aggrandizement."

Outside of TFA, the TFA hero teacher narrative was so common that the Assistant Dean of Yale Law School Asha Rangappa (2012) discussed this ubiquitous narrative trend in a blog post about the "TFA Essay" phenomenon. According to Rangappa, the TFA Essay depicts a bright, ambitious, idealistic CM who encounters problems as epitomized by a very troubled student. This student is a stereotype of urban or rural poverty, and it is up to the CM to save the illiterate troublemaker who is surrounded by drugs, violence, and gangs, and has only one parent. After working relentlessly and creatively, the CM helps the class to make incredible breakthroughs, pass the state test, and advance three grade levels. Then, the CM wants to take his rewarding experience and attend Yale Law School to enter the field of education policy. In this single story narrated by CMs, a hero enters, and through hard work and heart, saves his troubled students in a short amount of time, and after his TFA commitment is ready to do "more." Similar to the movie versions of the hero teacher narrative, the TFA Essay features an accelerated timeline, places greater responsibility on a single individual, and makes dramatic claims about students' growth trajectories. Through writing the TFA Essay and through reiterating the hero narrative in their various positions of future leadership, CMs perpetuate the hero narrative outside of TFA. Again, prescribing an untrue story as a model for success is problematic and sets quixotic expectations.

Damaging Effects of the Hero Narrative on CMs: Cognitive Dissonance, Disillusionment, Blame, and Burnout

The hero narrative has damaging effects on CMs. CMs connected the hero narrative to cognitive dissonance, disillusionment, blame, and burnout.

Cognitive Dissonance & Disillusionment

CMs joined TFA with particular expectations of how much change they could effect, how much they could control, and what they could accomplish through their hard work and heart. This hero teacher narrative was often reinforced by TFA and among CMs. But after they began working, CMs' experiences did not align with their expectations. Many CMs experienced a gap between the designated and actual narratives, a phenomenon Kramer (1974) called "reality shock." CMs used the word "shocked" to describe both their experiences in their classrooms and their experiences with TFA as an institution. Marie summarized, "We wasted a lot of time in our two years just dealing with shock. And that time could have been spent otherwise. And so much of it was just, 'Wow, what is happening?'"

CMs sought to make sense of the competing designated and actual narratives and experienced cognitive dissonance, defined by the APA as an internal incongruity experienced from holding contradictory beliefs (2014). Cognitive dissonance is a process of problem-solving. CMs struggled to reconcile their contradicting designated and actual narratives. For example, Ariel stated, "If I plan a lesson hastily, or don't handle a situation well, or have a bad observation, it is nearly impossible to reconcile that failure with the incredible amount of effort I put in every day." CMs expected to work hard and be successful teachers; failure was not part of their expected narrative, particularly not when they were putting in an "incredible amount of effort" and had track records of success.

CMs' expectations of what they could accomplish in their classrooms were often bolstered by what they had previously achieved before they began teaching. TFA recruits individuals "who have demonstrated outstanding achievement, perseverance, and leadership" (TFA, 2010). CMs' past records of achievement sometimes skewed their expectations of what they could accomplish in their classrooms and caused them additional shock and difficulty. Jane expounded, "People who they pick, Type A, highly motivated, highly successful, they're not used to feeling inadequate. And when the stakes are so high, that feeling of inadequacy takes on such an emotional and deep meaning that it's unbearable sometimes." Along these lines, Aiden described his own difficulty reconciling past successes with his limited success in his classroom:

> I have a very clear vision of what my classroom should look like and I am a perfectionist by nature, and it's very hard for me to see all the things that are not going how

I want them to go, and how I think they need to go for my students to succeed ... Personally, knowing that I've succeeded at so many other things in my life, this is a new avenue where my success is always limited and measured and relative. (Aiden)

Many CMs described experiencing an erosion of their beliefs and ideals in TFA. Their expectations had been detached from the realities of what they experienced as new teachers. The hero narrative CMs believed and had reinforced in TFA left CMs ill-equipped to face and operate in reality. Aiden described CMs' disillusionment with TFA's narrated mission after they began teaching:

> People come in having drunk the Kool-Aid. And I think you see an erosion of belief in that ... there are a lot of CMs who are giving up or surrendering on the mission. "One Day" has become an inside joke for people, where they chuckle at that principle. I think those ideas are very much eroded. At least within the Philadelphia corps culture, there's very little buy-in in terms of those corps values. Very little belief in them. (Aiden)

Marie and John both commented on the connection between oversimplified, idealistic expectations and the experience of disillusionment among CMs. Prior to TFA, Maggie and John had studied education and had spent time working in public schools in various capacities; they both credited these experiences with helping to adjust their expectations in TFA. According to Marie and John, CMs who had vague, abstract expectations of grandeur—of being "that girl from freedom writers" or "a great white knight on a shining horse"—experienced significant reality shock and disillusionment. John explained,

> I thought TFA had a culture of people who were in over their heads ... I was surprised by how many people seemed shell shocked. I expected that if we're recruiting across top colleges across the country from people who have achieved to a certain degree, I assumed people would come into this with their eyes open. I was surprised that not many people did ...

> I studied education policy in school fairly extensively, so I knew that these were systemic problems that were not going to go away overnight, that it wasn't up to me to fix the system. It was up to me to go into the system and do what I could to help the kids that I interacted with. A lot of people came into this thinking they were going to be a great white knight on a shining horse. Those were the first people to get their asses kicked. In fairness to them, they had spent their lives achieving at a certain level, and they thought this was going to be the same thing ... I experienced very little [negative] change in TFA because I experienced it from the 10,000-foot view and

> in the classroom, so when I got to TFA, it was ok. I don't think TFA really prepares its cohorts for that. At TFA, it's all sunshine and rainbows. (John)

As CMs experienced an erosion of their initial idealism due to struggles in the classroom, they described a shift towards focusing their energy more on daily survival rather than issues of systemic injustice. CMs experienced what is described as a crisis of competence: in the process of disillusionment, many new helping professionals begin to prioritize achieving an acceptable level of competence over their commitment to goals like helping people in need, working towards social change, or advocating for social justice (Cherniss, 1995, p. 18). CMs were struggling so much with day-to-day challenges that they had limited capacity to consider bigger-picture systemic change. For example, Nicole recognized acts of oppression based on racial and class identities and wanted to reflect critically on these dynamics, but lacked the space and energy to do so:

> I thought about race, class, and gender way more before I became a teacher. I had more mental space and energy for it. And I'm so sad, I just haven't thought about it as much. I start to almost not think about it as much, which is crazy, because I should, and I'm not color blind. (Nicole)

Jane described grappling with her limits and feeling disillusioned with TFA; her commitment to working towards social change shifted in nature to "just do what I can":

> I mean, how much can you do? At this point I'm just trying to be the best teacher I can be and I've forgotten about the achievement gap. Which is bad. I know it exists, but there's only so much I can do ... The whole idea of TFA I really don't agree with anymore. I would never tell anyone to do it. Just because—why would you put inexperienced teachers in the most high-need areas? It just doesn't make sense. That's the dissonance for me. I just don't understand—why would you put teachers who have the least tools with the kids who need the most? I just ... I just do what I can. (Jane)

Maggie described what she saw as a shift from idealism to cynicism among CMs. She stated that she thought TFA's rubrics were used to underscore ways CMs were not living up to the hero narrative, and that this contributed to the cynicism in TFA. Maggie stated that many of her fellow CMs became "jaded" by their TFA experience:

> ... because we were all bright, extremely empathic, idealistic people, they're just going to get a bunch of cynics. And [they're] going to get people who are going to shut [them] down. And guess what, when [TFA] sends out that mid-year survey that

TFA so dedicates its life to, TFA's not going to like those numbers. And guess what? TFA didn't like those numbers. (Maggie)

The hero narrative contributed to CMs' disillusionment with both TFA and TFA's mission of addressing educational inequity. Actual teaching did not align with their expectations. Many CMs felt unprepared to face the challenging realities they confronted daily, and their attitudes changed as they struggled to cope with reality. CMs expressed feeling misled by TFA's narrative and some thought that TFA "preyed on" their idealism. A number of CMs entered as passionate idealists who wanted to promote social justice, but shifted towards cynicism and prioritizing their daily survival.

Blame

CMs connected the hero narrative to messages and feelings of blame, failure, and judgment; related feelings of guilt and shame are explored in Chapter 5. Many CMs internalized a message that they needed to be a kind of hero to their students, and that if they were not actualizing their heroic potential it was because they were not working hard enough.

When asked what messages they perceived from TFA, CMs commonly responded that they were failing because they were not working hard enough:

We're failing in some way ... [and] we are "not working hard enough." (Stephen)

If you don't succeed, you're not trying hard enough. (Aiden)

If my students aren't achieving, then I'm not trying hard enough. (Taylor)

It's all your fault. You're not working hard enough ... if you cared about your students you would do more ... I feel like I give 110% and when I go with legitimate concerns, I'm not taken seriously. They just tell me to work harder. (Lola)

CMs also responded that they were to blame for any failures:

If things are not going well it is your fault. (Adrian)

I do feel that TFA messages that everything that happens in my classroom is my fault. (Ariel)

Everything in my class is my fault. On a more general scale, "everything is my fault" ... I do feel like TFA thinks I am a horrible teacher. (Kate)

If your students don't do well, it's your fault. If I am not teaching the way TFA wants me to, I am widening the achievement gap ... Like, "Oh, I'm not living up to their standards, I feel bad ... Oh, I'm not doing everything I can do ... Oh, I haven't updated my exit ticket in two days ... Oh my gosh, I'm the worst. I'm the worst teacher ever because I'm not showing them their progress in data. Of course it's important, but you know, I'm not fucking perfect. (Jane)

Additionally, CMs thought that when they failed, they were failing children:

Lives are counting on us as CMs. (Aiden)

I felt the pressure to do ... what TFA told me I had to do, because if I didn't, you know, children's lives were at stake. (Jane)

If I don't save the lives of all my children from poverty, I have failed. (Reagan)

Most CMs expressed feeling an enormous personal responsibility for whatever happened in their classrooms. Reagan felt like it was up to her to save the lives of all her children from poverty. Marie explained that TFA messaged that CMs are the driving forces in their classrooms in a way that could inadvertently teach CMs that they were to blame for everything and that they were failing children:

Especially as a first year teacher, you're already going to be competitive, and trying to show, "I'm not the worst person here!" But I feel like TFA almost made that even worse. It made the mission over-simplified. And in trying to teach teachers that "You are the driving force in your classroom," it also made it seem like "You are to blame for everything. If you ever mess up ever, then you're a terrible person." And that's clearly just not true. And I think having that message so heavily and turning CMs against each other made it like, "I'm better than you" and "This is why you're a bad person." And I don't think that's healthy for anyone involved.

I think trying to teach teachers that you're in control comes from a good place and to be a successful teacher you have to truly believe those things in some ways, but I don't think it's healthy to tell first-year teachers who you *know* are going to be terrible teachers—very few people can turn out to be amazing teachers their first year—I don't think it's fair to say that, "If your kids aren't making growth, you are at fault." And the emphasis is that *you're failing children* ... I don't think that's productive and I don't think that's healthy. (Marie)

CMs described the ineffectiveness of the hero narrative's blanket solution of working harder, and many felt like they were to blame when they did not live up to the hero narrative. The hero narrative places CMs in control of people, and "[CMs] forget that they don't have control over other people" (Maggie).

Moral Weight & Burnout

Feeling responsible to save children from poverty through hard work and heart put an enormous moral weight on CMs, which contributed to feelings of failure, exhaustion, and burnout in TFA.

Jane described her experience in TFA as "the greatest failure I've ever felt." The hero narrative emphasizes high stakes and moral responsibility in a way that intensifies failure. When Jane did not live up to the hero narrative, she expressed feeling like the enemy, a villain, a "shitty teacher that is not doing their job." The moral weight and feeling of perpetual inadequacy felt "unbearable sometimes":

> TFA puts such a moral weight on your job that maybe if you were a traditionally trained teacher it might not. But the moral weight is heavy and it adds; if your first year of teaching is 20 pounds on your shoulders, then TFA is an additional 20 pounds on your shoulders. It's the first time I've failed and the stakes are so high that that failure is the greatest failure I've ever felt. It's like going from a high of getting picked for this thing you think is great, that's hard to get into, and you're highly successful, and then they just bring you to the pits of failure like you've never experienced before, and that moral weight is unreal. You feel like you are part of the enemy. You feel like you are a shitty teacher that is not doing their job, when in reality, you're doing all that you can do, and there's a chance that you might be doing it better than other people. But in the realm of this organization, it's never enough. It's feeling perpetually inadequate. People who they pick, Type A, highly motivated, highly successful, they're not used to feeling inadequate. And when the stakes are so high, that feeling of inadequacy takes on such an emotional and deep meaning that it's unbearable sometimes. (Jane)

Maggie stated that "high ideals come at a very high price" and explained that idealism can further burden CMs even beyond what they might experience as a less idealistic first-year teacher. Maggie described how it was not the failures alone that CMs found difficult, but the weight of feeling insufficient, ineffective, and incapable. Many CMs who entered as idealists with high expectations for themselves experienced significant self-doubt, felt ineffective, and became jaded:

> Feeling insufficient, that's really hard to handle. The whole, "What the hell am I doing?" Every first-year teacher struggles with things to some different degree … it's going to call into question your ability to do this job, over and over and over again … And then you set yourself up for, someone comes in supposedly knows what they're doing and tells you you don't know what you're doing. You're going to be so low, your sense of self, your sense of ability. It's hard to recover from that … High ideals come at a very high price. And a lot of people aren't willing to—or aren't able to—pay for

it. Makes you jaded. It makes you really question how effective you are. It makes you wonder, "Why am I even staying?" This is ridiculous. This is too much. (Maggie)

Aiden explained that wrestling with these questions of personal responsibility and perceived failures can be "acutely hard" and "a recipe for burnout" in CMs' first year:

> It's really hard, and acutely hard when you're a first-year teacher and your classroom is not going how you want it to—it's a recipe for burnout. Wrestling with that question when things are not going well is really hard. It's hard to wrestle with when things are going amazingly well in your classroom, but when that's also happening in your first year teaching, it can be fatal. (Aiden)

Burnout is defined as a state of physical and emotional exhaustion caused by one's professional life; it is characterized by physical (e.g., fatigue, sleep difficulties), emotional (e.g., depression, anxiety, guilt, helplessness), behavioral (e.g., cynicism, substance abuse), work-related (e.g., feelings of inefficacy), and interpersonal (e.g., strained relationships) symptoms (Figley, 1995; Freudenberger & Richelson, 1980; Kahill, 1988; Maslach & Jackson, 1981; Maslach, 2003). Burnout is also linked to compassion fatigue, defined in Chapter 4 as the natural consequent behaviors and emotions resulting from knowing about a traumatizing event experienced by significant others (Figley, 1995, p. 7). Rather than a fixed condition, burnout is a process that begins gradually and becomes progressively worse (Figley, 1995, p. 11; Cherniss, 1980). The process of burnout includes erosion of idealism (Freudenberger, 1986; Pines, Aronson, & Kafry, 1981); Aiden stated that many CMs entered TFA with heroic expectations of what they could accomplish and experienced an "erosion of belief" after they started working.

Helping professionals who experience burnout tend to be overachieving, empathetic, and committed to their work (Freudenberger & Richelson, 1980; Ricket, 2013). According to Herbert Freudenberger (1980), one of the pioneers of burnout research, the youngest and most idealistic helping professionals who believe the hero narrative are often the first to burn out. Marie and John identified this trend in TFA: both observed that their peers who entered TFA with a strong hero narrative seemed to struggle the most. Marie explained, "Part of it is what people go in expecting. I noticed at the beginning that a lot of people I saw truly, truly struggling were the people who just didn't know how hard it was going to be from the get-go." Similarly, John stated, "A lot of people came into this thinking they were going to be a great white knight on a shining horse. Those were the first people to get their asses kicked."

The grandiosity of the hero narrative leaves little room for CMs to acknowledge or tend to their own needs. Additionally, the hero narrative enforces a kind of savior complex, in which CMs' worth depends on their capacity to save their students. CMs were intensely committed to their work, and their sense of self was heavily dependent on their capacity to perform. The commitment to work can particularly contribute to burnout when it is egoistic, meaning when the helping professionals' self-esteem is reliant on their work performance (Cherniss, 1995, p. 185). Relatedly, Bennett observed that he struggled less than the majority of his peers whose identities hinged on their classroom performance:

> I didn't put all my eggs in one basket. My own personal self-opinion of myself wasn't completely defined by how I performed in the classroom every day. Obviously it was my number one priority and I did my damndest to get as good as I could. But I would go home, and I would be able to laugh at things … I would make sure on weekends I would go out to adventure races, on long hikes. I got involved in acting again. I made sure that teaching wasn't the sole, only thing that I was doing … My saving grace was my ability to separate from work when I need to. (Bennett)

Some CMs, like Adrian, explicitly connected their depression, anxiety, fatigue, feelings of helplessness, strained relationships, need for therapy and medical prescriptions, or alcohol dependency to their experience of burnout in TFA. Dionne thought TFA and institutions like TFA that promote the hero narrative and "don't validate the humanity of teachers" consequently have "very high turnover, very high burnout."

There are ways TFA treats people as expendable since they can burn through a seemingly endless supply of new, idealistic recent college-graduates looking to make a difference in the world. However, burning through people has individual and systemic repercussions. Individually, CMs are valuable as people and as new teachers. Ignoring CMs' humanity is a misguided and ineffective means of addressing students' dehumanization in the education system.

Damaging Effects of the Hero Narrative on Systemic Change: Stereotypes, Doublespeak, & Euphemisms

There are several ways in which TFA's endorsement of the hero narrative actually works against TFA's purported hope for enacting positive systemic change. Systemically, burning through people wastes the precious resources of CMs. CMs have significant power and privilege which can be leveraged towards positive systemic change. The hero narrative pushes CMs into short attempted bursts at grandiosity rather than resilient, sustained partnerships in the movement for educational equity. Additionally, this hero teacher narrative promotes teacher burnout and attrition, thereby contributing to the transience and instability of what is already often an unstable environment.

Prescribing an untrue story has damaging effects on institutions and systems. Untrue stories misstate the challenges at hand, skew what resources are needed to address these challenges, and set unrealistic expectations of what can be accomplished. Collectively living into the hero teacher narrative can create a collective Quixote and cause harm where the intentions were to help. The hero narrative also reinforces the problems of stereotypes, doublespeak, and euphemisms.

Stereotypes

The hero narrative tells a single story. Telling a single story creates stereotypes. The hero narrative selects and fabricates aspects of reality by over-inflating the agency and power of CMs and undervaluing the agency and power of the students and communities CMs serve. In this way, idealism can reinscribe the very structure of oppression CMs are intending to address by abstractly treating those they work with as helpless objects. Conceptualizing students as people in need of saving denies students' agency. This narrative reduces unique people and groups of people to their perceived needs and creates two static roles of a savior and a victim. It is dehumanizing.

Stereotypes are tempting because they are a tool of convenience; when pressed for time or energy, or disinclined to engage deeply, stereotypes lend the sensory perception of understanding while projecting a false narrative (McMillan Cottom, 2014). Stereotypes present neatly pre-packaged interpretations of another person's identity and capability, often based on unexamined and problematic assumptions about a person's race and class. The stereotype of victim is laden with negative assumptions of students based on their race and class. These stereotypes are reductive, inaccurate, and problematic. Additionally, stereotypes are shown to have a wide range of negative impacts on the stereotyped person, including though not limited to stereotype threat[1] and psychophysical harm.[2] Educator and TFA alum Royal (2013) states, "There is a problem in assuming all poor people, all black people, all Latino people are the same and that the same thing will work everywhere for every situation where public education is a man-made disaster, like in my hometown, Philadelphia."

Reinforcing stereotypes of students who are predominantly poor and people of color reinforces a reductive narrative that poor people and people of color are inherently helpless and needy. Stereotypes curtail difficult conversations by highlighting the need of the victim without asking how this need came to be. It lends a narrative of explanation and understanding (as if being poor and a person of color were in and of itself an explanation for neediness) and obfuscates the reality of historic and systemic oppression (the systemic disadvantages people have faced based on racism and classism). Stereotypes do not acknowledge the conditions, the systemic theft and marginalization, and the longstanding history of racial and social segregation that contribute to the oppression of people groups (Coates, 2014a).

Discussing the struggles of students of color without discussing white privilege is problematic (Lapayese et al., 2014). The narrative of disenfranchisement is different than the narrative of oppression; one is spoken in the language of benevolent prescription, and the other in the language of restorative justice. TFA frequently described the problems poor students of color face without engaging with the other half of the discussion, the reality of white privilege; Jane positioned TFA's approach of addressing the educational inequity poor students of color face as "only half the battle. The other half is in the white privilege realm." In equating students of color with decontextualized disenfranchisement, students must be rescued from themselves. Focusing on students' disenfranchisement without recognizing the intent, agent, mechanism, or beneficiaries of the disenfranchisement leaves a lot of space for uninformed interpretations and encourages blaming students for their disenfranchisement (Freire, 1970, p. 21). TFA markets itself as a progressive education justice movement (Osgood, 2013; TFA: Our Mission, 2014), but TFA often recycles a narrative of disenfranchisement and charity rather than articulating a narrative of oppression and justice. Educational inequity is socially constructed; it is the workings and product of a man-made system. Addressing and overcoming systemic inequity requires justice, not charity. It is critical to examine the intent, agents, mechanisms, and beneficiaries of systems of oppression.

The hero narrative focuses on the decontextualized need for rescue and the abilities of the helpers in a way that can promote positive assumptions about CMs and reinforce negative assumptions about the people they are trying to help—poor people of color. Performing the hero narrative secures

CMs' identities as heroes through stigmatizing students as other. Othering students into an amorphous, racialized, helpless "them" reinforces the "need" for the heroes to prescribe solutions for students, thereby perpetuating systems of oppression. The narrative of disenfranchisement as an uncreated reality encourages CMs to work for rather than with the students and communities they serve. A helpless "them" requires benevolence and assistance, not justice or recognition as equals. Dehumanization emerges from people othering groups of people and interpreting them as subhuman.

TFA faces a double bind common to institutions created to help others: they want to be helpful, but they often carry into their endeavors problematic preconceived notions of the people they want to help. CMs are not immune from prejudice. Jane described ways TFA's messaging and structure inadvertently support stereotypes and assumptions that all children in poverty are the same. She also explained that CMs' struggle to survive as new teachers severely limits their ability to listen to and learn from their students, to move beyond these stereotypes:

> During institute, TFA really makes it easy to make assumptions about your kids. You assume someone's parent is in jail, you assume all these things … then I'm at a parent teacher conference and guess who walks in? A mom and a dad. Not all children growing up in poverty are the same. And I feel like that's a lot of what TFA preaches … The whole program really makes you make assumptions about the people you're going to be working with. And two, you're so overwhelmed your first year, you may not have time to understand the people—the kids—that you're serving. (Jane)

These stereotypes support deficit views of students. Jane, Nicole, Elliott, Lola, and Dionne discussed ways CMs make degrading assumptions and statements about their students' identities, a phenomenon exacerbated by the dynamic that most CMs were white and from wealthy backgrounds, while most of their students were black and from poor backgrounds. Nicole described the deficit model that TFA and CMs can reinforce, which positions CMs as heroes and their students as helpless victims in need of saving:

> I do feel like a lot of CMs feel like they're changing the world and their children *need* all the help they can get from the CM … And TFA says kids in these areas are kind of helpless. (Nicole)

Elliott explained that CMs' gross generalizations define students by what CMs perceive as students' lacks; Elliott called this "the dehumanization of students." It is problematic, patronizing, and arrogant for CMs to assume the right to define their students' identities with "they can't" and "they don't" statements. Students' perceived struggles and needs can be overinflated to the point where that becomes all the CM sees:

> I do get uncomfortable when a group of CMs come together and start the "they can't ..." or "they don't" game. Never heard of it? Here is what it sounds like: "They can't sit silently." "Yeah! They don't want to learn!" "Tell'em! They can't even read a sentence!" ... I don't think any of those comments are honest, and that's the issue. They can't read? They can read. These CMs are making gross generalizations ... Racial stereotypes like, "They're not even worthy." You hear a lot of CMs saying these things, "They can't read, they can't do this, they don't want to learn." I think comments like that are so degrading. Hopefully we can [change to] see students as people and not commodities. (Elliott)

Viewing students predominantly as an undifferentiated, helpless mass of need is already unproductive and harmful; this oppressive dynamic is exacerbated by decontextualized and often unacknowledged racialized assumptions (Rattansi, 2005, pp. 271–282). This reinforces a stereotype of a disenfranchised, helpless, incompetent student of color. Speaking of students' perceived needs as their defining identity employs a kind of metonymy, a tired trope in which a whole is defined and reduced to an externally perceived part. Though problematic, Lola confessed that this dynamic can be difficult to avoid in TFA: "I feel like I'm advancing negative stereotypes of African Americans ... I feel like I've started to believe in them and their ability less—that's tough to admit." The TFA experience positions CMs to witness students' disenfranchisement without necessarily recognizing the intent, agent, mechanism, or beneficiaries of this system; CMs are to serve a disenfranchised racialized "them" in a way that makes it difficult to recognize the humanity of their students.

Even attempts to help students develop positive attributes can inadvertently reinforce negative stereotypes. Dionne reflected on ways TFA positions students as needing to be taught grit, and she disagreed with this interpretation of students as lacking and the interpretation of her role as compensating for this lack. Grit, endurance, and perseverance are not new traits to poor students of color; these traits are not indigenous to CMs and foreign to their students. Dionne recognized that her students, out of necessity and survival, already possessed far more grit than acknowledged by the TFA-endorsed narrative. She also commented on the hypocrisy of TFA contributing to environmental instability which undermines the development of student grit and long-term investment:

I taught my kids about grit. Because at a PD, we decided to teach our students about grit. I struggled with it because I look at my students, and my students have mad grit. Just to get to school every day. Just to get to the train and to walk through the neighborhoods they walk through and get here. That's hard to do. And just to live some of the lives that they've lived—they have to persevere through so much. A lot of people say, "They give up so easily," or "blah blah blah" … Also, if you go through a program, or have a teacher, or anything else you get attached to leaving after two years, three years, how can you build grit through that? And TFA is contributing to that by putting teachers in classroom and sort of pushing them out, really. Our kids are used to constant fluctuation. In general, poverty and the structure of a lot of resources available to their community are stretched. It's way more difficult, if not impossible, to see things through. Because they're not adequately funded, or people leave, and there's turnover of staff. It's easier to have quote-unquote "grit" and stick through with something when things are consistent. And in poverty a lot of times, things are not consistent … So [students'] longevity is something not learned [from TFA and CMs], but it's out of necessity and survival …

[For example,] there's a kid who's trying to apply to high school, and he literally—the last [year-long] math teacher he had was in 6th grade! All of them left. He had three math teachers last year. So he's trying to figure it out, but 6th grade was three years ago! He's in 9th grade now and that 6th grade math teacher won't feel comfortable writing a recommendation any more, you know?

The question [of what grit is and how to build it] is a really important one, and grit is a new thing now in education—grit and teaching kids grit. I have … qualms [about reinforcing negative stereotypes] … I know that [my students] all are gritty in life. (Dionne)

Like Dionne, several CMs described the role reversal of learning grit and perseverance from their students. Contrary to the hero narrative, in environments of new scarcity, CMs described ways their students pushed CMs' understandings of grit and perseverance. CMs were older than their students, had track records of achievement in their respective affiliations, and were equipped with tools from elite institutions of higher education and TFA, and still they struggled to survive in their new school environments. Stereotypes do not acknowledge the reality that CMs were often negatively affected by their environments, that dehumanizing systems can affect all people and can also render CMs feeling powerless. CMs' struggle to survive in their schools underscores their students' necessary tenacity to survive or thrive despite a dehumanizing system. The shared challenge for CMs and students was learning how to sustain and channel this tenacity towards students' formal education.

Performing the hero narrative facilitates the inability or refusal to acknowledge various students' unique identities and experiences. It typecasts and flattens CMs and students—people—into clichés. And these clichés are not just problematic, they're false.

Further, the single story of the hero narrative generates the same solutions which include the same fallacies. Rangappa (2012) identified the "fairly predictable model" CMs recycled on their law school applications. Her deconstruction of the TFA Essay identifies a pattern of CMs perpetuating a single story that is predictable and detached from the complexities of reality. It is easy to parody a cliché. Rangappa's post illuminates how adherence to the single story generates uncreative, stereotypical solutions. If CMs internalize TFA's message that there is "nothing elusive" about education reform, then the solutions should all be the same; it becomes easy to hold fast to the meritocracy myth, to naively ignore historic oppression and social reproduction, to scapegoat structural educational inequity on lazy or uncaring teachers or incompetent students, to claim to be color-blind while holding racialized assumptions about those viewed as other, to perpetuate false narratives to the society outside of teaching who are eager to receive CMs' assessment of the problems of public education, to perpetuate systems of oppression. How a problem is positioned influences the type of solutions generated to address this problem.

Language helps to create and define identities (Butler, 1990). In the politics of representation, it is important to question who is able to exercise power and narrate another group's identity, and who is given the right to make decisions for another group. Stereotypes are a means of reproducing inequity, all while claiming heroic intentions. Stereotypes work against TFA's purported desire for positive systemic change because stereotypes reinforce the problem of dehumanization.

Doublespeak & Euphemisms

The generality of the hero narrative assumes noble intentions without requiring CMs to claim their various motivations or to say specifically what they mean.

CMs benefitted from TFA in ways that were often unspoken. TFA is known for being a highly competitive organization, and it is branded as an "ethical alternative to Wall Street for college seniors looking for a short-term commitment" (Royal, 2013). Additionally, TFA has established partnerships with a wide range of powerful institutions across various fields and in both the private and public sector (TFA: Graduate School and Employer Partnerships,

2013). CMs benefitted from TFA's prestige; its narrative of being a movement of intelligent, benevolent helpers; its network; and the new opportunities TFA helps connect its graduates to in the name of establishing leaders across fields who are committed to "ensure that all children can receive an excellent education" (TFA: Our Mission, 2013). In confidentiality, some CMs who had attended less prestigious universities for their undergraduate education confessed applying to TFAGP in part for the prestige of receiving an Ivy League degree from TFAGP's partnership with the University of Pennsylvania. CMs also borrowed the narrative of allegedly doing "more" for their former students in post-TFA interviews with prestigious banks, consulting firms, and law schools. CMs wanted to be able to say that they were part of and had completed their TFA commitment—"I want to say I was in TFA, I want to say I was an alum of TFA—legitimately" (Maggie).

Prestige attracts people with power and promises more power. The prestige and brand of TFA attracted and rewarded CMs. Prestige is a form of cultural capital; it is not inherently bad. Stewarded well, prestige and power can be leveraged to promote meaningful change. The hero narrative becomes problematic when it ignores the reality and social role of prestige and power while still bestowing additional prestige and power on CMs; when it euphemizes poverty with phrases like "the inner city" and abstracts students and communities into a noble cause of "closing the achievement gap"; when it objectifies one group of people for the benefit of another group of people through a sanitized, coded, covert process; when it claims a narrative of doing things exclusively for the benefit of students when in reality there are other motives and other beneficiaries; when it curtails important questions of who gets to tell the story of other people and for what purpose. Dionne commented on the doublespeak within TFA:

> When we're done with the program, we focus on CMs and the emphasis is less and less on the actual students … TFA doesn't take both CM responsibilities and limits into consideration. They have this focus on "student achievement, student achievement, whatever you need for students." One, I don't think that is actually the case. I think TFA is for the benefit of CMs. It greatly benefits CMs more than any other group. (Dionne)

As Dionne noted, there is an inconsistency, false humility, and dishonesty to claiming everything is "for students"; it ignores ways the program can benefit CMs over and more than the students and communities CMs serve. Similarly, Elliott questioned TFA's fast track to leadership and CMs' expedited career advancements; an increase in power and influence without an increase in wisdom is likely to cause more harm than help to the movement for educational equity. While certain career advancements for CMs could also theoretically benefit the movement for educational equity, CMs expressed uncertainty over this narrative. John questioned how much TFA benefits a community after CMs' two-year commitment: "What I don't see is [CMs] rebuilding a community to achieve change after they leave, either in education or some other policy state." In a message to potential TFA recruits, Royal (2013) stated, "Urban schools and classrooms don't need hyped-up heroes who burn out before their fire really gets going. We need resilient, lifelong educators who are focused on collective responsibility and the greater good. We need servant leaders, not self-serving saviors. In too many instances, Teach For America does more for those who join it than for the students and communities it hopes to serve. If you do choose to teach FOR America, please make sure your work improves more than just your life." CMs claiming they are participating in TFA solely "for students" is an exercise of power to do something *for* another group, and ignoring ways CMs benefit from TFA creates grounds for dishonest exchanges. Without naming all of CMs' motivations, at what point does TFA become a means for well-intentioned individuals to advance their careers while saying "for students" but meaning "for myself"?

Additionally, aggrandizing the cause of "for students" positions CMs as heroes instead of people with both important responsibilities and limits. CMs are people with limits. Ignoring CMs' limits or shaming CMs for their needs and struggles is unproductive; this contributes to problems such as CMs' negative life changes (see Chapter 3), a culture of teacher turnover and burnout, and the instability of high-poverty schools.

CMs need to engage in a process of recognizing and claiming their motivations and avoid relying on euphemisms. Language is important because it both communicates and shapes beliefs. Beliefs inform our ways of being and doing; as Lisa Delpit (1988) states, "We do not really see through our eyes or hear through our ears, but through our beliefs" (p. 46). The narrative told by stereotypes, clichés, and euphemisms silences important questions and diminishes the need for CMs to listen to others or critically reflect on CMs' roles as both advocates and benefitting participants in the systems that oppress the students they serve. Dehumanization and oppression are facilitated by and prefer abstraction, while extending care competently and well requires knowing particulars. Rather than indiscriminately buying into and benefitting from false and problematic narratives, CMs have the capacity to listen well, speak clearly, and grow as partner advocates. What would be the effect of an increasing number of CMs critically questioning ladders instead of climbing them?

Conclusion

Idealists are "people who want to do a good thing" (Lola). Many CMs came into TFA as idealists, and the culture of idealism was perpetuated through TFA slogans, programming, and CMs themselves. On an individual level, idealism has its strengths; working towards educational equity requires empathy, high standards, and some sense of personal dedication. Idealism can highlight the potential for positive change, provide a rudimentary vision of what needs to be accomplished, and remind individuals of their power and capacity.

However, lived reality did not align with the designated idealistic narratives. CMs are not saviors; they have both responsibilities and limits. Counter to the TFA hero narrative, Nicole asserted, "We are a small part of [students'] lives for a little bit. But we're not drastically changing their lives. And we're not saving anyone."

Prescribing and perpetuating an untrue story as a model for success is problematic. Individually and systemically, there are limits to idealism. Performing the idealistic hero narrative can do harm to both CMs and the people they are intending to serve, and idealism is insufficient to dismantle structural inequity. Individually, the hero narrative contributed to cognitive dissonance, disillusionment, blame, and burnout among CMs. CMs believed they were responsible for what happened in their classrooms and wanted to be effective teachers, but they struggled to interpret the reality that their efforts often did not achieve hero teacher effects. Systemically, the hero narrative promoted stereotypes, doublespeak, and euphemisms, which facilitate dehumanization, racist prejudices, and dishonest exchanges. These depictions express and reinforce oversimplified, inaccurate, and problematic narratives about CMs, the students they serve, and the nature of the problem at hand.

One of the central limits of idealism is that it treats structural inequity as a result of individual failure that can be wholly overcome by heroic effort. The hero teacher narrative presents educational inequity as separate from its relationship to historic and present power structures; this narrative euphemizes and presents the decontextualized problem of "the achievement gap" without questioning how this gap was created (TFA: Achievement Gap, 2014). The hero teacher narrative presents a narrative of disenfranchisement and ignores the intent, agents, mechanisms, and beneficiaries of systems of oppression.

It positions structural oppression, institutional racism, and historic inequity as obstacles to be overcome through personal, individual effort alone, and in doing so, it minimizes the need for systemic change. Educational inequity is socially constructed, and it needs to be addressed as such.

The hero narrative is reinforced and recycled in TFA, in what CMs identified as an issue of maturity for TFA as an institution. Applicable to both individuals and institutions, maturity is defined by Sfard and Prusak (2005) as the process of narrowing the gap between designated and actual narratives. TFA's hero narrative at best captures only partial truths and is in many ways divorced from the realities CMs experience. Idealistic CMs and the idealism of TFA need to mature to acknowledge and grapple with the reality of what is. Hope which acknowledges, grapples with, and addresses actual human conditions trumps idealism contrived from imagined human conditions.

Notes

1. Researchers Steele and Aronson (1995) found that stereotypes suggesting poor performance of certain groups can, when raised in a context involving the stereotype, disrupt performance of an individual who identifies with that group.
2. A growing body of literature shows discrimination can cause physical and emotional harm to the person discriminated against, a phenomenon termed "embodied inequality" (Anderson, 2013; Krieger, 1999). The stress from discrimination disproportionately affects people of color, and can increase the risk of depression, cardiovascular disease, breast cancer, and mortality (Silverstein, 2013).

· 8 ·

LISTENING AND LEARNING FROM COUNTERNARRATIVES

Moving From Idealism Towards Hope

Narratives shape how people see the world and direct peoples' actions. I began this research as a second-year TFAGP CM to better understand both the challenges CMs faced and why CMs struggled to narrate their lived experiences. With a focus on CMs as applied developmentalists, I listened for specific, immediate ways TFAGP could better supports CMs. The majority of my initial takeaways focused on what I viewed as urgent, individual-level, actionable steps for TFA (see Appendix D).

Similar to TFA's narrative, I also spoke of the challenges I witnessed as largely removed from the landscape and history of race, class, and power. I felt underprepared to engage in these complex dynamics, as I am still continually learning about the workings of socially constructed systems of advantage and disadvantage. Focusing on CMs as decontextualized applied developmentalists seemed more manageable, and more likely to yield popular, easy-to-endorse recommendations rather than raise political, potentially contentious questions. Asking questions with political implications seems fraught with public condemnation and ad hominem: people who ask questions with political implications often seem to be accused of not caring about or not believing in poor children of color, as evidenced both by CMs' interactions with TFA staff and the dominant discourse on education reform.[1]

This research process has challenged and changed my own understandings of educational inequity, education reform, and the differences between individual- and systemic-level work. Through listening to CMs' counternarratives and exploring the stories behind their stories, it became clearer that CMs' struggles were not only the result of a lack of support, but their struggles also stemmed from deeply flawed and damaging narratives. It became almost impossible to ignore the political underpinnings of CMs' counternarratives.

There is a gap between the dominant, idealistic narratives put forth by TFA and the realities many CMs experienced. Though TFA often paints a straightforward problem with a straightforward solution, CMs' counternarratives collectively problematize the standard, familiar narratives in TFA. Exploring the personal lent itself to seeing more clearly the political: what I had previously viewed primarily as an individual-level matter for CMs, I began to also recognize as a social, systemic issue with TFA and the dominant discourse on education reform.

Key Questions & Patterns

Several key questions and patterns emerged in this study. I begin with a focus on individual CMs in the first four bullet points:

- How should TFA respond to the complexity and depth of individual CMs' experiences? What is a compassionate and ethical response to human struggles as people work and learn in systems of inequity? CMs contended with a range of challenges during their two-year commitment. From their time in professional therapy, their personal reflection, and their independent research on the topic, CMs identified helplessness, depression, anxiety, primary trauma, Post-Traumatic Stress Disorder (PTSD), secondary trauma, and vicarious traumatization as part of their experiences in TFA. CMs also witnessed a range of their students' struggles, including trauma and behavioral health struggles. There was little acknowledgment—much less response to—these realities in TFA.
- What role should TFA take in supporting CMs through their two-year commitment? How much support should come from TFA and how much should come from a broader support network of family, friends, faith community, etc.? CMs' experiences in TFA with counseling, medical prescriptions, increased alcohol consumption, weight changes, strained relationships, fatigue, depression, trauma, and burnout raise questions

about TFA's role in supporting its CMs. Aiden stated, "CMs just need more support than they're receiving … CMs don't get the support they would need to drive the highest level of success." TFA blurs the line between employer and social impact community, and some CMs felt misled by TFA in what support they could expect as CMs; Drake stated, "My main issue is that the support [TFA] advertises is not the support we get."

- Where are CMs, as individuals and as a group, socially located? What are ways CMs' experiences parallel or diverge from students' experiences? How can CMs develop equity-oriented perspectives and ethically engage in the work of applied development? The process of CMs' identity development is complex and politicized. CMs struggled to understand their intersecting, developing personal and professional identities as new TFA teachers. CMs experienced a conflict between the nature of identity development as a process and a pressing, immediate need for improvement as new teachers. Additionally, many CMs felt ill-equipped to work through their questions about complex racial, class, cultural, and political dynamics experienced while teaching. CMs' social locations are significant as they seek to engage in the inherently political work of teaching and as they seek to address what is inherently a socially constructed inequity. However, CMs felt they lacked the language, time, and support to engage meaningfully in understanding their own identities independently or in relationship to their students' identities.

- What are CMs' primary responsibilities while they are in TFA? CMs' responsibilities and capacities were overstated on both an individual and systemic level, and they were blamed in TFA for a wide range of failures. Many CMs felt they could not individually address systemic injustice within their classrooms. Since TFA is evaluating and holding CMs accountable to certain standards, it is important for TFA to clarify CMs' responsibilities while they are in TFA.

Next, I transition to consider the broader narrative questions in the following five bullet points:

- What is educational inequity? TFA narrates educational inequity as "the achievement gap" and positions a historically and structurally rooted, man-made inequity as a natural phenomenon. Educational inequity has a legacy in the U.S.: students were historically advantaged or disadvantaged based on socially constructed systems of race, class, and gender (Anderson, 1989; Ladson-Billings, 2006; Fultz, 1995; Payne, 2008; Tyack, 2004). Some of these inequities have lessened in severity, but these systems still exist. How a problem is positioned influences the kinds of solutions generated to address the problem; the discourse around an achievement gap is different than the discourse around an education debt or opportunity gap. Educational inequity is part of and a product of a man-made system. Addressing it will require individual hard work and caring, but it also requires an examination of the broader system. The "achievement gap" is often presented as an isolated phenomenon, and it has become a misleading euphemism for the workings and product of historic oppression, structural injustice, and institutional racism. Focusing primarily on the decontextualized "achievement gap" precludes a need for systemic change and promotes short-term solutions without addressing the social construction of educational inequity. This discourse places all responsibility on individual poor students of color and their individual educators to simply try harder and care more as opposed to a discourse that also holds the larger society accountable for its historic and present marginalization of people by race and class, to the education debt the American public has accumulated and owes to entire groups of people and their subsequent generations (Coates, 2014b; Ladson-Billings, 2007). America has accrued an education debt.

- Can increasing individual educational access eliminate structural educational inequity? What are the distinctions between individual- and systemic-level responsibilities and impacts? By positioning CMs as teachers who are also tasked with "closing the achievement gap" (TFA: Achievement Gap, 2014), TFA blurs the line between individual and systemic responsibilities and impacts. The man-made problems of structural oppression, institutional racism, and historic inequity require both committed people to address the negative effects of these systems on individuals and committed people to address the system which continues to disadvantage groups of individuals. These people can work together and they are both working towards good, but it is important to understand the distinctions of these responsibilities. Teachers can serve a unique capacity by supporting students to gain both functional and critical literacy, to help students grow both academically and as advocates for educational equity (Freire, 1970; Giroux, 2004; Gutstein, 2006). Teachers can also provide needed insights into the

challenges and needs of students and teachers, and teachers can advocate for systemic change. However, within a classroom, a teacher's primary responsibilities are to his or her individual students. Increasing
individual educational access is rigorous, challenging, needed work.
Increasing individual educational access does not directly address the
systemic-level cause of inequity. Educational inequity in the U.S. is
not a problem of individuals' efforts or expectations, because it is not
an isolated problem of individuals, but a collective, systemic problem.
Educational inequity has structural roots, and it must be addressed
accordingly. Working on a systems level and an individual level are
both valuable and needed to address the same problem of injustice, but
one focuses on the structure of the man-made problem and the other
on the effects of the man-made problem.

- What is TFA's primary purpose? In TFA, there is a tension between
focusing on having an "immediate positive impact on their students" and fostering CMs as leaders to work across "all sectors" (TFA:
Achievement Gap, 2014). CMs are presented with an immediate need
for improvement as teachers placed in charge of classrooms, and they
are also called to address structural inequity. In response to critiques
that a revolving teacher corps cannot bring about long-term changes to
public education, Kopp stated, "I know we are not going to change the
education system with people teaching for two years. That's not what
we are trying to do." Kopp explained that TFA's mission is to recruit
enterprising college graduates who will contribute to the field of education even if they do not continue in the classroom (Lerer, 2012). CMs'
experiences help to illustrate the problem of TFA's at times conflicting
intentions. Examining TFA's discourse and trainings, CMs questioned
whether TFA as a program was prioritizing the students in CMs' classrooms or functioning primarily as a cross-sector leadership training
program. The foci and trainings for individual-level and systemic-level
work in the field of education are connected yet distinct. While there
is theoretical value in creating a network of leaders across sectors with
educational experience and who advocate for educational equity, many
young, inexperienced teachers already leave urban underfunded schools
at alarming rates. As a group, CMs questioned whether their participation in a two-year alternative certification program such as TFA exacerbated a pre-existing systemic problem of high teacher attrition rates
in underfunded schools. Additionally, through their participation in a

program that placed them as teachers, but defined "more" as leaving the classroom, CMs questioned whether they were collectively denigrating and deprofessionalizing teaching. Both individual- and systemic-level work are valuable and needed in the movement for educational justice, but the primary purposes, responsibilities, and practices of each are differentiated. TFA's purpose and role in the movement for educational justice needs to be critically examined and clarified.

- In the politics of representation, who is able to exercise power and narrate another group's identity, and for what purpose? The single story told through the "TFA script" misrepresents reality and overlooks the important questions of what knowledge gets collected and prioritized, how phenomena are interpreted, and who has right to authorship. Language helps to create and define identities (Butler, 1990). TFA faces a double bind common to institutions created to help others: they want to be helpful, but they often carry into their endeavors problematic preconceived notions of the people they want to help. CMs are not immune from prejudice. Additionally, TFA positions CMs to witness students' disenfranchisement without necessarily recognizing the intent, agent, mechanism, or beneficiaries of advantaging/disadvantaging systems; CMs are to serve a disenfranchised, racialized "them" in a way that makes it too easy for CMs to reinforce uninformed prejudices about students and their communities. CMs described forming problematic conclusions from their experiences focusing on students' disenfranchisement in TFA. Stereotypes reinforce deficit views of poor students of color, reify systems of oppression, and work against TFA's purported desire of effectively addressing educational inequity. Stereotypes express and reinforce oversimplified, inaccurate, and problematic narratives about CMs, the students they serve, and the nature of the constructed problem at hand.

- How do CMs' struggles impact TFA's narrative and theory of change? TFA often speaks in absolutes and reinforces the meritocracy narrative through slogans such as "Work Hard, Get Smart," "Nothing Elusive," and "No Excuses." In contrast, though many CMs worked hard and experienced varying levels of success as determined through improved students' test scores, CMs commonly described their experiences in TFA with the words "shame," "failure," and "isolating." CMs were older than their students, were recruited for track records of achievement in their respective affiliations, and were equipped with tools from elite institutions of higher education and TFA, and still they struggled to survive in their new school environments. Many CMs articulated that the greatest power they possessed was to leave the school system. How does this reality problematize TFA's narrative, the meritocratic bootstrap theories of change, and the dominant discourse on education reform?

Discussion of Key Questions and Patterns: Individual, Institutional, and Systemic

If TFA and CMs—as an institution, helping professionals, and advocates for systemic change—are to meaningfully participate in a movement towards educational equity and justice, how TFA and CMs "help" matters. TFA must listen to and learn from both the experiences of CMs and from the experiences of students and their communities. There are limits and consequences to TFA's prescription of untrue narratives. Untrue narratives—whether oversimplified, incomplete, exaggerated, or alienated from reality—misrepresent the challenges at hand, skew what resources are needed to address these challenges, and misstate what can be accomplished through the prescribed method. TFA's epistemology needs to seek out, include, and learn from the perspectives of those directly affected by its claims, including those belonging to its CMs. CMs' counternarratives help to construct a fuller historical account of events and encourage new practices to emerge. In this section, I discuss the implications of CMs' counternarratives, beginning first with individual-, then institutional-, and finally systemic-level implications.

CMs were struggling in TFA, and CMs are significant as individual people and in their roles as new teachers. CMs found the work of addressing educational inequity in their classrooms to be elusive and at times incomprehensible; they worked hard and still experienced both significant failures and unexpected negative life changes. Consistent themes emerged within this sample group of 26 CMs. After joining TFA, 35% began professional counseling; 27% began taking prescription medications to address depression, anxiety, and trauma; 38% experienced increased alcohol consumption and dependency; 42% experienced major weight changes; 46% experienced strained relationships; and 73% experienced physical fatigue, some to the point of requiring medical attention. CMs identified primary trauma, Post-Traumatic Stress Disorder (PTSD), secondary trauma, and vicarious traumatization as part of their experiences in TFA. CMs described feeling helpless, isolated, guilty, ashamed, and like failures. These patterns are problematic for CMs as people, regardless of their professional positions. These patterns are also problematic for CMs as teachers, as they are given significant responsibility to teach and extend care to their students. It is difficult for CMs to extend the best care possible to students when many struggled to care for themselves on a fundamental level.

CMs are also significant in their roles as advocates for educational equity. As individuals who are recruited and trained to "lead an educational revolution in low-income communities across the country" (TFA: Our Mission), it is critical for CMs to grapple with the realities they experience and witness. For the personal to illuminate the political, and for CMs' advocacy to bear witness to reality and support their students and communities, CMs must engage in the deeply human work of critical action-reflection. As Freire (1970) notes, "Human existence cannot be Silent, nor can it be nourished by false words, but only by true words, with which men and women transform the world. To exist, humanly, is to name the world, to change it ... Human beings are not built in silence, but in word, in work, in action-reflection. But while to say the true word—which is work, which is praxis—is to transform the world, saying that word is not the privilege of some few persons, but the right of everyone. Consequently, no one can say a true word alone—nor can she say it for another, in a prescriptive act which robs others of their words" (pp. 88–89). It is a human imperative to name the world.

In naming lived experiences, there is a difference between prescription and description: description honors the existence of a story and presents interpretation without denigrating the existence of other stories, while prescription forces one story to become everyone's story. Chimamanda Adichie states, "Power is the ability not just to tell the story of another person, but to make it the definitive story of that person" (2009). This is the particular power of hegemonic practices (the social, cultural, ideological, or economic influence exerted by a dominant group) and neocolonialism, both of which are predicated on oppression of a person or peoples.

CMs and TFA must engage in a process of description. It is problematic and ineffective to prescribe onto others what does not even work for CMs and without recognizing students and their communities as primary stakeholders and authors of their own narratives. Without a committed practice of action-reflection, it would be easy for TFA and CMs to promote hegemonic practices and neocolonialism, to bolster deficit views of students and their communities, and to extend false generosity while reinforcing the very structures CMs seek to dismantle.

As CMs experience some of the complex effects of systemic poverty, oppression, and injustice, they are in a position to name their own experiences and stand in solidarity with many of their students. Students do not require CMs' stories to legitimate their lived experiences; and as people who are opting into the public school system, CMs' experiences as a group are different than their students'. But as students' lived stories are real and powerful, in humble partnership, CMs' lived stories can also be transformative. Perhaps among the greatest contributions CMs as a group can offer the movement for educational equity are their own honest stories working in dehumanizing systems, because these stories are real. When CMs begin to adopt false narratives about who they are in relation to their students, they might become entrapped in the narrow dynamic of helper-helped. Within the structures of helper-helped, every individual is prescriptively reduced to their role in this rigid dichotomy. People are not meant to be reduced and controlled in this way, even in, or perhaps especially not in, the name of helping. The human work of naming our world, transforming our schools and educational systems, and laboring for equity and justice is everyone's work and privilege; it is not and cannot be treated as a possession of elite parties. Rather than perpetuating a problematic dominant narrative or pretending that they are not deeply affected by the reality of systemic injustice, CMs can give testimony to the reality that they are affected as both subjects with agency and hope, but also sometimes affected as dehumanized individuals with limited control. As individuals and as a group, CMs must commit to speaking their own narratives with honesty and humility, to listen and support those they serve to name the world, and to labor in the shared movement that all true narratives might construct a fuller account of experience and inform better individual and systemic practices.

In the effort to do "more," powerful entities like TFA have as much potential to harm as they do to help the people they serve. As TFA continues to expand in scope and influence, CMs' counternarratives become increasingly important; CMs' counternarratives collectively articulate specific changes needed within TFA. Critical reflection on its CMs' experiences can help TFA to shift from recognizing phenomenon as isolated and individual to noticing patterns of what is social and systemic in nature (Crenshaw, 1991, pp. 1241–1242). CMs and educators often possess insightful, salient critiques of their work contexts and preparation programs. Rather than interpret struggles as excuses or shame CMs into silence, TFA needs to gather data on CMs' well-being and provide support accordingly, invite CMs as co-partners in constructing meaning of their experiences, and invite the personal to illuminate the political. Omitting CMs' counternarratives limits both TFA's maturity and growth, and the depth and range of TFA's discourse on educational reform. It is important for TFA as an institution to listen and incorporate these critical reflections into their narratives, to narrow the gap between designated and actual narratives.

TFA's narrative—including the way TFA defines change—is both rooted in and also shapes the dominant discourse on public education. CMs' counternarratives present a critique to both the way TFA approaches systemic change, and also to the way dominant American cultural narratives position working in poor and under-resourced communities.

Idealism can reinforce a dominant narrative that is detached from reality and history in a way that undermines the purpose, relevance, and effectiveness of idealists' efforts. Idealism and individually-applied meritocracy narratives are insufficient to dismantle structural inequity. It is irresponsible and ineffective to position systemic change as a matter of scaling up individual caring and effort. It is unacceptable and unproductive to publicly discuss the disadvantages some groups of people face without also discussing the same system that simultaneously advantages other groups of people. CMs' counternarratives collectively challenge dominant discourse's definition of "more."

Untrue dominant narratives can cause harm where the intentions were to help; this reality is reflected in a larger pattern of service and aid (Crawford-Garrett, 2013; Easterly, 2006; Fikkert & Corbett, 2009; Polman, 2011). International aid organizations, religious institutions like churches, local service corps, other alternative teaching certification programs, and other helping institutions face thematically similar challenges in learning to competently and ethically engage in the work of applied development, in reconciling how to extend help without reinforcing pre-existing inequities or creating deficit ideologies, in learning to constructively partner with the people they serve. Every act of applied development is an act of interpretation and requires systematic deconstruction. Both individuals and institutions—consciously or subconsciously—have a set of underlying ideological beliefs, which drive their actions. How helping institutions position and approach change involves a series of ethical decisions, as peoples' lives are the foci of these programs, policies, and practices (Nakkula & Ravitch, 1998).

When it comes to recognizing and dismantling systems of oppression, TFA and CMs have at least as much—if not more—to learn from their students and their communities as students and their communities have to learn from TFA and CMs. Perspectives that are excluded by the official narratives—primarily those belonging to the people who are disadvantaged by and labor against systems of oppression, and secondarily the people who stand in solidarity with them—are necessary to developing ethical stances and practices in the movement for educational equity.

If able to wrestle with the tensions between their designated and actual narratives, TFA can make a meaningful contribution to the dominant discourse on improving the quality of care helping professionals and helping institutions extend; on how to listen to and support helping professionals; and on how to ethically, constructively partner with people who are already recognizing and responding to the reality of injustice.

If left unchallenged and unchanged, it is questionable whether TFA's current discourse and approach are suited to addressing educational inequity. TFA needs to fundamentally restructure conversations around how they engage in this pressing work, how to respond to the complexity of what CMs and their students experience, and how to address the particular histories and dynamics of power which undergird educational inequity.

Conclusion

Acknowledging and responding to individuals' experiences in systems of oppression are requisites to engaging humanly in the work of applied development. Teachers, particularly young and inexperienced teachers working in urban under-resourced schools, will continue to abandon these jobs, unless there is a forum for this sort of teacher reflection and responses to these realities. Powerful institutions will continue to prescribe problematic and potentially detrimental narratives without systematic deconstruction of their ideologies and practices. The kind and quality of help individuals and institutions extend is a matter of ethical importance.

TFA has a number of strengths, but CMs' experiences indicate that TFA's approach is in many ways disconnected from reality. In both a theoretical and a very practical sense, CMs' counternarratives are a necessary part of cultivating a deeper understanding of what many joined TFA hoping to address. CMs' counternarratives challenge TFA's idealistic narratives to grow in context, nuance, and inclusivity. Both CMs as individuals and TFA as an institution must commit to listening and supporting those they serve to name the world; to make the unconscious conscious and situate themselves in the historic and present realities of systemic oppression; to recognize the politicized nature of social justice; to speak their own narratives with honesty and humility; to develop a stance of working alongside with rather than for the students and communities they serve; and to labor in the shared movement that all true narratives might construct a fuller account of experience and illuminate more egalitarian and equitable practices.

Hope comes from a place of reality. In examining their lived realities and articulating a need for change, CMs' counternarratives also testify to the possibility of change. As de Beauvoir (1947) affirms, "It is in the knowledge of the genuine conditions of our lives that we must draw our strength to live and our reason for acting." It is only from a place of reality that constructive change takes root and equity-oriented perspectives and practices develop. In an ongoing process of growth, there is a collective invitation to a different way of seeing and a different way of naming the world.

Note

1. CMs' descriptions of these dynamics are detailed in Chapters 2, 5, and 7. This dynamic also emerges in TFA CEO Villanueva Beard's 2014 response to people who critique TFA, in the Gates Foundation's Irvin Scott's charge against Anthony Cody for acknowledging social privilege and inequity, and generally among some "No Excuses" reformers to Social Context reformers (Thomas, 2013; Villanueva Beard, 2014). Other educators and advocates, like Camika Royal, who raise important political questions have been accused of being "anti-education reform" (Royal, 2012a).

APPENDIX A

Titles & Acronyms

A brief description of the titles and acronyms used in the book:

All-Corps Saturdays (ACS): Mandatory, all-day Saturday trainings through CMs' two-year commitment.

Charter Management Organization (CMO): CMOs are nonprofits that operate multiple charter schools. Charter schools receive public funding but are privately run separate from the public school system.

Corps Member (CM): TFA teachers are called corps members during their two-year commitment.

Graduate School of Education (GSE): Teach For America Greater Philadelphia partners with the University of Pennsylvania Graduate School of Education.

Manager of Teacher Leadership and Development (MTLD): Each corps member is assigned an MTLD through Teach For America.

Penntor: Penn Graduate School of Education mentor assigned to individual CMs through the Penn GSE/TFA partnership.

School District of Philadelphia (SDP): The SDP is the school district that includes all public schools in Philadelphia. In 2014, Philadelphia had 218 SDP schools and 86 charter schools.

Summer Institute or **Institute:** Five-week summer training prior to the first year in which newly accepted CMs take responsibility for a four-week summer school class, participate in grade- and subject-specific group trainings, and attend seminar-style workshops.

Teach For America (TFA): Teach For America is a national teacher corps which selects graduates from many of the nation's most selective universities and places them in urban and rural schools serving predominantly poor students of color.

Teach For America Greater Philadelphia (TFAGP): A regional chapter of Teach For America, TFAGP was established in 2003 with an initial corps size of 120 CMs. In 2014, TFAGP had 1,120 alumni in the region. TFAGP was formerly referred to as the TFA Mid-Atlantic office, which included school placements in Philadelphia, Camden, and Delaware (Teach For America: Greater Philadelphia, 2015).

Teaching as Leadership (TAL): CMs were required to read a book titled *Teaching as Leadership* (2010) before entering the corps. TAL refers to both that book and to evaluative metrics developed from the book's framework.

TFANet: TFA's general online resources for CMs.

APPENDIX B

Journal Reflection

Analysis in this book is done through my perspective and lens. I want to disclose more explicitly where I am rooted in this paper, and how I came to develop some of my research questions. This is a journal reflection I submitted to an Inquiry into Practice class with Professor Alice Ginsberg at the Penn Graduate School of Education in December 2012.

December 4, 2012

Many of my questions the first semester of my second year have had to do with understanding my own and other new teachers' responses to the questions of, "Who am I? What is my identity, what is my identity as a teacher, and what is my identity in relationship to my students? What am I doing here? Who am I to be doing this? Can I do this? Do I want to do this? What is the effect my environment and work have on me, and what effect do I have in my class-room?" and the difficulty with which these questions are asked, answered, or left unanswered. Entries in my journal reflect the difficulty with which teach-ers answer these questions—it is a painful process and a lot of peoples' sense of self, their intellectual and emotional health, and their evaluation of their work seems to hinge on the responses to these questions.

In my journal I noted the additional stressors that many new TFA teachers seem to face as they begin teaching in Philly. Transitioning out of college and into a work environment has enough of its own challenges, add to that trying to make sense of an environment that largely contains many falsehoods in its system (so, people trying to make sense of things that maybe just don't make sense), and then you have a slew of young TFA teachers struggling to survive and experiencing varying levels of cognitive dissonance. In listening to my own and other TFA teachers' articulations of their answers to the above questions, I have noted that part of the pain in this process is the inability to name precisely what it is that makes this job so difficult. There is so much that seems to be weighing on young teachers, and yet the narratives being fed to us about who we are, who we should be, who our students are, who they should be, and so forth all do not seem to align with many peoples' daily experiences. It is alienating to know that you are exhausted but not be able to share why, to be known by others in that way, to know yourself in that way, to be able to express yourself, to be understood in a safe environment. As a first-year TFA teacher, S. shared with and asked me right before fall break, "Am I supposed to be this sad? I'm not sure if I should quit. I've never been this miserable in my life. I cry every single day—no, really. Every single day. Is this normal?" We were meeting informally over a quick cup of coffee—she was a close college friend of one of my closest friends from home, so though I did not know her well, I said I would be happy to meet her to talk through some of her first-year experiences. In our meeting, she expressed that even though she felt like she didn't have time to talk with me and almost couldn't make space in her weekend, she also felt like she couldn't not talk about "all of this." Even though we barely knew each other and only knew each other through a close mutual friend, she clearly expressed a desire to be known, to know if she made sense, to know if she was not alone in her wanting to quit and feeling like a complete failure. Throughout our short conversation, I could hear her wrestling with the questions from the first paragraph, and being pained by the answers she didn't have and by the ones she did.

S. was not the only person I've noted expressing this kind of incomprehensible internal struggle. So many CMs from my year could not make sense of how exhausted they were from working in the classroom last year. It's almost like people couldn't say how tired they were, so it came out in dreams and jokes. Throughout the summer, there would be a couple half-jokes tossed around in e-mails among friends, "Now I finally feel like a human again" or "I'm so worn out I don't even want to get off of the couch or stop watching

TV" or "Oh my god, it's like I've got PTSD or something." I wonder why the primary forum for discussing this kind of exhaustion was in the form of jokes. While peoples' conscious minds may not seem to fully own how challenged and worn down they felt, their dreams reflect that there is a very real part of them (even if it is subconscious) that knows the trauma is not a joke. On the first All Corps meeting we had back from summer, I noted to a friend that I woke up at 3am and 5am on the first day before school with nightmares of my class being out of control. In my dream, I was shouting to be heard, almost pleading, and no one could hear me. Objectively, my classroom has never looked like that (or at least, not according to my formal evaluations from my school principal, informal feedback from veteran teachers, and TFA evaluations). But I wonder how many times it has felt that way to me. And I know that is something I have feared as a teacher—to be trying so hard to connect and yet be still discounted, ignored, ineffective. As I shared this quietly in the hallway, another TFA person was shocked and joined in, and then another, and soon the hallway had several people sharing about the morning before their first day back in the classroom. Every person who heard that conversation shared that they woke up some time in the middle of the night with some kind of nightmare. There were at least 5 other people who stopped, heard, and identified with this experience. One teacher dreamt she was drowning. Another teacher dreamt she was being attacked by bloodied knives and guns. A third just woke up startled and couldn't fall back asleep, and a fourth barely slept at all to begin with. A fifth teacher did not share the specifics of his nightmare, but volunteered that he also woke up multiple times in the middle of the night with some fear of what the next day would bring. While all of these teachers wanted to be back and came back for a second year, they also clearly grappled with understanding what this year would mean for them, particularly considering what last year had meant.

In addition to the jokes and dreams, there also seem to be a number of TFA teachers who are drinking to black out, which may or may not be another symptom of some of the same causes of those jokes and dreams. My non-TFA friend who went out with TFA teachers one Thursday night shared that, "I have never seen people drink so hard throughout all of our undergrad years at Penn unless they had just finished their LSATs or MCATs. I can't believe there are TFA people drinking like this several times a week. Did you know that they're basically drinking to black out like at least three times a week?" I reflected on her comment in my journal that I wonder what about our current lives and work environments are making it so that people would rather drink to black out and not be present than be present and want to face reality. Many CMs seem to have a lack of mental health resources (maybe because they are paying off loans, or because of the stigma, or because of perceived time constraints) in a way that seems to parallel many of my students' experiences. In a school with over 500 students, my school has one counselor's salary. In my not even one and a half years at Global Connections Charter School,* I have seen 3 different school counselors: the first was disconnected from most students and was fired, the second was fired for reasons not disclosed to students or staff, and the third has just entered mid-year. For both CMs and my students, there does not seem to be a person seeking them out or seeking to provide counsel on self-care and mental health. I brought up this concern in one of my Penn TFA classes last year, and there was an immediate response of loud, awkward, uncomfortable laughter—people were familiar with the phenomenon of drinking to black out because of new teacher stress, but no one knew how to respond to it in a healthy way. Another TFA colleague, A., was angered by this and quietly told the class that she did not think this was a laughing matter, and that "mental health is not something to be laughed at." Our class ended on that note, and I haven't heard of teacher health being brought up in a large group conversation since. I brought this concern up in a small group with my MTLD, O. He said he appreciated the important insight. Then he, like many other people affiliated with TFA, left Philly to a "higher" leadership position to do "more" in a different city.

While many expressions of stress, fatigue, fear, and struggle with understanding one's experience as a teacher have been indirect (jokes, dreams, drinking to black out), I have also heard some direct expressions. Last week, a colleague and third-year TFA teacher came to my room in tears—"I do not think I can do this. I don't know if I can make it into my third year at this place with my mental health intact." Other TFA teachers have started counseling for their first time ever or have started on anti-depression medication for their first time ever.

All these narratives indicate to me that it is hard to name the subjective experiences of teaching. It is elusive. We are enmeshed in a system in which we are both the helper and the helped; the oppressor and the oppressed. Who are we? It is painful and difficult to name the ways we are hurt or hurting others. It just is. And it impacts how we view ourselves, how we think others will view us, our chances and developing a career we'd like, etc.

So many CMs feel helpless and ineffective, like failures—it is hard to exist humanly and name the world, much less change it. When there is such a glaring inequity and deep need that is witnessed, it is almost seems logical in the moment to cut the reflection out of the work of action-reflection. However, this is the right of all people, including students, and including Teach For America CMs. And the reflection should not just be what sounds good or what fits in best with a career plan or with what we think others want to hear. Without honest reflection, people struggle to understand, much less control, their actions, which then in turn can easily contribute to unhealthy drinking patterns, nightmares, and so forth. Maybe these are some ways our selves are telling us that we're not ok; that this way of being, this way of thinking and treating ourselves, our stories, our students' stories—it's not ok.

The trend is that people are struggling. And their inability to talk about their experiences—with others or with themselves—is an issue. One way or another, everyone responds to the realities surrounding them. Many of the CMs are having positive responses: enjoying getting to know students, developing relationships, becoming involved and learning about how to partner with their students and communities, seeing significant academic gains, etc. But there are also an overwhelming number of problematic responses that are even more concerning because they do not seem to be being addressed or even named—the binge drinking, the nightmares, the trauma.

I've never so directly tried to run up against a long-standing, powerful, hegemonic system before, much less tried to do so from my own effort alone. I've read some of my own experiences into the high turnover rate—sometimes it has felt like the greatest power I have is in leaving this environment. In some ways, this is humbling because I've acknowledged the even clearer falsity of the strict meritocratic kind of thinking—if as someone who is twice as old as my students and readied with so many of dominant-culture's finest endorsed resources (e.g., a Penn undergraduate and soon-to-be master's)—if in evaluating my students' school situations I feel my greatest power is in leaving, how is one of our dominant cultural narratives expressing that my students should be picking themselves up by their bootstraps? The fact that some students survive and graduate from such a brutal system is testament to a miracle and their own tenacity, strength, and beyond-the-odds kind of experience. So very little of what I've daily experienced of the school system seems to set students up for survival, much less success. Though this knowledge can be humbling, it has also been dehumanizing—I am again forced to ask the question, "Who am I here? Can I do this? Do I want to do this?"

Many of my own entries about my own health and some of my colleague's health reflect how poverty in our school is subjectively experienced by some teachers and some students. Factors in the physical environment and more elusive culprits seem to affect everyone—it oppresses students, the community, administration, veteran teachers, new teachers, etc. I've taken note of various teachers who, despite being effective in raising students' scores and developing a positive relationship with students, are setting their hopes on leaving at the end of their second year. According to second-year M., "I just don't know if I can do this anymore. I want to be here, but this job is eating at me." When I asked another CM, D., before our Penn class how she was doing, she responded with a half laugh at first, but still seriously, "I feel like I'm on drugs. I'm so tired." When asked why, she said, "It's everything. My school is crazy, it's TFA, it's classes ... People kept asking me today if I was crying. I think my eyes are tearing up because I'm just so tired ... though I also cried three times today." A first-year TFA CM at my school shared, "Our MTLD saw my list of things to do. I made the list because I wanted our meeting to be efficient and helpful, and I shared that I didn't know when I could do all these things. She told me I should do it on my Sundays. Does she not get it? I mean, maybe it's because she taught in Houston 5 years ago?" While she did not explicitly state it, another question I heard through our conversation was, "I am working so hard. How is this not good enough? How am I supposed to live through this?" A second-year teacher, B., said, "It's heart-breaking seeing where some of our students are. Look at my Spanish kids. Look at some of your students. What can we actually do here. I mean, part of seeing this makes me want to stay, but I don't think I have it in me, y'know?" Across various people I've spoken with and written about in my journal, I'm noting that while many think this job is worthwhile, few are approaching this as a life-long endeavor, or even a 2+ year endeavor. Additionally, it's not because they would not want to stay longer. The way it is spoken about, the TFA teachers seem to be questioning the sustainability of their own efforts. Hearing these reflections, I'm left wondering about the unnamed factors that make this job so difficult, what resources are currently available to teachers, what ways our experiences parallel and do not parallel student experiences, and also what things could be done to address some of these issues. Additionally, I wonder how exploring another set of perspectives could add to the understanding of what it is many people came into TFA hoping to help address. While I believe strongly in people's agency, the value of grit and perseverance, and the deep need for structural changes in the movement for educational equity, I think some honest reflections could problematize the sometimes over-simplified narratives surrounding educational inequity and the popular solution of, "Work Hard, Get Smart."

APPENDIX C

Data Analysis

I drew on four overlapping methodological and philosophical orientations as a means for data analysis: Inquiry Stance, Critical Pedagogy, Counternarratives, and Ethnographic Methods.

Inquiry Stance

To investigate the complexity of the phenomena observed within TFA, I adopted an inquiry stance. With the ultimate goal of improving the professional practice, this work investigates intersecting layers of complexity in the field—cultural, contextual, positional, political, historical, and institutional (S. Ravitch, 2014, pp. 7–9). An inquiry stance generates contextualized knowledge and problematizes hegemonic standard narratives; it seeks to link individuals within their micro-contexts to the macro-context of larger groups and social movements seeking to address educational inequity (Cochran-Smith & Lytle, 2009, p. viii). An inquiry stance is integral to action research. This study initially focused on not only generating knowledge, but also influencing the practices of TFA as an institution, particularly how they related to CMs' lived narratives when CMs did not align with dominant reform narrative.

Critical Pedagogy and Counternarratives

To better work with, rather than for, the many already laboring for educational equity and justice, I adopted Paulo Freire's school of critical pedagogy. Critical theory helps to "recognize as social and systemic what was previously understood as isolated and individual" (Crenshaw, 1991, pp. 1241–1242) and critical pedagogy includes: "Habits of thought, reading, writing, and speaking which go beneath surface meaning, first impressions, dominant myths, official pronouncements, traditional clichés, received wisdom, and mere opinions, to understand the deep meaning, root causes, social context, ideology, and personal consequences of any action, event, object, process, organization, experience, text, subject matter, policy, mass media, or discourse" (Shor, 1992, pp. 129–130). This philosophy and social movement is characterized by "action-reflection" and praxis work; the ends to this method are not only to generate meaningful, contextualized, oppressed-people-led systemic change, but also to develop critical consciousness in individuals (Freire, 1970). Critical consciousness includes power awareness, the recognition of dominance and power dynamics within society; critical literacy, the in-depth process of action-reflection; permanent desocialization, understanding and challenging political limits on human development; and self-education, the organization to develop critical thought and action (Shor, 1992, pp. 129–130). This critical consciousness is necessary for both those who are oppressed by the unjust systems and those who seek to partner meaningfully with them in the shared work of restorative justice.

Guided by critical pedagogy principles, I sought to understand more the depth and range of experience within the corps and invited CMs to name their lived experiences beyond any dominant myths, surface meanings, official pronouncements, traditional clichés, or received wisdom. Counternarratives are an active expression of critical pedagogy which allow for those excluded by dominant narratives to identify and interpret their experiences. Counternarratives resist 1) "the modernist predilection for 'grand,' 'master,' and 'meta' narratives" and 2) "the 'official' and 'hegemonic' narratives of everyday life: those legitimating stories propagated for specific political purposes to manipulate public consciousness by heralding a national set of common cultural ideals" (Giroux, 1996, p. 2). These little stories present an expression of Foucault's counter-memory: the contextualized examination of not only what is remembered and forgotten, but how history—the collective memory—is crafted, the agenda behind its creation, and its authorship. These localized "little stories" have the power to interrupt the grandiosity of the metanarrative, advocate for a fuller, more truthful representation of reality, and encourage new practices to emerge.

Ethnographic Methods

Though this is not a traditional ethnography in length or form, I approached my data from an "ethnographic perspective" (Crawford-Garrett, 2013, p. 7). Characteristic of an "ethnographic perspective," I utilized theories of culture and inquiry practices derived from anthropology and sociology to guide this research (Green & Bloome, 1997). Specifically, I utilized qualitative research tools of thick description, member-checking, external audit, peer debriefing, and theory triangulation to analyze this data (Denzin, 1978).

I invited CMs to provide detailed accounts of their experiences and their interpretations of their experiences. To support research credibility, I conducted member-checks in which I consulted interviewees to review their working themes. Interviewees were presented with preliminary findings and given the opportunity to address any misinterpretations of their interviews and provide any additional information prompted by the playback process (Lincoln & Guba, 1985). This feedback was incorporated into the final narrative.

A number of colleagues provided additional perspectives on analyses and aspects of inquiry that might otherwise have remained implicit within my researcher positionality (Lincoln & Guba, 1985, p. 308). These colleagues included: university professors, teachers in TFA who did not participate in this survey, critical theorists who studied urban education and TFA, and friends from my undergraduate years at Penn who majored in a range of subjects. These individuals' questions and reviews served as a form of peer-debriefing and external audit.

APPENDIX D

Recommendations to TFA Staff on What Can Be Done to Better Support TFA Greater Philadelphia CMs

This study's findings and the following outline of suggestions have been presented to the regional chair and leadership team of TFA Hawai'i in August, 2013; presented to Greater Philadelphia CMs, GSE staff, and TFA staff at the 2013 Penn GSE/TFA Capstone Conference; and shared with the TFAGP staff.

These are some immediate and actionable changes needed to better support CMs as individuals, as potential lifelong advocates for educational equity, and as current teachers. TFA needs to gather information on CMs' actual experiences, engage in a process of critical action-reflection, and prioritize CMs' mental health:

- Gather information on CMs' mental health.
  - For an organization that deeply values and emphasizes the importance of data collection, it is amazing that little to no data is collected on CMs' mental health. How are CMs, the supposed leaders of this educational revolution, actually doing? Aiden stated, "With the organization and the staff as a whole … I think that there is a certain culture that does try and stifle that kind of conversation [on behavioral health]. I think bringing this kind of conversation into daylight could help. It's a hard to tackle."

- o Add a page on mental health to the mandatory TFA survey so that the organization can know and address the struggle on a broader basis if needed. The survey I created was open to all 2011 and 2012 Greater Philadelphia TFA CMs, but there is a possibility that those who responded might have come from a somehow self-selecting population (maybe they had especially bad experiences they wanted to share, or maybe people who have had the toughest experiences did not have time to respond, etc.). The question of how CMs are doing needs to be explored throughout the whole corps.
- Incorporate this information in a process of action-reflection.
  - o The findings from this study serve as a starting place. TFA needs to explore and narrow the gap between the narratives they are propagating and the realities many CMs are experiencing.
  - o Develop a system and process for critical reflection because the identity of TFA as an institution needs to mature.
- Foster an environment open to talking about mental health and empowering CMs to ask for help when they need it for themselves.
  - o Possible introduction at TFA Summer Institute to what some of CMs' struggles outside of the classroom have been like while they served in TFA. Have older classes of CMs share some of what they have struggled with and some healthy methods of coping (e.g., finding a counselor, finding a running buddy, asking friends and family for support early on, etc.). Use some of this data to start conversations with CMs to help prepare them for the challenges ahead.
    - E.g., Dane Galloway, another CM who did not participate in this study but read the study findings, utilized this data to facilitate conversations on mental health with new CMs. He served as a Corps Member Advisor for two summers after completing his TFA commitment, and he utilized this study's findings to introduce CMs to some potential challenges and encourage them to reach out for help if they needed it in the future. He stated, "I have shared some of [your findings] with my CMs in hopes that they will feel more empowered to reach out."
  - o Dionne stated, "TFA does not want to talk about mental health of CMs. When brought up I have had little to no response." Other CMs have echoed similar sentiments.
  - o In a public forum, acknowledge that generally CMs are struggling and commit to providing support. Both the responses and the thanks

several corps members extended to me after an initial posting of my findings, it is clear that these narratives are resonating with people. There is value in being able to identify our stories and share them, in acknowledging the obstacles encountered, and in co-constructing identity.

- Create a database of resources outside of TFA.
  - How can others be involved? Community mentors, corps members helping each other, etc. Connect or inform CMs about specific opportunities from outside organizations that are about their own self-care.
    - E.g., Vineyard Community Church's Restore group. Taken from their flyer: "Restore is a group designed for people who work with people and communities in crisis, such as social workers, counselors, childcare providers, teachers, and community workers. The group will facilitate community, allow for personal reflection, provide times to share, and practice soul-sustaining exercises."
- Create specific partnership between TFA and Penn Counseling and Psychological Services (CAPS) so CMs can receive counseling if they need it (CAPS is open to all Penn students and included in the general tuition, but TFA teachers cannot make the current hours of 9am–5pm because they are still at work).
  - Deanna Santoro, a CM who did not participate in this study but read the study findings, suggested group counseling in a specific TFA and CAPS partnership. She stated, "Since CAPS' current hours are hard, if not impossible, for many TFA teachers to make, can there be a group counseling session once every two weeks or once a month?" This could help normalize some peoples' experiences and combat some of the isolation and personal shame described in survey and interviews.
  - Provide counselor referrals; find counselors who have a deeper understanding of TFA and how to support people in service positions.
- Be sensitive to the fact that many CMs have felt guilty, ashamed, and like failures. Set ground rules, norms, and best practices for conversations between TFA staff and CMs. Provide training for MTLD on how to provide constructive feedback as a supervising mentor figure. Encourage MTLDs to problem solve with CMs.
  - E.g., When CMs share with staff that they are struggling, the first question should not be, "Do you care about your students?" CMs

shared feeling attacked in their interactions with TFA staff. Develop practices of asking questions and inviting critical reflection without making CMs feel attacked.

- o CMs explained what they wanted from their relationship with MTLDs and TFA staff: support and a relational process of action-reflection. CMs expressed wanting constructive conversations rather than scripted directives.
- Normalize the experience of trauma if it occurs for individual CMs.
  - o When speaking about her own traumatic experiences and responses, Kate asked, "I've been wondering, is this normal? ... it makes me feel better to know I'm not alone." TFA needs to include programming on trauma to help normalize CM experiences. Understanding the emotions and normal responses that follow a disaster or other traumatic event can help people cope with challenging and complex feelings, thoughts and behaviors—this can aid in the process of recovery. TFA could work with a mental health professional to aid in this process.
  - o Clinical psychologist Dr. Barry Jacobs described that his first step he takes in addressing someone who has experienced trauma is to "Identify what happened to this patient as traumatic, and tell her acute anxiety was an understandable response" (Graham, 2013). In addressing people who experience trauma, it is important to normalize their experiences so those people do not feel isolated and can seek healing. University of Colorado psychology professor Dr. Sara Qualls noted, "I think that a piece of the trauma reaction that is so devastating is the intense privacy of it" (Graham, 2013). CMs commented on the pervasiveness of isolation in TFA.
- Provide differentiated support for CMs, and make concerted efforts to provide support to CMs who express requiring additional support.
  - o CMs described wanting differentiated support. Some preferred less contact with TFA staff, while others wanted more feedback on how to improve instruction. Aiden suggested, "Target MTLD time to CMs who are struggling most and need it most."
- Create structural space for CMs to reflect critically on their experiences in a safe environment.
  - o This can be in the form of a class, a specific group, or sessions available on All-Corps Saturdays.
  - o Ground rules, norms, and expectations can be established to create a safe space. Former CMs can come in to speak about their experiences,

or videos could be shown of former CMs discussing their experiences honestly and constructively.

- Encourage CM self-care through language and programming.
  - One of the three-prongs of TFA's Mission Statement is "Investing in Leaders." Currently, many CMs feel guilty and ashamed by their own standards and guilty and ashamed from comments made by staff members. Many CMs do not have the time or the capacity to take care of themselves, and they were interpreted as selfish if they tried. This lack of self-care is affecting their well-being as individuals and as teachers. Dionne stated, "Reflecting on this interview and your research, the organization needs to focus more on corps members' work-life balance and ensuring that corps members are having a healthy balance because we're good teachers when we're happy and content with our lives." CMs commented that we are better teachers when we take care of ourselves. There is sacrifice involved in any service job. But what is extended needs to be replenished somehow. Without healthy self-care, there is even greater burnout and turn-over not to "do more" but just to get out for self-preservation.
  - Other organizations such as Apple have "wellness" staff, individuals dedicated to helping promote the mental and physical well-being of their company employees. While we do not have the resources to have a built-in gym, nutritionists, personal trainers, or other amenities offered in many corporate settings, if TFA wants to invest in their leaders, they need to encourage and remind the leaders to invest in and care for themselves. We do not need a lot of money to change our stance on and our language around self-care.
  - E.g., TFA could facilitate wellness groups run by TFA alum. Maybe TFA alum in the area can host different activity groups such as a running group, or a yoga group, a baseball game once a month, or some activity which would be helpful to TFA CMs' well-being.
    - A friend and fellow CM at my school and I signed up for Broad Street Run and it was a great commitment and encouraging accountability system. Maybe there can be a TFA Broad Street Run team. There was a kickball team started by one of the 2011 CMs. The Corps Member Advisory Council is part of a mentor-mentee group that is starting. There are things being done on this front.
  - TFA has such a name brand and a robust marketing team that many larger corporations are aware of and supportive of TFA. Maybe some

organizations would be interested in donating a once-a-month work-out class, or transportation to a nearby hike, etc.

- The Phillies donated tickets to TFA this past year and many CMs said it was one of their best experiences in TFA—they were able to bring a student and a friend, and it was a great way to relax, spend quality time with a student outside of school, enjoy themselves, and recharge.

- Prioritize CM health by assigning a person to this role.
  - Possible hires include an in-house counselor, or someone who is familiar with trauma and can help connect CMs to the resources they need, facilitate wellness events, work on developing groups for CMs, etc. Maggie stated, "If TFA truly were smart and were honest with themselves, what they've lost track of is those numbers don't mean jack if you've got a bunch of disgruntled employees. And that's what we are. They need a dean of culture. Someone apolitical, neutral to the mission, and really focuses on the lives of young CMs who are troubled. I had no idea how much work this is, and they need to say that without being shut down and judged. They need to hire a therapist."

- Consider other structures of teaching
  - E.g., Robin suggested, "Make CMs co-teachers for a year. Eliminate the sink or swim. I would not have been a teacher if not for TFA. People who want to do this should have access, but you do need that first year of co-teaching. I would have slept better if I knew that there would be someone in the room. I've noticed people who stay are co-teachers with veterans."
    - Two TFAGP CMs were featured in a piece on co-teaching classrooms: http://www.nbcphiladelphia.com/news/local/Local-Charter-Employs-Teach-For-America-Corps-to-Provide-Co-Taught-Classrooms-235132661.html

- Invite and encourage CMs to critically reflect on TFA's pedagogy and what needs to change.
  - There was one meeting with Wendy Kopp about the growth of TFA, but some CMs felt it was exclusive, secretive, and did not allow for anything actionable.
    - E.g., Give this data to a group of CMs and hear their responses. Create open task groups to problem-solve and interpret group data. When I posted this data, some CMs I do not usually talk

with started asking me or mutual friends questions about the data. When I interviewed people, there were definite reactions and thoughts of how to make sense of this data. Multiple individuals reached out after I posted initial findings—they had questions, suggestions, and possible solutions.

○ Encourage critical reflection throughout all levels of TFA and allow the personal to illuminate the political. In his second year working as a Corps Member Advisor, Dane stated, "I'm trying really deliberately to ground my coaching methods in the reality that good teaching is actually much more complex than just 'hard work' and 'discipline' and that stress is real, but that it's possible to teach sustainably and avoid (or channel and dismantle) that shame, failure, and isolation. The idea that teaching is purely meritocratic is similarly misleading as saying our students' success depends solely on how hard they work."

APPENDIX E

Elle's E-mail

I spoke with Elle* several times and received her permission to attach her letter in my appendix as an example of communication between CMs providing constructive feedback to TFA staff. I explained to her what Jane had said of her, and invited her to respond. The following is an e-mail she wrote to staff, prefaced by an introduction to why she wrote the letter.

As some background information to understand aspects of Elle's letter:

- Elle was part of the 2013 TFA corps and left TFA after her first semester teaching.
- Elle was not among the 26 CMs officially interviewed for this study, though two CMs in this study referenced her in their interviews.
- Elle was trained to teach Algebra 2 at summer institute, but was placed to teach high school biology in her first year. She had limited experience in this assigned subject.
- TFA staff questioned why she could commit to ten years in the military but not one in TFA.
- *Steve, TFA's manager of veteran recruitment, asked Elle to help recruit veterans. Elle agreed to help as a thank you to Steve for his support, but she felt like a hypocrite for recruiting others to a program she was considering quitting.

- Courtney Lemon-Tate is a non-TFA science teacher who taught at Elle's school. Lemon-Tate has an undergraduate and graduate degree in Biology. In addition to those degrees, she also obtained her Pennsylvania teacher certification traditionally through a state-approved program at Ursinus College.

Elle's introduction to her letter to TFA staff

December 22, 2014

I will say, that as nice as it was and is to receive the praise from my coworkers, as I've told them multiple times, I was never "in danger." Yes, I was deployed twice at the time I joined TFA, but the nature of my job always put me at a safe distance from what many veterans had to endure.

I will also say that many of my experiences in TFA were actually more stressful than things I encountered in the Air Force, so "Jane" and all the rest should not sell themselves short. For all the respect you say they have for me, I have it for them in return. They have all done what I could not—finished their two year commitment.

As for what prompted me to respond to TFA with this letter, I think it was a direct response to Dayna's* question, why I could do ten years in the military, but not one in TFA (by the way, I'm not the only vet who walked away from TFA). It came down to a simple answer: training. The military isn't easy, but they provide you with the tools you need for success. In contrast, I kept asking for the resources I needed from TFA and not getting them. There were those who went above and beyond to help (my Penntor Lori, Penn professors, Lemon-Tate), but never those who promised it from the beginning: TFA. I found it mind-boggling that after all these years in existence, TFA didn't have a continuity book of curriculums for people in my situation. When I asked if we could get it from people at schools with curriculum (such as Mastery Charter Schools), I was pretty much told it was not possible due to proprietary reasons. I wondered if it's about ALL children deserving a good education, why are we essentially allowing competition between private businesses (charter schools) getting in the way of that? I could go on, but I'll stop there before I write 3 pages.

Really, what it all boiled down to for me is I started feeling like part of the problem and not the solution. I was another crappy teacher placed there temporarily until the assembly line replaced me and I was taking my frustrations out partly on the students. The kids deserved better than that.

Quitting TFA was a tough decision for me, but necessary for where I was in my life. I hope getting the MSW and staying involved as well as keeping in touch with former students will help me one day put aside the guilt of leaving, but it's always something that will nag at me. I don't think it's fair to CMs that invested so much emotionally to feel this way. I don't think TFA makes you feel like this on purpose, it's bred out of frustration with the system as a whole and they're only doing what they think they need to in order to get people to stay. I think, however, they could take a lesson from the military when people leave. (And I can't speak for everyone's experience, just mine). When I left after 11 years (the goal for most is 20, so I did about half), I was told, "Thank you for your service. You have chosen to do what only 1 percent of the population does, we wish you well in your future endeavors."

Elle's letter to TFA staff

---------- Forwarded message ----------
From: **Elle***
Date: Sun, Nov 17, 2013 at 3:40 PM
Subject: feedback for yesterday
To: Dayna*, TFAGP staff
Cc: Steve*, TFA's Manager of Veteran Recruitment

Dayna,

I want to apologize if yesterday my tone at ACS seemed like I was ungrateful or complaining.

You were seriously asking me suggestions for improvement, which I appreciate, and I was so frustrated I did not fully articulate what I think could help (I also didn't want to monopolize the conversation).

I am including *Steve on this because he has asked to include him on issues I'm facing, and there is also something I want to come clean on.

You had asked us what did we expect when we joined TFA?

Honestly, I expected to be taught how to teach. The reason I went with TFA instead of just sticking to TTT (Troops to Teachers) is that the idea of a "teacher bootcamp" and "mentors" seemed like what I needed to be the best teacher I could be. I wanted the best chance to be effective in the classroom as I possibly could. That's why I joined TFA. Institute was a valuable experience, but did not teach me how to teach. The constant deadlines meant that

I was always treading water. I was in survival mode. I also did not have nearly as much "real time coaching" as I thought I would. My CMA seemed confused that I did not understand the math I was teaching.

Steve* had recently asked me to participate in a webinar telling veterans why they should join TFA. I gladly accepted because Steve* has been a good support for me and I wanted to return the favor. However, participating in the webinar made me feel like a hypocrite, since I had just a few days before that contemplated leaving the program because I was overwhelmed, and as much as people like my Penntor and fellow teachers at my school tried to help, I just felt like I didn't leave my last job only to step into another one that made me as miserable as this one often does.

So, you asked us what TFA could do to help:

1) Use the vast network of people that have taught in the past and are teaching now to help those that are currently teaching. As some other CMs have mentioned, we are told not to "reinvent the wheel" but there is not much of a wheel provided for us. As we stated, boosting up the TFANet with resources we can use will alleviate the stress of planning lessons in subjects that some of us are learning ourselves. For a lot of the resources, there are no answer keys, so I have to research the information myself, which takes time. I understand your sentiment of "we did it in the past, you can do it," but my issue with this train of thought is a few things:

A) Just because some have struggled in the past does not mean those now should struggle. I used to hear the same sentiment about boot camp, survival school, and numerous other military trainings I have been through ("I did it, you should do it too."). Yes, it is true that adversity builds character, I'm not denying that, but the problem with this reasoning is it makes it about the CM, and not the students they serve. For every week that I spend hours scouring the internet, or peeling through my external hard drive for the resources that fellow teachers (4 so far) have given me, I can't help but think this is time I could be using to stay on top of my Penn studies (which have gone to the wayside) or analyzing the data that you requested, or honestly grading my students work instead of giving them credit for trying (because I didn't have time to read all of it.) You ask us to backwards plan, and honestly, it makes perfect sense to me, it's how we would gear up for deployments. The problem is that in order to backwards plan, I need to know what the finish line looks like, and I have no clue.

B) This idea that that struggle is necessary to build a good teacher is part (not all, but certainly part) of the reason why people don't stay after 2 years, or for that matter, didn't make it through the first 2 months. They're burnt out. A little bit of stress builds character, grit, and resilience. Too much stress breaks people. What is the end goal?

So, why do we have teacher A at school X with a curriculum not sharing that info with teacher B at school Y? (some of us do it informally, but why doesn't TFA step in and help? What, is there no way for first year CM to network with second years in their same subject area? Further, why does a teacher who is going to teach Biology in the fall teach Algebra 2 at Institute when this is their main chance to practice before the real thing (train like we fight?) (my situation) or even worse, a person who does not know Spanish teaching Spanish (which happened to a person at my institute this summer, I stopped feeling bad for myself when I heard that.). Are we just filling in boxes to say we have a training program or are we really trying to help build teachers? Why are we not shown an exemplar? In my old training it was called demo perf. You watch how it's done, then you do it yourself, and are debriefed. Here, we just expect people to do it themselves. Yes, I observed a teacher at Ridely High School before Institute, but watching suburban honors biology students was not going to prepare me for teaching kids that are a few grades behind in reading.

2) Put the focus on teaching. Learning the social issues is important, because we don't exist in a vacuum, but it seems the vast majority of mini clinics, ACS talks, and the Penn classes focus on social issues, instead of the teacher training we could use.

I appreciate what you and Lori try to do for me, please don't think that I don't, but it should not have been 10 weeks into my school year before I was able to sit down with a science teacher (that Lori set me up with) to bounce ideas off. Mary and Tim (Penn GSE methods class instructors) are great, but we often don't have time in methods class to do it either.

Finally, (because this e-mail is already too long, and I apologize), I found the programming at ACS also sending mixed messages. The majority of the optional PD was geared around "what are you going to do after TFA?" We don't even hide the fact that we don't expect people to stay, that it's a pipeline of fresh faces that will be easily replaced.

Is TFA really focused on the kids and their education, or is it a Leadership Training program? (more and more, it sound like the latter to me). If a social justice leadership program is what TFA wants to be, perhaps it's time to separate the missions and have 2 sister organizations. Teach first, then work on staff to gain that leadership experience. If not staff work, other sub organizations that can address the other issues our students face (malnutrition, after-school programs, etc.).

Also, thank you for stepping in and trying to work with my school. It is reassuring that we are not left to languish in a broken school by ourselves, and that folks are advocating for us.

So far, 8 teachers have quit since September, the morale is abysmal. It's good to know it is on TFA's radar.

If there is more to the picture that I don't see, please let me know. I want to understand how everything works. And thank you for all you do.

v/r
Elle

BIBLIOGRAPHY

Adichie, C. (2009, July). Chimamanda Adichie: The danger of a single story [Video file]. Retrieved from http://www.ted.com/talks/chimamandaadichiethedangerofasinglestory.

Anderson, J. D. (1989). *The education of Blacks in the South, 1860–1935*. Chapel Hill, University of North Carolina Press.

Anderson, J. D. (2002, February 28). *Historical perspectives on Black academic achievement*. Paper presented for the Visiting Minority Scholars Series Lecture. Wisconsin Center for Educational Research University of Wisconsin, Madison.

Anderson, K. F. (2013). Diagnosing discrimination: Stress from perceived racism and the mental and physical health effects. *Sociological Inquiry, 83*(1), 55–81.

Anyon, J. (1980). Social class and the hidden curriculum of work. *Journal of Education, 52*(1), 67–93.

Ayers, W. (2001). A teacher ain't nothin' but a hero: Teachers and teaching in film. In Joseph, P. B., & Burnaford, G. E. (Ed.), *Images of schoolteachers in America* (pp. 201–210). Mahwah, NJ: Lawrence Erlbaum Associates.

Ball, D., & Cohen, D. (1999). Developing practice, developing practitioners: Towards a practice-based theory of professional education. In G. Sykes & L. Darling-Hammond (Eds.), *Teaching as the learning profession: Handbook of policy and practice* (pp. 3–32). San Francisco: Jossey-Bass.

Barnett, B. M. (1993). Invisible southern black women leaders in the civil rights movement: The triple constraints of gender, race, and class. *Gender & Society, 7*(2), 162–182.

Barnum, M. (2013, February 28). It's time for Teach For America to fold—former TFAer. *The Washington Post*. Retrieved from http://www.washingtonpost.com/blogs/answer-sheet/wp/2013/02/28/its-time-for-teach-for-america-to-fold-former-tfaer/

Beckert, S. (2014, December 12). Slavery and capitalism. *The Chronicle Review*. Retrieved from http://m.chronicle.com/article/SlaveryCapitalism/150787/

Blackburn, R. T., & Fox, T. G. (1983). Physicians' values and their career stage. *Journal of Vocational Behavior, 22*, 159–173.

Blanchard, O. (2013, September 23). I quit Teach For America: Five weeks of training was not enough to prepare me for a room of 20 unruly elementary-schoolers. *The Atlantic*. Retrieved from http://www.theatlantic.com/education/archive/2013/09/i-quit-teach-for-america/279724/

Blow, C. (2014, December 7). A new age of activism: From Eric Garner and Michael Brown to the ballot box. *The New York Times*. Retrieved from http://www.nytimes.com/2014/12/08/opinion/charles-blow-from-eric-garner-and-michael-brown-to-the-ballot-box.html?r=0

Boyd, D., Grossman, P., Lankford, H., Loeb, S., & Wyckoff, J. (2006). How changes in entry requirements alter the teacher workforce and affect student achievement. *Education Finance and Policy, 1*(2), 176–194.

Boyle, L. (2013, July 24). Huffpost: Why are we burning Teach For America at the stake? [Web log]. Retrieved from http://www.huffingtonpost.com/lauren-boyle/in-defense-of-teach-for-a1b3635955.html

Broussard, M. (2014, July 15). Why poor schools can't win at standardized testing. *The Atlantic*. Retrieved from http://www.theatlantic.com/features/archive/2014/07/why-poor-schools-cant-win-at-standardized-testing/374287/

Brown, C. S. (2002). *Refusing racism: White allies and the struggle for civil rights*. New York: Teachers College Press.

Burgo, J. (2013, May 30). The difference between guilt and shame. *Psychology Today*. Retrieved from http://www.psychologytoday.com/blog/shame/201305/the-difference-between-guilt-and-shame

Butler, J. (1990). *Gender trouble: Feminism and the subversion of identity*. New York: Routledge.

Carnevale, A., & Strohl, J. (2010). How increasing college access is increasing inequality, and what to do about it. In R. Kahlenberg (Ed.), *Rewarding strivers: Helping low-income students succeed in college* (pp. 71–190). New York, NY: The Century Foundation.

Carter, S. C. (2000). *No excuses: Lessons from 21 high-performing, high-poverty schools*. Washington, DC: Heritage Foundation.

Cervantes, M. (2003). *Don Quixote*. London: Penguin UK.

Chappell, B. (2014, April 27). Minneapolis renames Columbus Day as Indigenous People's Day. *National Public Radio*. Retrieved from http://www.npr.org/blogs/thetwo-way/2014/04/27/307445328/minneapolis-renames-columbus-day-as-indigenous-peoples-day

Cherniss, C. (1980). *Professional burnout in human service organization*. New York: Praeger.

Cherniss, C. (1995). *Beyond burnout: Helping teachers, nurses, therapists, and lawyers recover from stress and disillusionment*. New York: Routledge.

City Year: Our Approach (2014). In *City Year* online. Retrieved from http://www.cityyear.org/philadelphia/our-work/our-approach

City Year: Starfish Story (2014). In *City Year* online. Retrieved from http://www.cityyear.org/about-us/culture-values/founding-stories/starfish-story

Clozel, L. (2012). Teach For America adjusts with Philadelphia school district cuts. *The Daily Pennsylvanian*. Retrieved from http://www.thedp.com/article/2012/11/teach-for-america-shifts-focus-to-charter-schools

Coates, T. N. (2014a). The case for reparations. *The Atlantic, 21*, 90–101.

Coates, T. N. (2014b, June 4). The radical practicality of reparations. *The Atlantic*. Retrieved from http://www.theatlantic.com/business/archive/2014/06/the-radical-practicality-of-reparations/372114/

Coates, T. N. (2014c, June 23). How racism invented race in America. *The Atlantic*. Retrieved from http://www.theatlantic.com/politics/archive/2014/06/the-case-for-reparations-a-narrative-bibliography/372000/

Coates, T. N. (2014d, November 26). Barack Obama, Ferguson, and the evidence of things unsaid. *The Atlantic*. Retrieved from http://www.theatlantic.com/politics/archive/2014/11/barack-obama-ferguson-and-the-evidence-of-things-unsaid/383212/

Cochran-Smith, M., & Lytle, S. (2009). *Inquiry as stance: Practitioner research for the next generation*. New York: Teachers College Press.

Connelly, M., & Clandinin, J. (1999). *Shaping a professional identity: Stories of education practice*. London, ON: Althouse Press.

Crawford-Garrett, K. (2013). *Teach For America and the struggle for urban school reform: Searching for agency in an era of standardization*. New York: Peter Lang Publishing, Inc.

Crenshaw, K. (1991). Mapping the margins: Intersectionality, identity politics, and violence against women of color. *Stanford Law Review, 43*(6), 1241–1299.

Damast, A. (2012, March 26). Q&A: Teach For America's Wendy Kopp. *Bloomberg Businessweek*. Retrieved from http://www.businessweek.com/articles/2012-03-26/q-and-a-teach-for-americas-wendy-kopp#p2

Darling-Hammond, L., Holtzman, D. J., Gatlin, S. J., & Heilig, J. V. (2005). Does teacher preparation matter? Evidence about teacher certification, Teach For America, and teacher effectiveness. *Education Policy Analysis Archives, 13*(42), 1–50.

Davies, E., Freiman, L., & Pitingolo, R. (2011). *A lost decade: Neighborhood poverty and the urban crisis of the 2000s*. Washington, DC: Joint Center for Political and Economic Studies.

de Beauvoir, S. (1947). *The ethics of ambiguity*. Secaucus, NJ: Citadel Press.

Decker, P. T., Mayer, D. P., & Glazerman, S. (2004). The effects of Teach For America on students: Findings from a national evaluation. Washington, DC: Mathematica Policy Research, Inc. Retrieved from http://www.mathematica-mpr.com/~/media/publications/PDFs/teach.pdf

DeFleur, M. L. (1964). Occupational roles as portrayed on television. *Public Opinion Quarterly, 38*, 57–74.

Delpit, L. (1988). The silenced dialogue: Power and pedagogy in educating other people's children. *Harvard Educational Review, 58*(3), 282.

Demby, G. (2014, July 29). What we see in the Eric Garner video, and what we don't. *National Public Radio*. Retrieved from http://www.npr.org/blogs/codeswitch/2014/07/29/335847224/what-we-see-in-the-eric-garner-video-and-what-we-dont

Denzin, N. (1978). *Sociological methods*. New York: McGraw-Hill.

Depression. (2013). In *American Psychological Association* online. Retrieved from www.apa.org/topics/depress/index.aspx

Doyle, K. (2015, February 11). Teacher depression may affect child learning. *Reuters*. Retrieved from http://www.reuters.com/article/2015/02/11/us-mental-health-teacher-depression-idUSKBN0LF27620150211

Easterly, W. (2006). *The white man's burden: Why the West's efforts to aid the rest have done so much ill and so little good*. New York: Penguin.

Ellen, I. G. (2010). Continuing isolation: Segregation in America today. In J. H. Carr & N. K. Kutty (Eds.), *Segregation: The rising costs for America* (pp. 261–278). New York: Routledge.

Farr, S. (2011, August 26). *Instruction with investment in mind video Justin Meli and 3rd grade class high quality resolution*. [Video file]. Retrieved from https://www.youtube.com/watch?v=M-wh1tDXpe7I

Farr, S., & Teach For America (2009). Teaching as leadership: Ms. Lora's story. In *Teaching As Leadership* Online. Retrieved from: http://www.teachingasleadership.org/sites/default/files/Ms.Lora.Story.pdf

Farr, S., & Teach For America (2010). *Teaching as leadership: The highly effective teacher's guide to closing the achievement gap*. San Francisco: Jossey-Bass.

Featherstone, H. (1993). Learning from the first years of classroom teaching: The journey in, the journey out. *Teachers College Record, 95*(1), 93–112.

Feiman-Nemser, S. (2003). What new teachers need to learn. *Educational Leadership, 60*(8), 25–29.

Figley, C. R. (1995). *Compassion fatigue: Secondary traumatic stress disorders in those who treat the traumatized*. New York: Routledge.

Fikkert, B., & Corbett, S. (2009). *When helping hurts: Alleviating poverty without hurting the poor … and Yourself*. Chicago, IL: Moody Publishers.

Finn, P. J. (1999). *Literacy with an attitude: Educating working-class children in their own self-interest*. Albany State University of New York Press.

Fiske, S. (2010). Envy up, scorn down: How comparison divides us. *American Psychologist, 65*(8), 698–706. doi: 10.1037/0003-066X.65.8.698

Forbes: The 50 Largest U.S. Charities (2013). In *Forbes* online. Retrieved from http://www.forbes.com/companies/teach-for-america/

Foucault, M. (1977). *Language, counter-memory, practice: Selected essays and interviews*. Ithaca, NY: Cornell University Press.

Freire, P. (1970). *Pedagogy of the oppressed*. New York: Herder and Herder.

Freudenberger, H. J., & Richelson, G. (1980). *Burnout. The high cost of high achievement*. New York: Anchor Press.

Freudenberger, H. J. (1986). The issues of staff burnout in therapeutic communities. *Journal of Psychoactive Drugs, 18*(2), 247–251.

Fultz, M. (1995). African American teachers in the South, 1890–1940: Powerlessness and the ironies of expectations and protests. *History of Education Quarterly, 35*(4), 401–422.

Gandhi, L. (2013, October 14). How Columbus sailed into U.S. history, thanks to Italians. *National Public Radio*. Retrieved from http://www.npr.org/blogs/codeswitch/2013/10/14/232120128/how-columbus-sailed-into-u-s-history-thanks-to-italians

Garbarino, J. (1995). The American war zone: What children can tell us about living with violence. *Journal of Developmental and Behavioral Pediatrics*, 16(6), 431–435.

Garbarino, J. (2000). The effects of community violence on children. In J. P. Shonkoff & S. J. Meisels (Eds.), *Handbook of early childhood intervention* (pp. 412–428). New York: Cambridge University Press.

Garrow, D. (1978). *Protest at Selma: Martin Luther King, Junior, and the Voting Rights Act of 1965.* New Haven, CT: Yale University Press.

Gil, E. (1996). *Treating abused adolescents.* New York: Guilford Press.

Gilens, M. (2005). Inequality and democratic responsiveness. *Public Opinion Quarterly*, 69(5), 778–796.

Giroux, H. (1996). *Counternarratives: Cultural studies and critical pedagogies in postmodern spaces.* New York: Routledge.

Giroux, H. (2004). Teachers as transformative intellectuals. In A. S. Canestrari & B. A. Marlowe (Eds.), *Educational foundations: An anthology of critical readings* (pp. 205–212). Thousand Oaks, CA: Sage Publications, Inc.

Giroux, H. (1983). *Theory and resistance in education: A pedagogy for the opposition.* New York: Bergin & Garvey.

Goodman, J. F. (2013). Charter management organizations and the regulated environment: Is it worth the price? *Educational Researcher*, 42(2), 89–96.

Goodman, J. F. (2014, September 10). The high cost of no excuses. *Edushyster*. Retrieved from http://edushyster.com/?p=5616

Graham, J. (2013, January 30). For some caregivers, the trauma lingers. *The New York Times*. Retrieved from http://newoldage.blogs.nytimes.com/2013/01/30/for-some-caregivers-the-trauma-lingers/

Green, E. (2014, July 23). Why do Americans stink at math? *New York Times*. Retrieved from http://www.nytimes.com/2014/07/27/magazine/why-do-americans-stink-at-math.html

Green, J., & Bloome, D. (1997). Ethnography and ethnographers of and in education: A situated perspective. In J. Flood, S. B. Heath, & D. Lapp (Eds.), *Handbook of research on teaching literacy through the communicative and visual arts* (pp. 181–202). New York: Macmillan.

Gutstein, E. (2006). *Reading and writing the world with mathematics: Toward a pedagogy for social justice.* New York: Routledge.

Haberman, M. (1991). The pedagogy of poverty versus good teaching. *Phi Delta Kappan*, 73(4), 290–294.

Haley, A., & X, M. (1964). *The autobiography of Malcolm X: As told to Alex Haley.* New York: Ballantine Books.

Hanigan, J. (1984). *Martin Luther King, Junior and the foundations of nonviolence.* Lanham, MD University Press of America, Inc.

Hedges, C. (2010). *Death of the liberal class.* New York: Nation Books.

Henry, G. T., Thompson, C. L., Bastian, K. C., Campbell, S. L., Patterson, K. M., & Chapman, A. (2012). *UNC teacher quality research: Teacher portals effectiveness analysis.* Chapel Hill: The University of North Carolina at Chapel Hill Carolina Institute for Public Policy.

Hidden Curriculum (2014). In *The glossary of education reform*. Retrieved from http://edglossary.org/hidden-curriculum/

Hill, B. (2014, August 29). Negrophobia: Michael Brown, Eric Garner, and America's fear of black people. *Time Magazine*. Retrieved from http://time.com/3207307/negrophobia-michael-brown-eric-garner-and-americas-fear-of-black-people/

Ingersoll, R. M. (2001). *A different approach to solving the teacher shortage problem*. Seattle, WA: Center for the Study of Teaching and Policy.

Ingersoll, R. M. (2004). *Why do high-poverty schools have difficulty staffing their classrooms with qualified teachers?* Washington, DC: Center for American Progress.

Jesness, J. (2002). Stand and deliver revisited. *Reason, 34*(3), 34–39.

Kahill, S. (1988). Symptoms of professional burnout: A review of the empirical evidence. *Canadian Psychology, 29*(3), 284–297.

Kim, J. Y. (1999). Are Asians black? The Asian-American civil rights agenda and the contemporary significance of the black/white Paradigm. *Yale Law Journal*, 2385–2412.

Kopp, W. (2003). *One day, all children …: The unlikely triumph of Teach For America and what I learned along the way*. Cambridge, MA: Perseus Books Group.

Kovacs, P. (2011, December 13). Teach For America "research" questioned. [Web log]. Retrieved from: http://www.washingtonpost.com/blogs/answer-sheet/post/teach-for-america-research-questioned/2011/12/12/gIQANb40rO_blog.html

Kozol, J. (2005). *The shame of the nation: The restoration of apartheid schooling in America*. New York: Crown Publishing.

Kramer, M. (1974). *Reality shock*. St. Louis: C. V. Mosby.

Krieger, N. (1999). Embodying inequality: A review of concepts, measures and methods for studying health consequences of discrimination. *International Journal of Health Services, 29*, 295–352.

Laczko-Kerr, I., & Berliner, D. C. (2002). The effectiveness of Teach For America and other under-certified teachers: A case of harmful public policy. *Education Policy Analysis Archives, 10*(37), 1–42.

Ladson-Billings, G. (2006). From the achievement gap to the education debt: Understanding achievement in U.S. schools. *Educational Researcher, 35*(7), 3–12.

Ladson-Billings, G. (2007). Gloria Ladson-Billings reframes the racial achievement gap. In *Keynote address given at the 2007 Urban Sites Conference of the National Writing Project, Washington DC*. Retrieved from http://www.nwp.org/cs/public/print/resource/2513

Lanier, H. K. (2010). What Jaime Escalante taught us that Hollywood left out: Remembering America's favorite math teacher. *Education Week, 29*(29), 32.

Lapayese, Y., Aldana, U., & Lara, E. (2014). A racio-economic analysis of Teach For America: Counterstories of TFA teachers of color. *Perspectives on Urban Education, 11*(1). Retrieved from http://www.urbanedjournal.org/archive/volume-11-issue-1-winter-2014/racio-economic-analysis-teach-america-counterstories-tfa-teach

Lee, J. (2002). Racial and ethnic achievement gap trends: Reversing the progress toward equity? *Educational Researcher, 31*(1), 3–12.

Lerer, J. (2012, March 9). Wendy Kopp responds to TFA Critics at Ed School. *The Harvard Crimson*. Retrieved from http://www.thecrimson.com/article/2012/3/9/kopp-teach-for-america

Levy, P. (1998). *The civil rights movement*. Westport, CT: Greenwood Publishing Group.

Lewis, H. B. (1974). *Shame and guilt in neurosis*. Oxford, UK: International Universities Press.

Lincoln, Y., & Guba, E. (1985). *Naturalistic Inquiry*. Newbury Park, CA: Sage Publications.

Lorde, A. (1984). *Sister outsider*. Trumansburg, NY: Crossing Press.

Martin, R. (2014, November 30). Feelings on Ferguson reflect deep racial divide. *National Public Radio*. Retrieved from http://www.npr.org/2014/11/30/367544580/feelings-on-ferguson-reflect-deep-racial-divide

Maslach, C. (2003). *Burnout: The cost of caring*. Los Altos, CA: ISHK.

Maslach, C., & Jackson, S. E. (1981). The measurement of experienced burnout. *Journal of Occupational Behavior, 2*, 99–113.

McAdam, D., & Brandt, C. (2009). Assessing the effects of voluntary youth service: The case of Teach For America. *Social Forces, 88*(2), 945–970.

McIntosh, P. (1988, July). "White privilege: Unpacking the invisible knapsack." *Peace and Freedom Magazine*, July/August 1989, 10–12.

McLaren, P. L. (1989). *Life in schools: An introduction to critical pedagogy in the foundations of education*. New York: Longman.

McLean, L., & McDonald Connor, C. (2015). Depressive symptoms in third-grade teachers: Relations to classroom quality and student achievement. *Child Development*. doi: 10.1111/cdev.12344.

McMillan Cottom, T. (2014, September 22). What Rhimes with bad cultural analysis? [Web log]. Retrieved from http://tressiemc.com/2014/09/22/what-rhimes-with-bad-cultural-analysis/

Miner B. (2010). The ultimate superpower: Supersized dollars drive waiting for 'superman' agenda. *Rethinking Schools, 25*(2), 1–11.

Mueller, B., & Southall, A. (2014, December 13). *25,000 march in New York to protest police violence. The New York Times*. Retrieved from http://www.nytimes.com/2014/12/14/nyregion/in-new-york-thousands-march-in-continuing-protests-over-garner-case.html

Murnane, R. J., & Phillips, B. R. (1981). What do effective teachers of inner-city children have in common? *Social Science Research, 10*(1), 83–100.

Muse, Q. (2013, July 16). Philly's Teach For America chapter feels the layoff pinch. *NBC News*. Retrieved from: http://www.washingtonpost.com/blogs/answer-sheet/wp/2013/02/28/its-time-for-teach-for-america-to-fold-former-tfaer/

Naison, M. (2011, July 18). Why Teach For America is not welcome in my classroom. *LA Progressive*. Retrieved from http://www.laprogressive.com/teach-america/

Nakkula, M. J., & Ravitch, S. M. (1998). *Matters of interpretation: Reciprocal transformation in therapeutic and developmental relationships with youth*. San Francisco: Jossey-Bass.

National Center for Education Statistics (2013). *Performance of U.S. 15-year-old students in mathematics, science, and reading literacy in an international context: First look at PISA 2012*. Retrieved from http://nces.ed.gov/pubs2014/2014024rev.pdf

National Commission on Teaching and America's Future (2003). No dream denied: A pledge to America's children: Summary report. Washington, DC: Author. Retrieved from http://nctaf.org/wp-content/uploads/no-dream-deniedsummaryreport.pdf

Neufeld, S. (2014, November 10). Can a teacher be too dedicated? *The Atlantic*. Retrieved from http://www.theatlantic.com/national/archive/2014/11/can-a-teacher-be-too-dedicated/382563/

Orwell, G. (1950). *1984*. New York: Penguin Group.

Osgood, K. (2013, June 30). At the chalk face: An open letter to new Teach For America recruits [Forum]. Retrieved from http://atthechalkface.com/2013/06/30/an-open-letter-to-new-teach-for-america-recruits/

Payne, C. (2008). *So much reform, so little change: The persistence of failure in urban schools*. Cambridge, MA: Harvard Education Press.

Pearlman, L. A., & Saakvitne, K. W. (1995). Treating therapists with vicarious traumatization and secondary traumatic stress disorders. In C. R. Figley (Ed.), *Compassion fatigue: Coping with secondary traumatic stress disorders in those who treat the traumatized* (pp. 150–177). New York: Brunner/Mazel.

Pines, A., Aronson, E., & Kafry, D. (1981). *Burnout: From tedium to personal growth*. New York: Free Press.

Planty, M., Hussar, W., Snyder, T., Provasnik, S., Kena, G., Dinkes, R., KewalRamani, A., & Kemp, J. (2008). *The condition of education 2008* (NCES 2008-031). National Center for Education Statistics, Institute of Education Sciences, U.S. Department of Education: Washington, DC.

Polman, L. (2011). *The crisis caravan: What's wrong with humanitarian aid?* London: Picador.

Post-Traumatic Stress Disorder. (2013). In *American Psychological Association* online. Retrieved from http://www.apa.org/topics/ptsd/

Prince, C. (2003). *Higher pay in hard to staff schools*. Lanham, MD: Scarecrow Press, Inc.

Rangappa, A. (2012, July 11). P. S. Boot Camp II: Outsmart, outwrite, outlast (a.k.a. The TFA Essay). [Web log]. Retrieved from http://blogs.law.yale.edu/blogs/admissions/archive/2012/07/11/p-s-boot-camp-ii-the-tfa-essay.aspx

Rattansi, A. (2005). The uses of racialization: The time-spaces and subject-objects of the raced body. In K. Murji & J. Solomos (Eds.). *Racialization: Studies in theory and practice*. New York: Oxford University Press.

Ravitch, D. (2014a, October 16). Julian Vasquez Heilig: Why TFA is a problem, not a solution [Web log]. Retrieved from http://dianeravitch.net/2014/10/16/julian-vasquez-heilig-why-tfa-is-a-problem-not-a-solution/

Ravitch, D. (2014b, February 23). Teach For America: Newark: 700 teachers may be laid off and replaced by TFA [Web log]. Retrieved from http://dianeravitch.net/category/teach-for-america-tfa/

Ravitch, S. (2014). The transformative power of taking an inquiry stance on practice: Practitioner research as narrative and counter-narrative. *Perspectives on Urban Education. 11*(1). Retrieved from http://www.urbanedjournal.org/sites/urbanedjournal.org/files/pdf_archive/2%20Ravitch%20POUE%20Volume%2011%202014.pdf

Rich, A. (1976). *Of woman born: Motherhood as experience and institution*. New York: W.W. Norton.

Richardson, J. (2014, November 18). The phrase "drank the Kool-Aid" is completely offensive. We should stop saying it immediately. *The Washington Post.* Retrieved from http://www.washingtonpost.com/posteverything/wp/2014/11/18/the-phrase-drank-the-koolaid-is-completely-offensive-we-should-stop-saying-it-immediately/

Ricket, A. (2013, December 23). The myth of the hero teacher. Teaching Tolerance. Retrieved from http://www.tolerance.org/blog/myth-hero-teacher

Rigole, N. (2011). Becoming the generalized other: An analysis of the narratives of Teach For America teacher-bloggers. *Middle-Secondary Education and Instructional Technology Dissertations.* Paper 86.

Rockoff, J. (2004). The impact of individual teachers on student achievement: Evidence from panel data. *American Economic Review, 94*(2), 247–252.

Rogers, S. (2013, February 27). The civil rights movement of our time? Not yet. [Web log]. Retrieved from http://www.teachforamerica.org/blog/civil-rights-movement-our-time-not-yet

Rothstein, R. (2012a). A comment on Bank of America/Countrywide's discriminatory mortgage lending and its implications for racial segregation. *Economic Policy Institute.* Retrieved from http://s3.epi.org/files/2012/bp335.pdf

Rothstein, R. (2012b, February 3). Racial segregation continues, and even intensifies: Manhattan Institute report heralding the "end" of segregation uses a measure that masks important demographic and economic trends. *Economic Policy Institute.* Retrieved from http://www.epi.org/publication/racial-segregation-continues-intensifies/

Royal, C. (2012a, July 12). Swift to hear; slow to speak: A message to TFA teachers, critics, and education reformers. *Huffington Post.* Retrieved from http://www.huffingtonpost.com/camika-royal-phd/teach-for-america_b_1669121.html

Royal, C. (2012b, November 9). Please stop using the phrase "achievement gap." *Good.* Retrieved from http://magazine.good.is/articles/please-stop-using-the-phrase-achievement-gap?full_site=1

Royal, C. (2013, November 26). I won't say 'don't join Teach For America' (Yet). *Good.* Retrieved from http://magazine.good.is/articles/i-won-t-say-don-t-join-teach-for-america-yet

Rubinstein, G. (2011, October 31). Teach for us: Why I did TFA, and why you shouldn't. [Web log]. Retrieved from http://garyrubinstein.teachforus.org/2011/10/31/why-i-did-tfa-and-why-you-shouldnt/

Rubinstein, G. (2012a, July 3). Ms. Lora's tall tale. [Web log]. Retrieved from http://garyrubinstein.teachforus.org/2012/07/03/ms-loras-tall-tale/

Rubinstein, G. (2012b, September 7). My review of "Won't Back Down." [Web log]. Retrieved from http://garyrubinstein.teachforus.org/2012/09/07/my-review-of-wont-back-down-spoiler-alert/

Rubinstein, G. (2013a, March 20). TFA sponsors reform propaganda videos. [Web log]. Retrieved from http://garyrubinstein.wordpress.com/2013/03/20/tfa-sponsors-reform-propaganda-videos/

Rubinstein, G. (2013b, June 11). National Education Policy Center: My experience at a #TFAListen event. [Web log]. Retrieved from http://nepc.colorado.edu/blog/my-experience-tfalisten-event

Sawhill, I. V., & Morton, J. E. (2007). *Economic mobility: Is the American dream alive and well?* Economic Mobility Project. Retrieved from http://www.brookings.edu/views/papers/sawhill/200705.pdf

Schoen, D. (2014). National attitudes around education issues, improvements and institutions: Conducted August 2014. Chicago, IL: Education Poll. Retrieved from http://343jii21 wly33h03em3o8es6.wpengine.netdna-cdn.com/wp-content/uploads/2014/10/EdPostpoll-detailed-findings-final.pdf

Seidel, A. (2014, July 18). The teacher dropout crisis. *NPR Education.* Retrieved from http://www.npr.org/blogs/ed/2014/07/18/332343240/the-teacher-dropout-crisis

Serko, L. (2013, March 28). Teach For America expands to allow junior applicants. *The Daily Pennsylvanian.* Retrieved from http://www.thedp.com/article/2013/03/teach-for-america-expands-to-allow-junior-applications

Sfard, A., & Prusak, A. (2005). Telling identities: In search of an analytic tool for investigating learning as a culturally shaped activity. *Educational Researcher, 34*(4), 14–22.

Shernoff, E., Mehta, T., Atkins, M., Torf, R., & Spencer, J. (2011). A qualitative study of the sources and impact of stress among urban teachers. *School Mental Health, 3*(2), 59–69.

Shor, I. (1992). *Empowering education: Critical teaching for social change.* Chicago: University of Chicago Press.

Silverstein, J. (2013, March 12). How racism is bad for our bodies. *The Atlantic.* Retrieved from http://www.theatlantic.com/health/archive/2013/03/how-racism-is-bad-for-our-bodies/273911/

Sondel, B., & Kretchmar, K. (2013, December 9). School of Education alums explore Teach For America's impact during WISCAPE forum. *WISCAPE: News.* Retrieved from https://wiscape.wisc.edu/wiscape/news/2013/12/16/school-of-education-alums-explore-teach-for-america's-impact-during-wiscape-forum

Steele, C. M., & Aronson, J. (1995). Stereotype threat and the intellectual test performance of African Americans. *Journal of Personality and Social Psychology, 69*(5), 797–811.

Steinberg, M. P., & Quinn, R. (2014). An urban myth? New evidence on equity, adequacy and the efficiency of educational resources. Retrieved from https://www.cpre.org/sites/default/files/workingpapers/2029_anurbanmyth12-21-2014steinbergquinn.pdf

Stringfellow, W. (1994). *A keeper of the word: Selected writings of William Stringfellow.* Grand Rapids, MI: Wm. B. Eerdmans Publishing Co.

Students Resisting Teach For America (2014, July 21). Resources. [Forum]. Retrieved from http://studentsresistingtfa.k12newsnetwork.com/why-resist-tfa/

Sue Lehmann Excellence in Teaching Awards (2013). In *Sue Lehmann Award* online. Retrieved from http://www.suelehmannaward.org/about

Tangney, J. O., & Stuewig, J. (2004). A moral-emotional perspective on evil persons and evil deeds. In A. G. Miller (Ed.), *The social psychology of good and evil* (pp. 327–355). New York: Guilford Press.

Teach For America (2010). Teach For America announces the schools contributing the most graduates to its 2010 teaching corps [Press Release]. Retrieved from http://www.teachforamerica.org/achievement-gap

Teach For America. (2014, January 13). *A new mandate for public schools*. [Video file]. Retrieved from https://www.youtube.com/watch?v=yKIEVztLKz4

Teach For America: Application (2013). In *Teach For America* online. Retrieved from https://www.teachforamerica.org/online/info

Teach For America: Graduate School and Employer Partnerships (2013). In *Teach For America* online. Retrieved from https://www.teachforamerica.org/why-teach-for-america/compensation-and-benefits/graduate-school-and-employer-partnerships

Teach For America: Our History (2013). In *Teach For America* online. Retrieved from https://www.teachforamerica.org/our-organization/our-history

Teach For America (2014). *The Big 7*. Philadelphia, PA: Teach For America.

Teach For America: The Achievement Gap (2014). In *Teach For America* online. Retrieved from http://www.teachforamerica.org/achievement-gap

Teach For America: Our Mission (2014). In *Teach For America* online. Retrieved from http://www.teachforamerica.org/our-mission

Teach For America: Our Organization (2014). In *Teach For America* online. Retrieved from http://www.teachforamerica.org/our-organization

Teach For America: Research (2014). In *Teach For America* online. Retrieved from http://www.teachforamerica.org/our-organization/research

Teach For America: Salary and Benefits (2014). In *Teach For America* online. Retrieved from http://www.teachforamerica.org/why-teach-for-america/compensation-and-benefits/salary-and-health-benefits

Teach For America: Greater Philadelphia (2015). In *Teach For America* online. Retrieved from https://www.teachforamerica.org/where-we-work/greater-philadelphia

Teach For America: Who We Look For: The Importance of Diversity (2014). In *Teach For America* online. Retrieved from http://www.teachforamerica.org/why-teach-for-america/the-corps/who-we-look-for/the-importance-of-diversity

Tennyson, T. (2013, October 4). Teach For America: Remember the 'I Quit Teach For America' essay? Here's the counterpoint. 'I stayed.' [Web log]. Retrieved from http://www.teachforamerica.org/blog/remember-i-quit-teach-america-essay-heres-counterpoint-i-stayed

Thernstrom, A., & Thernstrom, S. (2004). *No excuses: Closing the racial gap in learning*. New York: Simon and Schuster.

Thomas, P. (2013, January 22). Is poverty destiny? Ideology v. evidence in education reform. [Web log]. Retrieved from http://radicalscholarship.wordpress.com/2013/01/22/daily-kos-is-poverty-destiny-ideology-v-evidence-in-education-reform/

Thomas, P., Porfilio, B. J., Gorlewski, J., & Carr, P. R. (Eds.). (2014). *Social context reform: A pedagogy of equity and opportunity*. New York: Routledge.

Timmerman, M. (2011, September 29). TFA: A Corporate Approach. Why 18 percent of last year's graduating class applied to teach in America's worst schools. *The Harvard Crimson*. Retrieved from http://www.thecrimson.com/article/2011/9/29/tfa-harvard-students-education/

Tracy, J. L., & Robins, R. W. (2004). Putting the self into self-conscious emotions: A theoretical model. *Psychological Inquiry, 15*, 103–125.

Trauma. (2013). In *American Psychological Association* online. Retrieved from http://www.apa.org/topics/trauma/

Ture, K., & Hamilton, C. V. (1992). *Black power: The politics of liberation*. New York: Vintage.

Tyack, D. (2004). *Seeking common ground: Public schools in a diverse society*. Cambridge, MA: Harvard University Press.

Urahn, S. K., Currier, E., Elliott, D., Wechsler, L., Wilson, D., & Colbert, D. (2012). Pursuing the American dream: Economic mobility across generations. Retrieved from http://www.publicradio.org/marketplace-archive/pdf/pewamericandream.pdf

U.S. Department of Education (2009, February 9). *Secretary Arne Duncan speaks at the 91st Annual Meeting of the American Council on Education*. Retrieved from http://www.ed.gov/news/speeches/secretary-arne-duncan-speaks-91st-annual-meeting-american-council-education

Valencia, R. (2005). The Mexican American struggle for equal educational opportunity in Mendez v. Westminster: Helping to pave the way for Brown v. Board of Education. *The Teachers College Record, 107*(3), 389–423.

Valle, V. (1988, March 17). Real-life flashbacks to 'stand, deliver'. *The Los Angeles Times*. Retrieved from http://articles.latimes.com/1988-03-17/entertainment/ca-19961stand-deliver-real

Villanueva Beard, E., & Kramer, M. (2014, March 4). Co-CEOs Matt Kramer and Elisa Villanueva Beard discuss challenges and opportunities ahead at Teach For America. [Web log]. Retrieved from http://www.teachforamerica.org/blog/co-ceos-matt-kramer-and-elisa-villanueva-beard-discuss-challenges-and-opportunities-ahead-teach

Washington, J. (1986). *A testament of hope: The essential writings and speeches of Martin Luther King, Junior*. New York: HarperCollins Publishers.

Wolfe, B., & Haveman, R. (2001). Accounting for the social and non-market benefits of education. In J. Helliwell (Ed.), *The contribution of human and social capital to sustained economic growth and well-being*. Vancouver, BC: University of British Columbia Press. Retrieved from http://www.oecd.org/innovation/research/1825109.pdf

Žižek, S. (1989). *The Sublime Object of Ideology*. London: Verso.

INDEX

C

Studies in the Postmodern Theory of Education

General Editor
Shirley R. Steinberg

Counterpoints publishes the most compelling and imaginative books being written in education today. Grounded on the theoretical advances in criticalism, feminism, and postmodernism in the last two decades of the twentieth century, Counterpoints engages the meaning of these innovations in various forms of educational expression. Committed to the proposition that theoretical literature should be accessible to a variety of audiences, the series insists that its authors avoid esoteric and jargonistic languages that transform educational scholarship into an elite discourse for the initiated. Scholarly work matters only to the degree it affects consciousness and practice at multiple sites. Counterpoints' editorial policy is based on these principles and the ability of scholars to break new ground, to open new conversations, to go where educators have never gone before.

For additional information about this series or for the submission of manuscripts, please contact:

Shirley R. Steinberg
c/o Peter Lang Publishing, Inc.
29 Broadway, 18th floor
New York, New York 10006

To order other books in this series, please contact our Customer Service Department:

(800) 770-LANG (within the U.S.)
(212) 647-7706 (outside the U.S.)
(212) 647-7707 FAX

Or browse online by series:
www.peterlang.com